Better, Bolder, Different

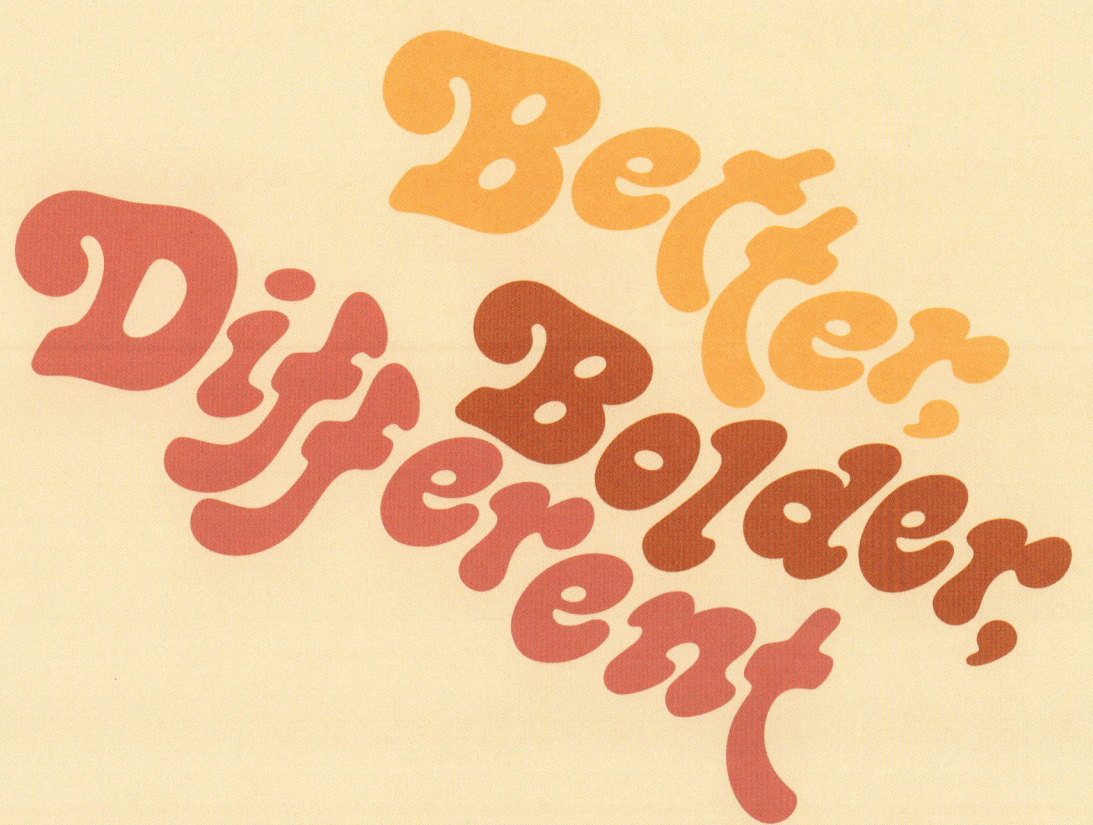

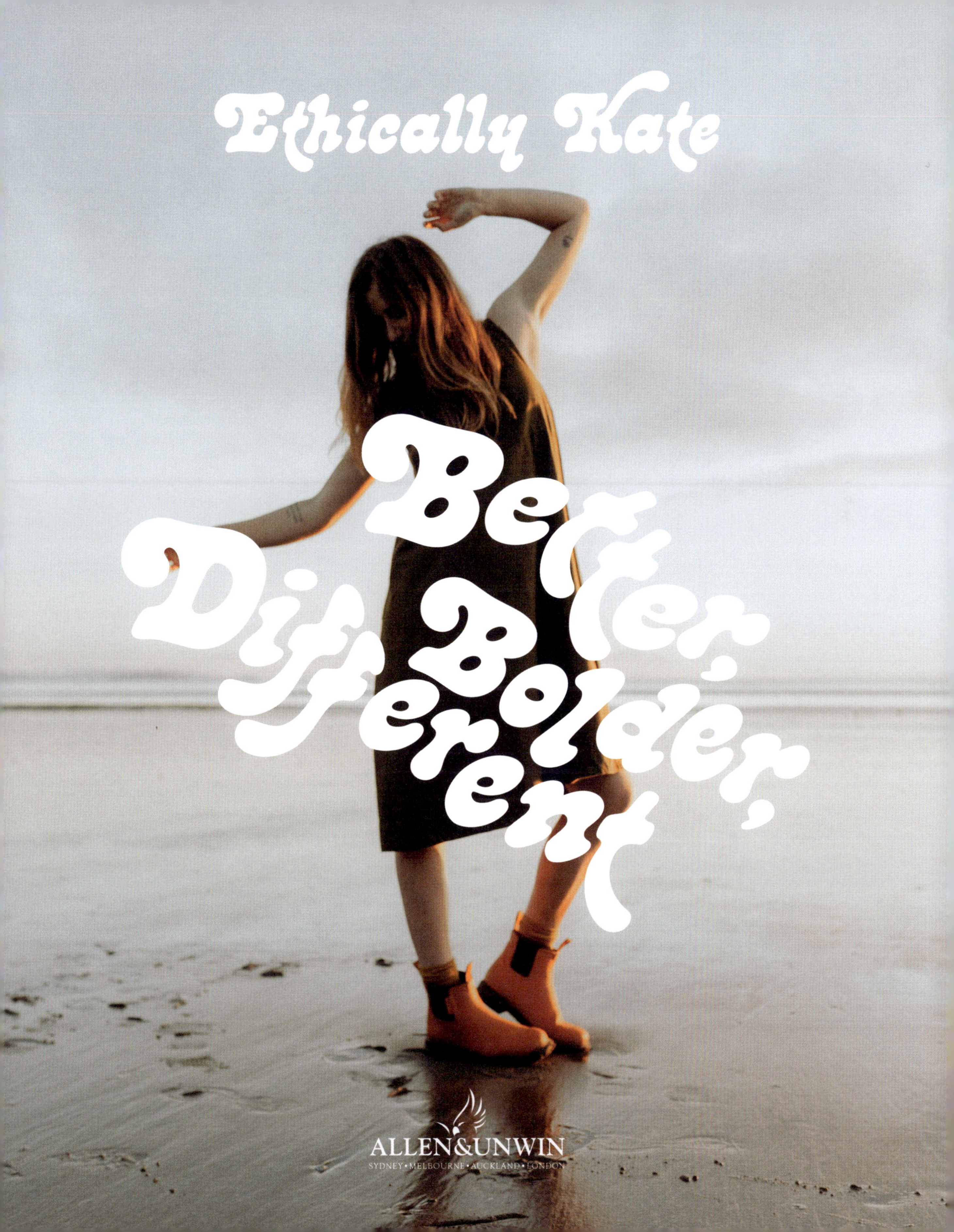

Ethically Kate

Better, Bolder, Different

ALLEN&UNWIN
SYDNEY • MELBOURNE • AUCKLAND • LONDON

First published in 2022

Text © Kate Hall, 2022

Photography © Melissa Palmer, except page 134 (Dorian Gaseling), 2022

The information contained in this book is for general information purposes only and is not meant to substitute professional advice.

All rights reserved. No part of this book may be reproduced or transmitted in any form or by any means, electronic or mechanical, including photocopying, recording or by any information storage and retrieval system, without prior permission in writing from the publisher.

Allen & Unwin
Level 2, 10 College Hill
Auckland 1011, New Zealand
Phone: (64 9) 377 3800

Email: info@allenandunwin.com
Web: www.allenandunwin.co.nz

83 Alexander Street
Crows Nest NSW 2065, Australia
Phone: (61 2) 8425 0100

A catalogue record for this book is available from the National Library of New Zealand

ISBN 978 1 99100 609 7

Design and illustrations by: Megan van Staden
Set in 10/15 pt Galaxie Copernicus
Printed and bound in C&C Printing Co Ltd

10 9 8 7 6 5 4 3 2 1

Contents

Introduction *7*

Me *15*

Wellbeing *31*

The 3 Ss: sleep, stuff, self *63*

Connection *113*

Food *145*

Clothes *193*

Conclusion *231*

Thank you, so much *236*

Notes *238*

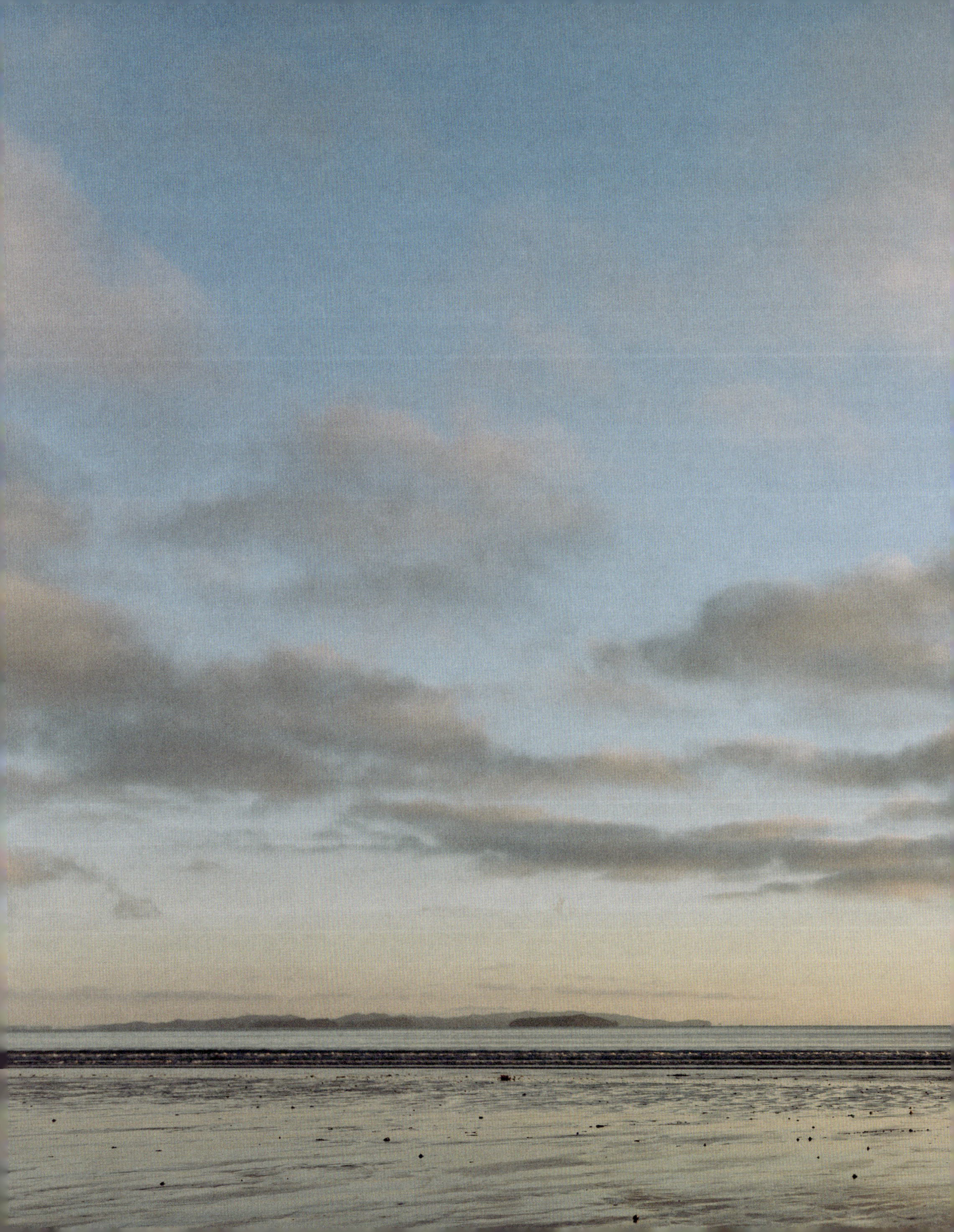

Introduction

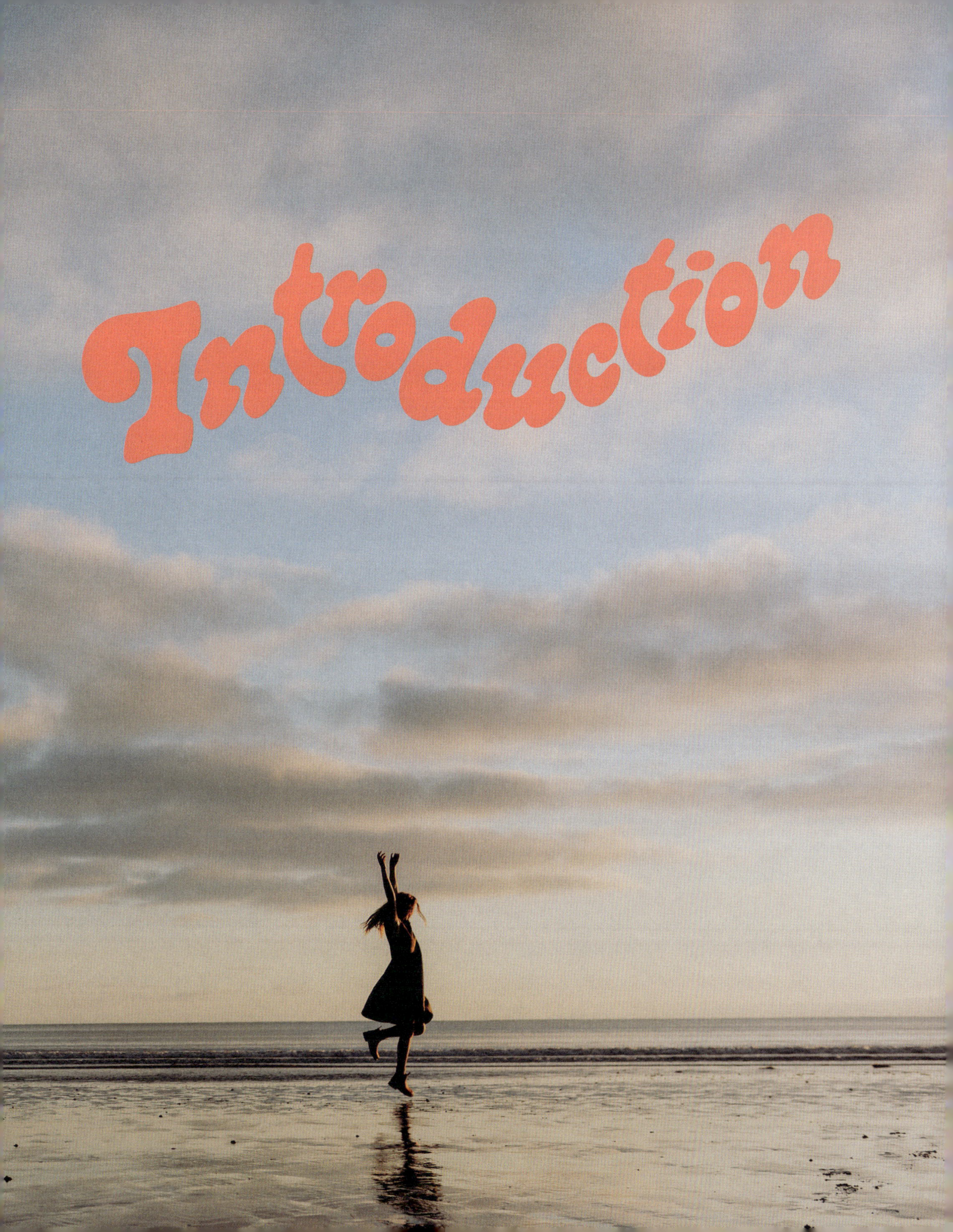

'Life's short, you're going to die, so why does all that stuff really matter?' It's nearly midnight on 31 December 2017. I'm in the middle of a field, sitting at a picnic table with a stranger: a sober musician. One of the only sober people at the festival. My passion for making the world a better place has come up in conversation. I've discussed why I visit packaging-free grocery stores, why my drink bottle does not look like his, and the environmental activism I've dedicated my life to. His response is a laugh, followed by words that essentially tell me my life's work and future dreams are pointless.

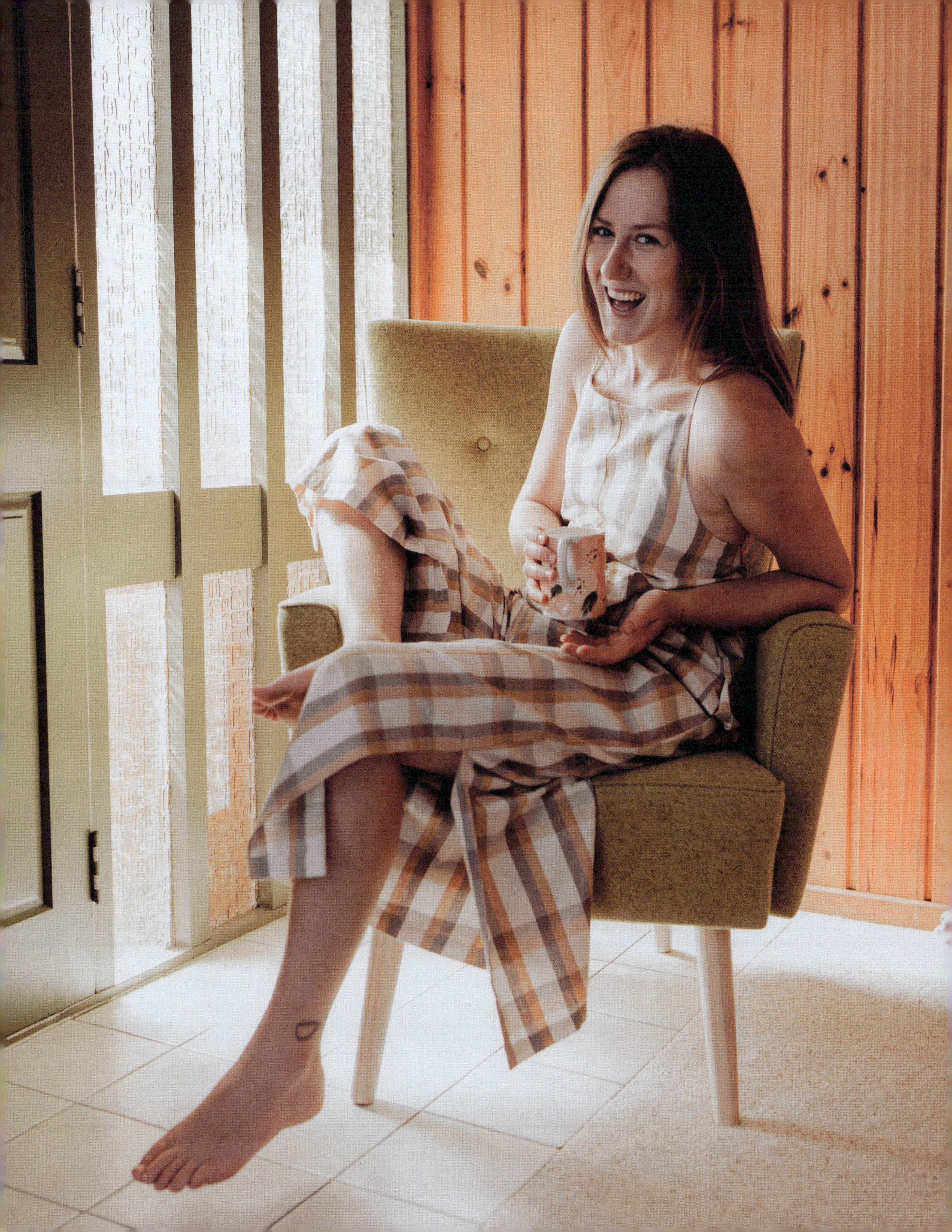

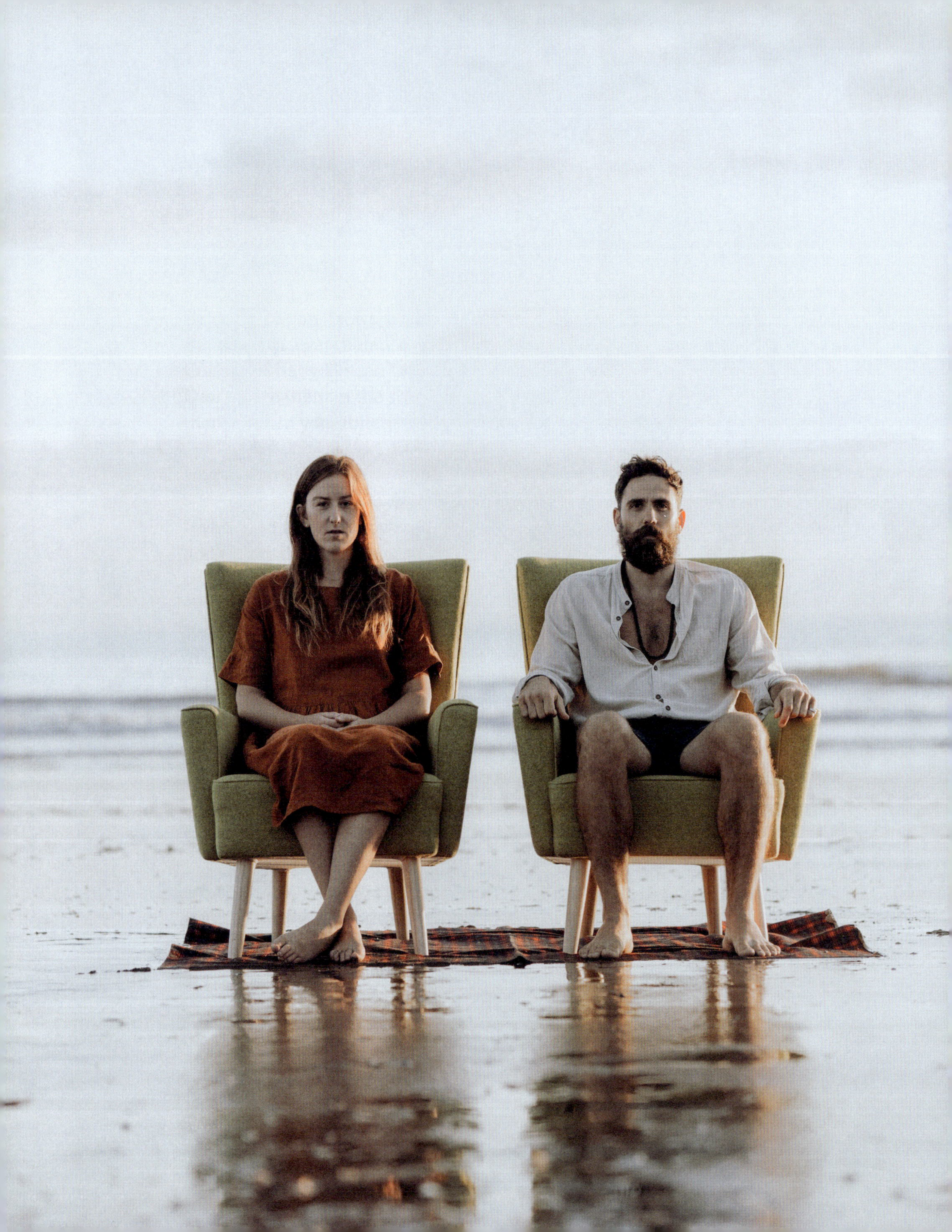

And my response to him — after a brief moment of wanting to throw the picnic table in the air and scream — is 'Life *is* short, I *am* going to die, so all this stuff *really* matters.'

The story you've been told that caring about the environment and living with less waste involves wearing hemp sacks and giving up everything that brings you joy is a myth. Since 2015, that's exactly what I've done and there's nothing but colourful clothes in my wardrobe and a smile on my face. Making daily decisions with people and the planet in mind has been better for my mental and physical health, my relationships, my savings — and everything in between. No matter what you think the state of the climate is right now, whether you think it's absolutely fine or you acknowledge we're in a climate crisis, I firmly believe living life with these values is the best way to live, and I'm here to explain why.

This book is not a how-to. I believe how-to guides can be dangerous. They assume all humans share the same culture and have the same goals and desires. Instead, this book is my philosophy on living, presented in a practical way to help you throw some of my ideologies and ways of living into your own life. I am acutely aware that I'm a white, middle-class, child-free woman living with lots of privileges. But I'm also of the belief that everyone, everywhere, can live life a little better.

And better is enough. Too often the sustainable-living rhetoric includes absolutes, perfection, instructions, and prescriptive rights and wrongs. But that completely disregards the complexity of humanity. First and foremost, our current societal systems in the Western world make it hard, nearly impossible, for someone to live totally within their values. It's never okay to pop a blanket rule over any way of living.

Before I encourage someone to shop at a packaging-free store instead of the supermarket, I must first ask how they are doing.

Before I inspire someone to reconsider how often they drive their car, I must first understand their accessibility needs and capabilities.

Before I reassure someone of the benefits of purchasing ethical fashion garments instead of buying fast fashion, I must first acknowledge their financial situation.

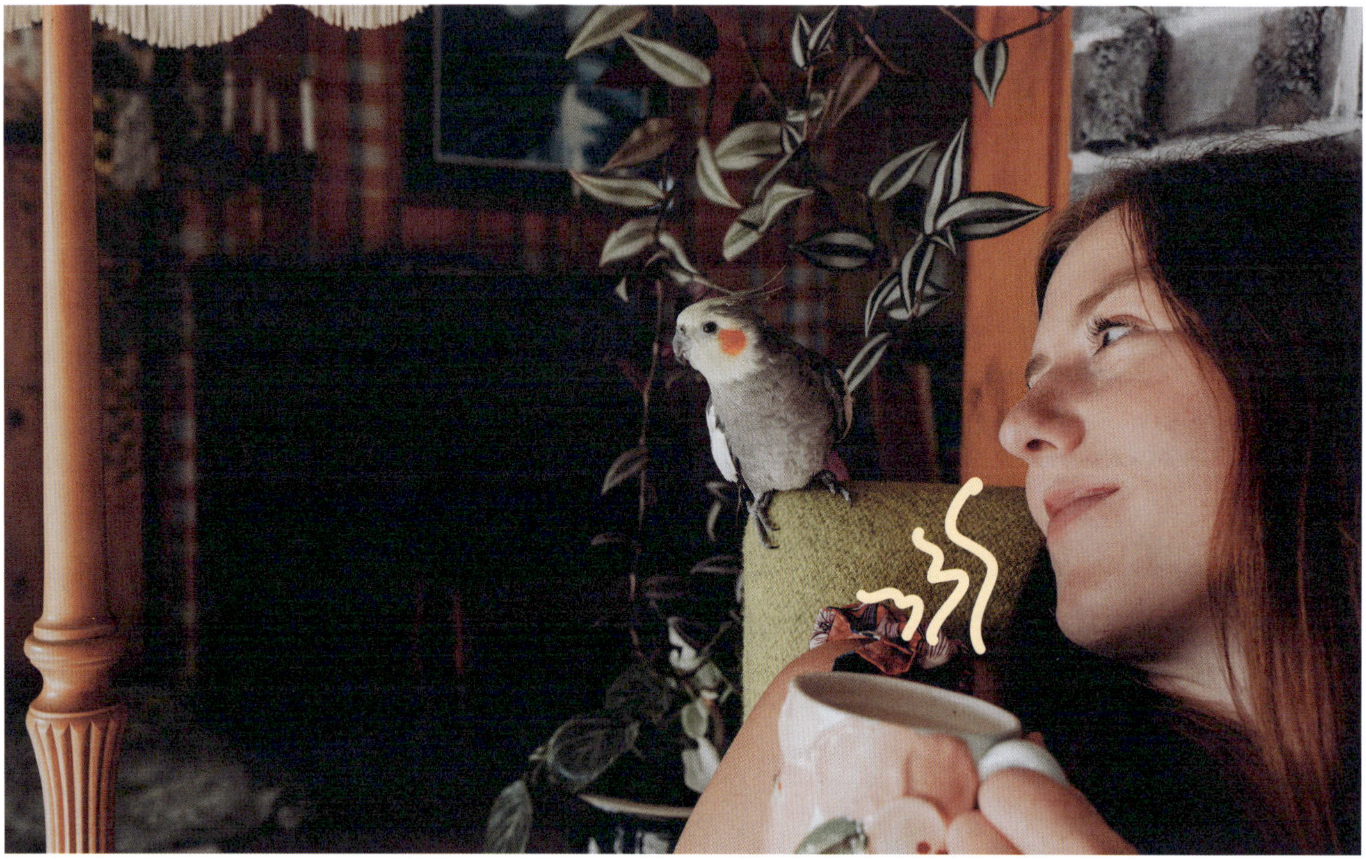

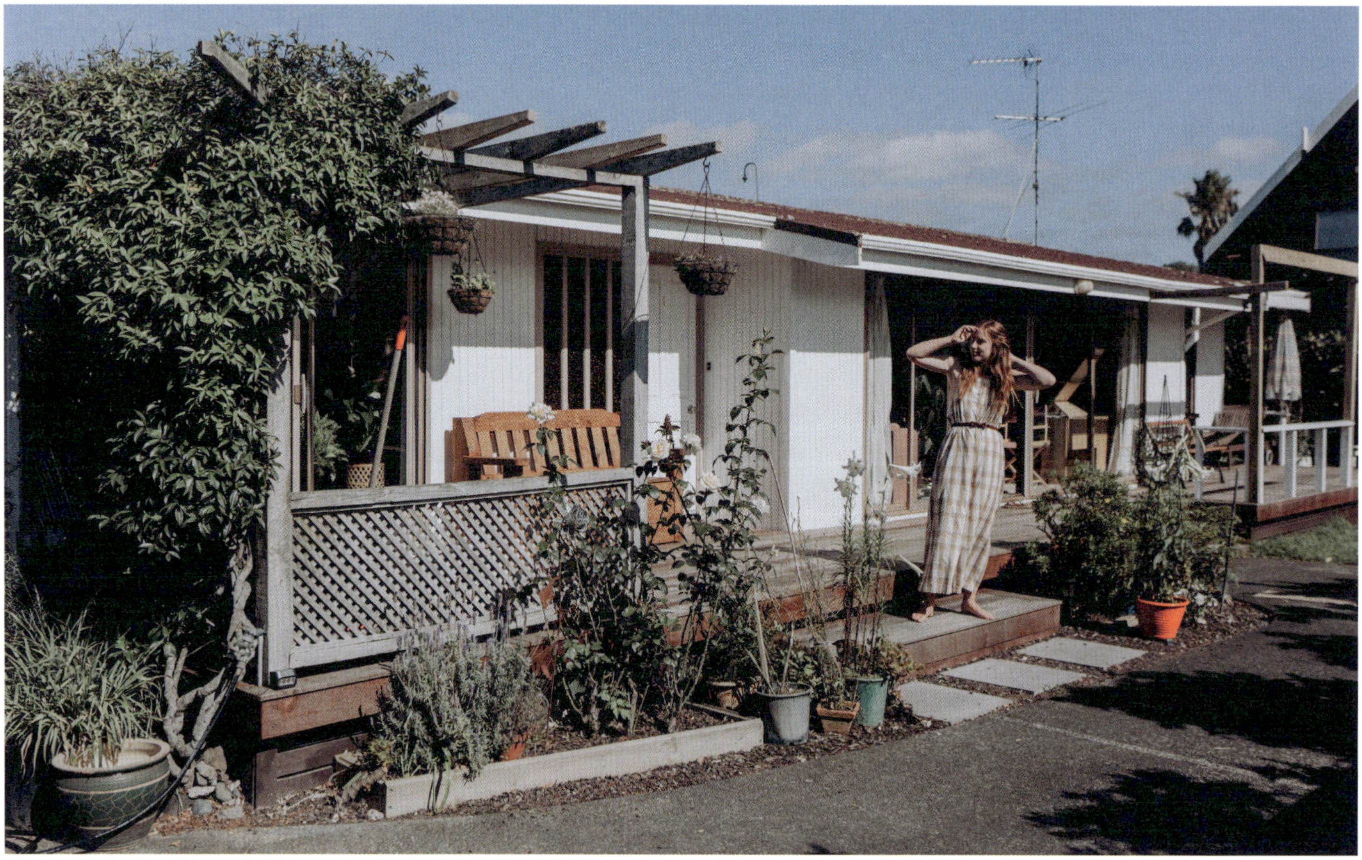

Before I recommend someone use a menstrual cup, I must first understand their cultural values.

Before I tell someone to go outside and enjoy nature, I must first consider that they may be stuck in a city.

So, my hope for you throughout this book is that you adopt philosophies, question your mindset, realise your potential for an excellent life, and act on it. I also secretly hope you, my dear readers, start a global trend of sleeping upside down on Thursday nights — but you can make that call in the Connection chapter.

A note on the term 'sustainability': When people think about the word 'sustainability' they think of the colour green. They think of orangutans, wild forests, vegetable gardens and ocean plastic. They think of activists lining streets with billboards saying 'CLIMATE STRIKE' and refer to their friends who wash their hair only with camomile tea (which I've heard is great btw). The word sustainability has been taken over by green things; it's lost its strong meaning that has nothing to do with being green.

Sustainable refers to something that can happen over and over again with little or no negative effects. Zero degradation. Sustainability means resilience, ongoing habits and the longevity of systems. If something is sustainable, it means it can continue. When the word sustainable is used throughout this book, remember it refers to sustainable health (am I doing things for my body that I can happily continue?), sustainable finances (am I spending in a way that's possible for me to repeat this over and over again?), and of course sustainable for communities and the environment (are my habits positively affecting people and the planet?).

Lastly, I didn't want to write a book. Over the years people have read my writing and naturally asked me if that was coming next, but I told them a book would be wasteful and unsustainable. I hated the thought of my book sitting in the back of a dusty second-hand-shop store-room in several decades' time. But when the wonderful team at Allen & Unwin asked me to write one, I was challenged to think again. I asked myself, what if all your favourite authors had not written books? I couldn't bear the thought — I adore books. So I said yes. Please treasure it.

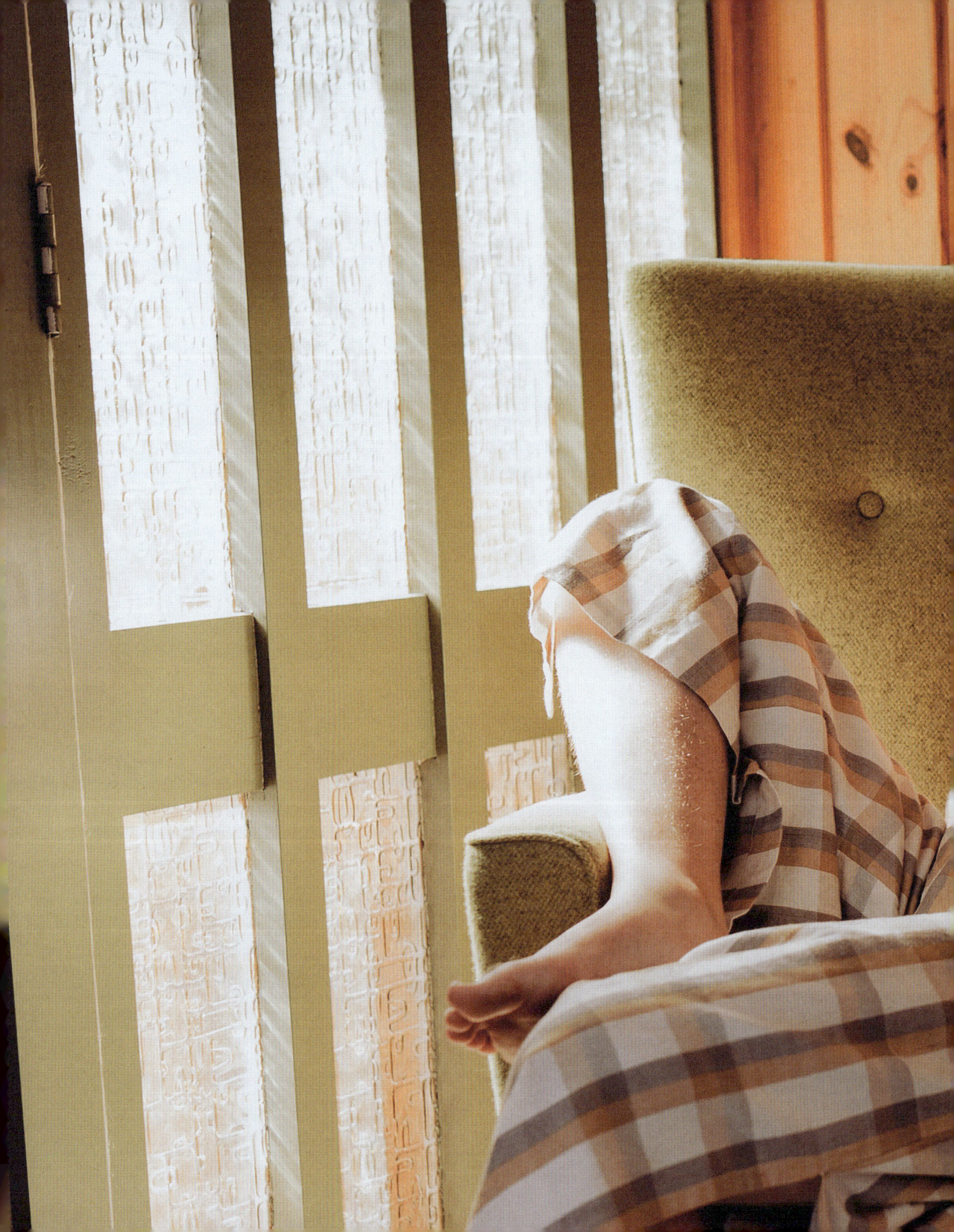

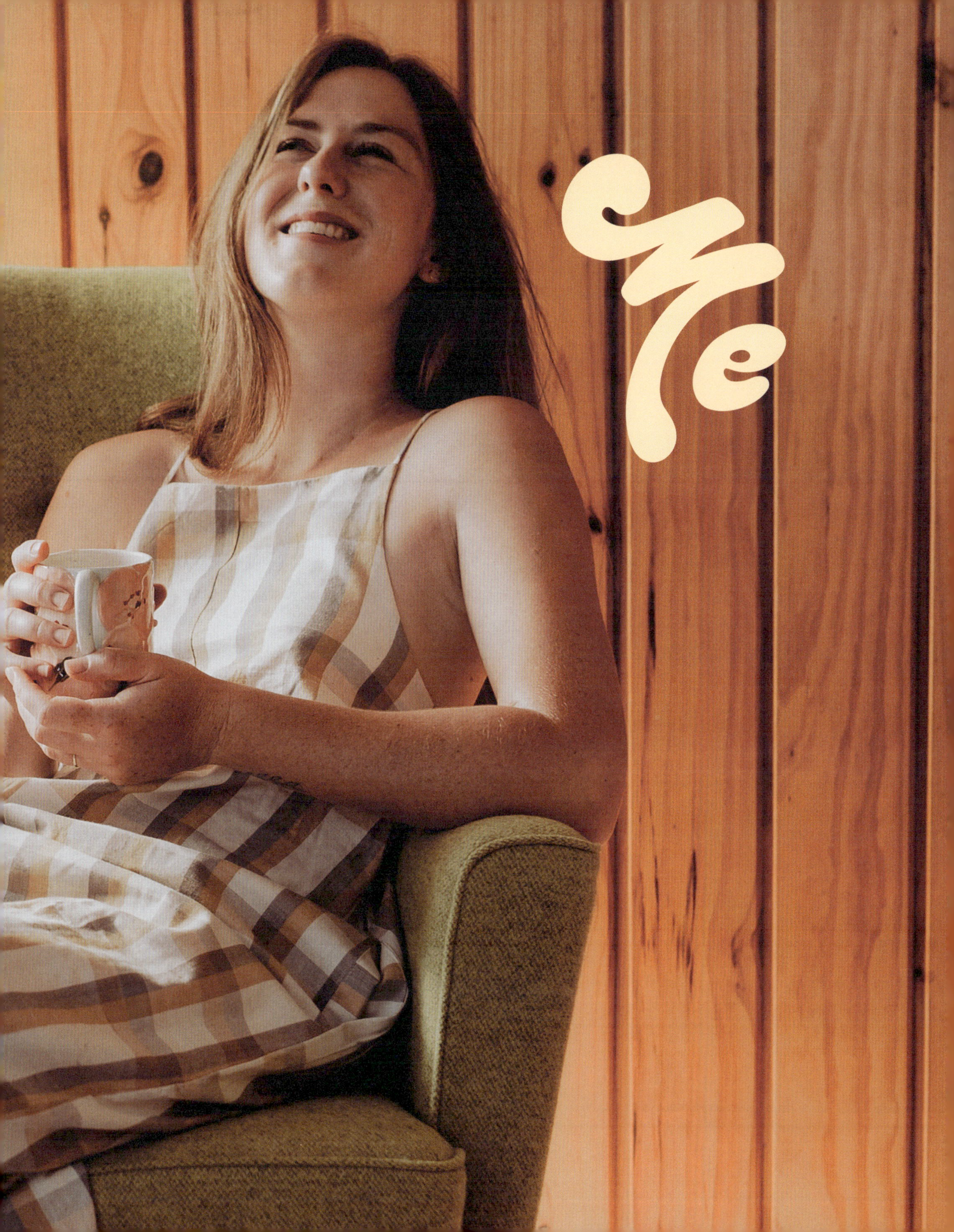
Me

Unless you've followed me online, met me in person or watched me over-share on social media, you'll be wondering who the heck I am. I'm Kate, an environmental activist and educator. I write, I speak, I literally do anything that helps people and the planet thrive together. I live on the Hibiscus Coast, a beach-laden peninsula about an hour north of Auckland City. Being just 300 metres from the ocean, my husband Tim and I can sometimes hear the waves crashing as we go to sleep.

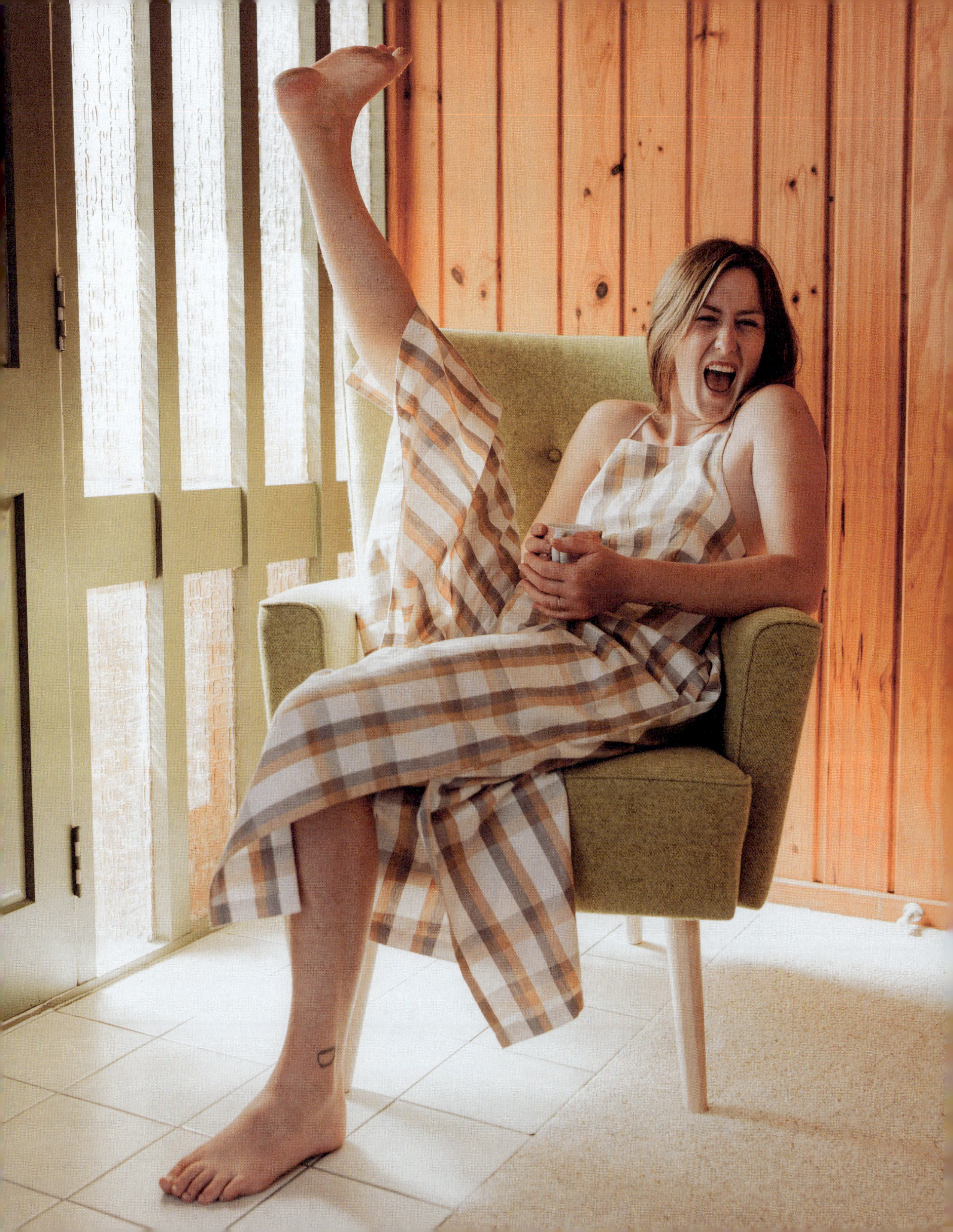

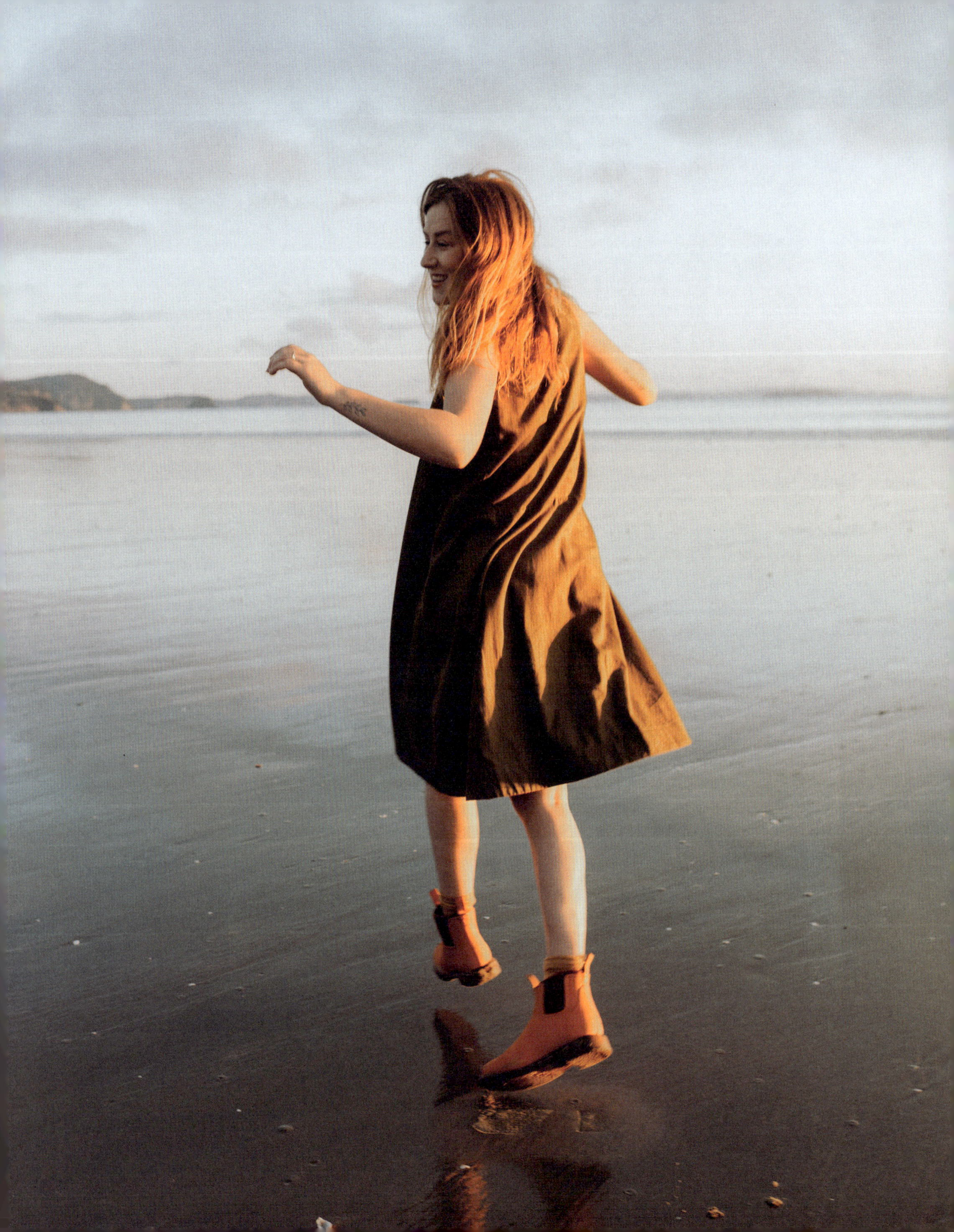

We share our home with a young labradoodle, Tchaikovsky (affectionately known as Chai), and a hand-raised cockatiel, Zugda, who fill any silence in our home and make sure there's always something to do.

I'm one of those annoying people who bounce out of bed in the morning with a smile on their face and walk to the beach to see the sunrise. I sleep really well, I eat healthily, I meditate and I have lots of energy. See what I mean? Annoying. That's not to say I don't have my bad days, but you'll soon find out my tricks for living this way.

Our home is an old 1960s showhome, known to some as The Rose Garden. It's housed many different people, hosted numerous flamboyant gatherings, and is the mini-suburban-homestead of my childhood dreams. When I'm not sitting in my office at the beloved Rose Garden writing blog posts, columns for media platforms, presenting online to businesses, consulting through zoom, or creating social media content, I am out speaking to community groups or businesses, attending exciting events or hosting my own. On the weekends you'll find Tim pottering by the passionfruit vine while I host a virtual workshop on how to make kombucha in our kitchen. On a rare weekend 'off', I'll tend to my wild vegetable garden and read a book in the sun. I might darn my socks while watching Netflix, then snuggle up in front of our outdoor fire with friends.

Throughout this book I'll be telling a lot of personal stories and sharing my thoughts around important topics. It's important that you know who I am and where these ideologies come from.

I'll start from, roughly, the beginning.

Growing up

For the first sixteen-and-a-half years of my life, I wanted to be a vet. I adored animals, loved science and my dad and grandfather were vets. Our house was a zoo: rats, birds, rabbits, cats, dogs and the occasional tadpole or fish. Under Dad's tutelage, my speciality was treating sick birds brought to us when storms hit or tides washed baby blue penguins onto the shore.

We lived in the worst house on the best street, a 'bach' my parents slowly renovated, which was also, coincidentally, 300 metres from the beach. As a family of five in a three-bedroom house with one small bathroom that housed the shower, toilet and sink, we lived in relatively close proximity. We had to get an extra cabin plopped on our lawn because my older brother, Isaac, literally outgrew his bedroom as he hit six foot four.

As a kid, I did all the clichéd things that would be the making of an eco-inspirer and sustainability educator. I made moss gardens with my nana. I was part of the 'Wild Flower Society' and filled our entire garden with all sorts of flowers, depending on the season. I walked on the beach in the mornings and evenings with Mum and our dog. We also had constant fun. We went on night-time hikes, had dance parties after dinner, and Dad would dress up as 'Uncle Steve' and arrive on our doorstep wearing a blonde wig and glasses for a hilarious evening. My younger sister, Georgia, and I were constantly dressed up in costumes and diligently tending to our imaginary horses.

Most nights growing up, as I went off to sleep I watched Dad reading through the slightly open bedroom door, or listened to my mum play the cello. Sometimes both. Dad read us books before bed every night, and Mum made a lot of our food from scratch. The television was never in the main lounge room and screens were not allowed on Sundays. Sometimes we'd pick Dad up from the beach after he commuted across the bay on his windsurfer, other times I'd spend days at his vet clinic 'helping' with the animals.

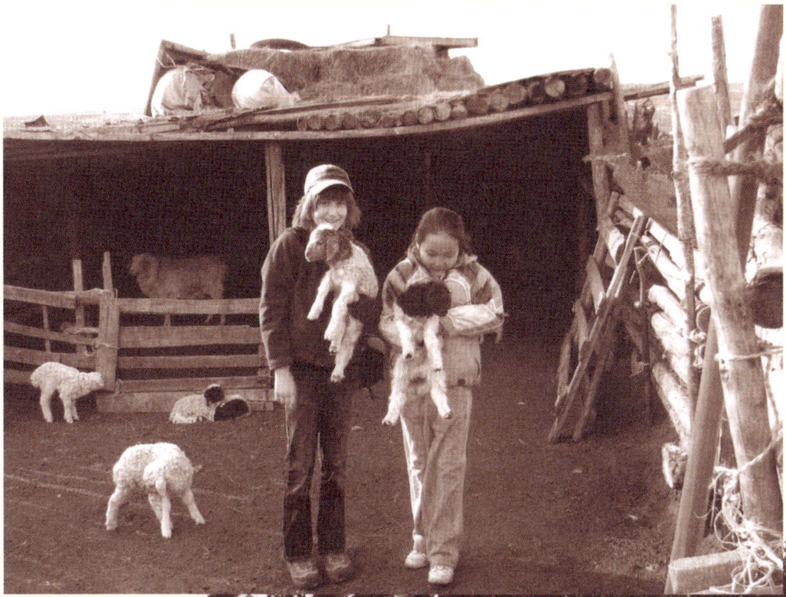

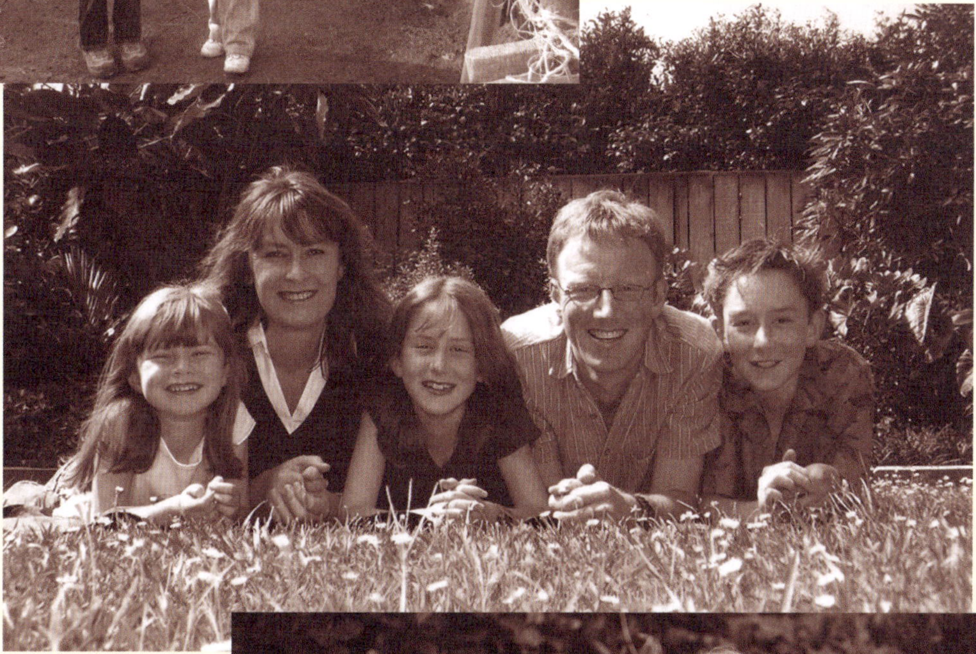

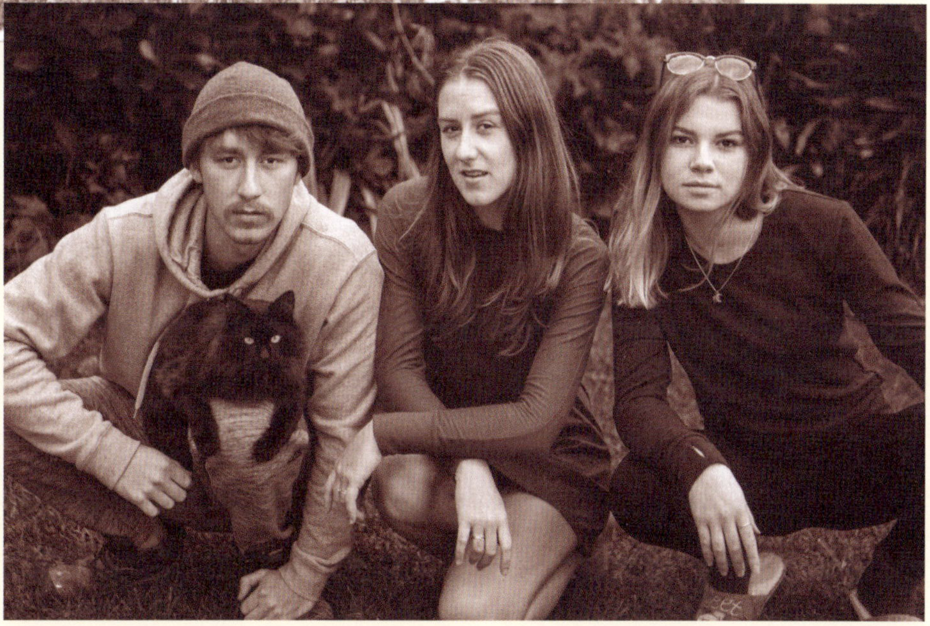

Top: Life in Mongolia.

Middle: With the family.

Bottom: Isaac, me and Georgia.

Responsibility addict

I started my first business when I was eight years old; it was called 'Kate Care'. I had a logo, brochures and an incredibly sophisticated lined journal where I kept my accounts in order.

My services included feeding cats, collecting mail, walking dogs, mowing lawns and watering plants. I remember one summer, when I was around eleven years old, I had the keys to about ten homes in my area for doing all sorts of jobs while the owners were away. These homes were mansions, holding huge responsibilities. I adored it. Responsibility makes my heart hum, and that was one of the first moments I remember patting myself on the back and acknowledging my entrepreneurship.

Now that I reflect on it, giving an eleven-year-old the keys to your house while you're away for several weeks seems explicitly unwise. But I wasn't like most eleven-year-olds. It was rare that I would connect with people of my own age; I found myself craving the company of my parents' friends far more than my own. Now I am married to a man seven years older than me and some of my current best mates experienced life for many years before I was born.

When I was fourteen years old I managed a holiday home. I cleaned it from top to bottom, and managed the people who came to stay. When the owner, Arielle, rented out the house to a permanent renter, she came by to pick up the keys and conclude our working arrangement. I gave her back the keys, and in return Arielle gave me life advice that I will never forget: 'Kate, you must remember to stop and smell the roses.'

I'm a responsibility addict. I am obsessed with lists and achievements. My time management and planning abilities are my greatest strengths, but they also come with the cost of rarely being in the moment. Arielle noticed this, and her advice is a lesson I remind myself of regularly.

Mongolia

I had to dedicate a specific section for this part of my life. There's a reason I have a tattoo in another language on my arm.

When I was nine years old, my family lived in Mongolia for a year and a half, and it permanently changed who I am — for the better. In case you don't know where Mongolia is (I didn't), it's the country wedged between Russia and China. My dad worked there as a volunteer vet, teaching other vets, and my mum homeschooled me and my siblings. Even though we were only there for a short time, I was obsessed with the country. I learnt some of the language, I became fascinated with the culture, and I went on lots of adventures with Dad when he worked outside the city. I didn't want to leave.

As a kid from an isolated and privileged part of the world, spending time living in a country like Mongolia was formative, to say the least. Walking to the shops involved being aware of pickpockets and fearing for your life when you crossed a road. We were homeschooled alongside others from all over the world and suddenly exposed to a lifestyle completely opposite to our sheltered lives in Aotearoa New Zealand. One day, my brother walked my sister to a friend's house only 200 metres away and had to karate-chop the arm of a man who grabbed my sister's forearm. Isaac dragged Georgia away and they ran. My mum's fanny pack was slit open with a knife as we walked through a crowd at a festival. Pedestrian crossings were less safe to walk over than just crossing the road.

Basic needs were also harder to get. Even though we lived in an apartment in the capital city, most of the time we bathed in a bucket. We'd boil the kettle several times to get hot water, and washing wasn't an everyday thing. We had modern toilets in our home, but when we travelled in the countryside, I quickly learnt how to pee in a bush. With Mongolia being ranked as having some of the worst toilets in the world and the alternative being a sketchy long drop (essentially a hole in the ground with two slats to stand on), this skill came in handy. It still does!

In summary, Mongolia taught me to grow up quickly. My worldview was immediately changed and challenged. I became aware of our global community, I was encouraged to think differently and it was one of the experiences that started my passion for living sustainably.

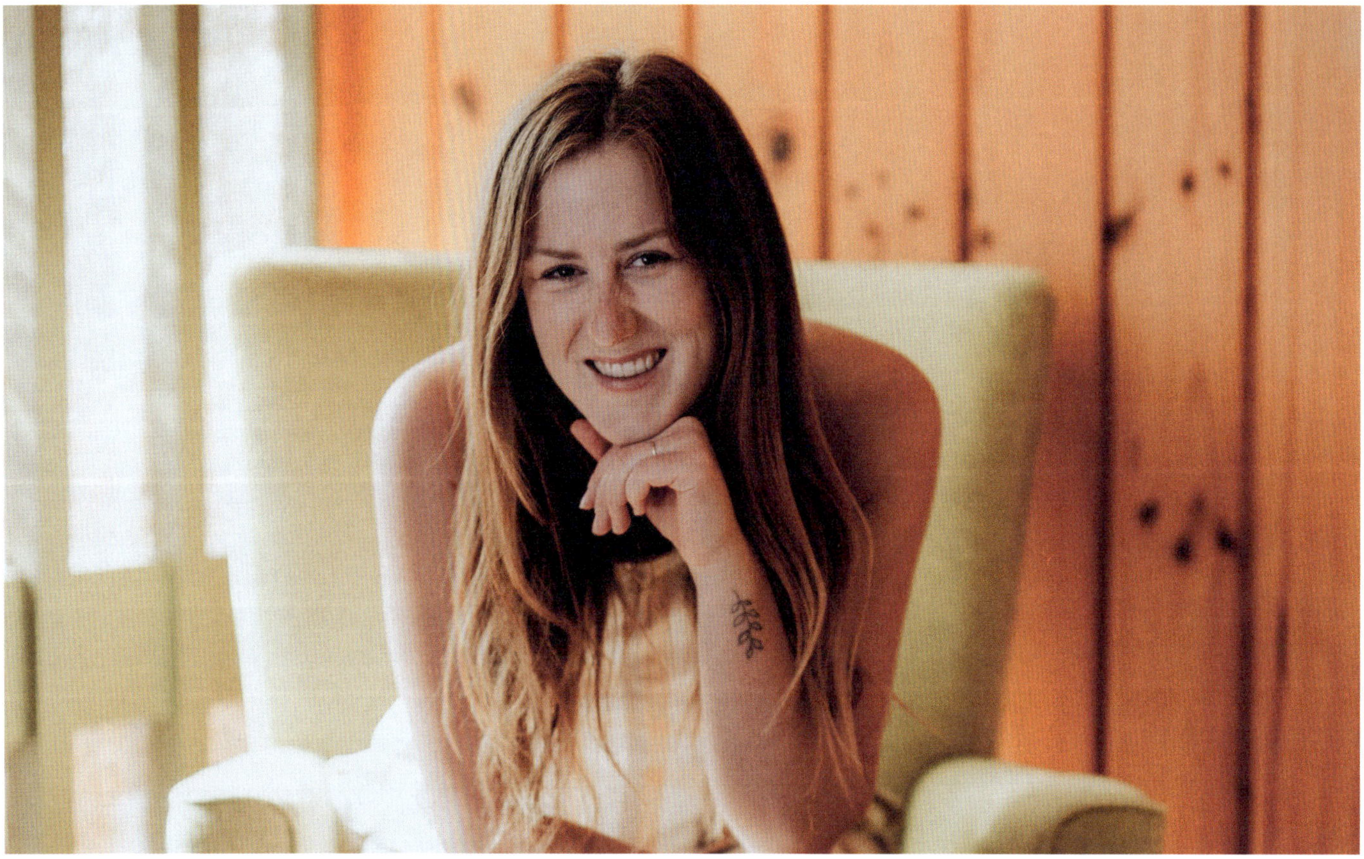

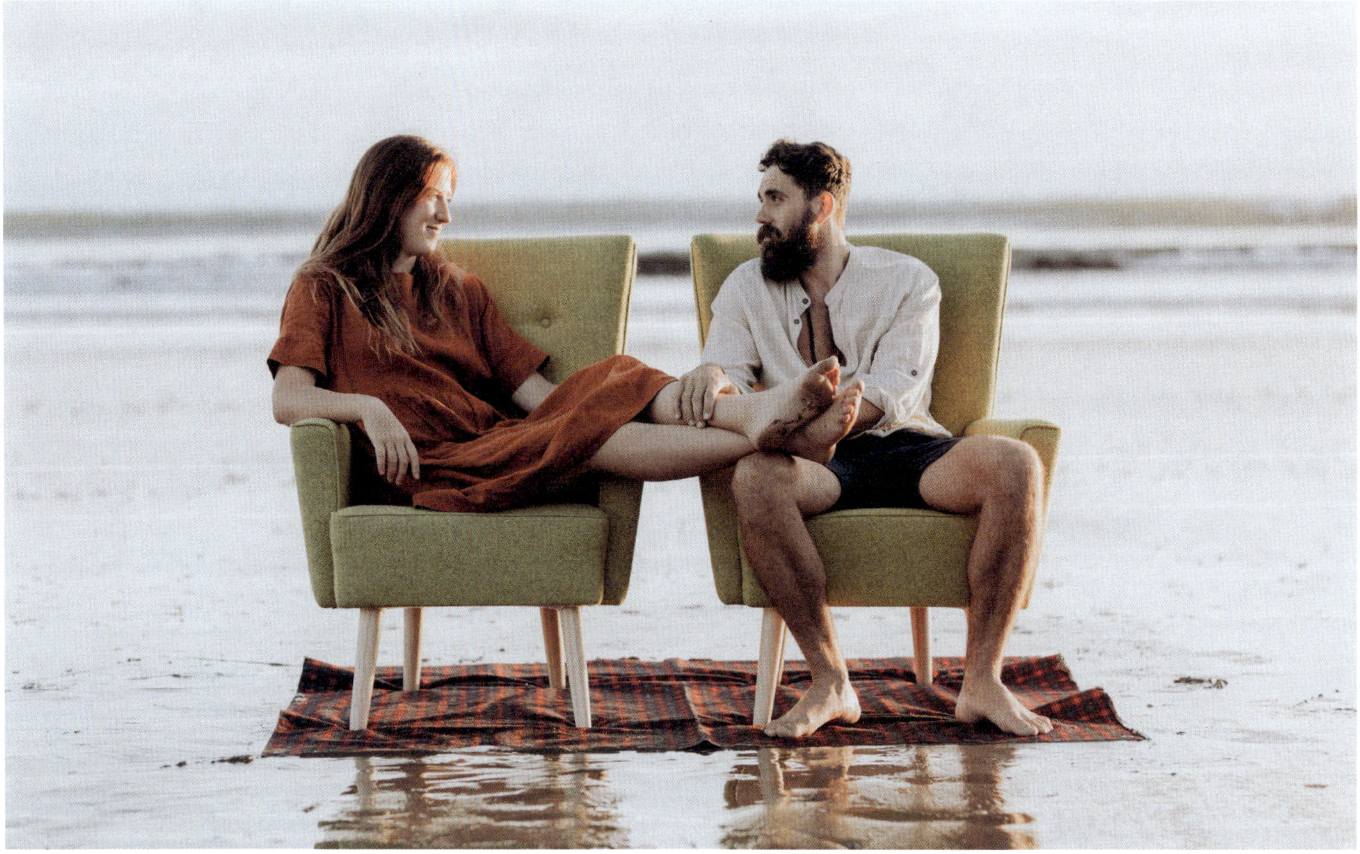

Study, work and falling in love

With my plans to be a vet strongly rooted in my mind, I took all the sciences at school. I loved and aced them. I was also the top of my fabric cohort, the only Pākehā girl in the Māori-language class, and generally treated school like my kingdom. I had close relationships with my teachers and knew at least a few people from each clique. Even the cool kids. School sucks for many students; for me it was heaven on earth.

In 2013, at the age of sixteen, I came to realise there were more options than being a vet. I also met Tim, and as friends we started playing music together at pubs, weddings and markets. Although I loved high school, it got to the point where someone would ask me what I did, and I would describe my work as a nanny and a musician, then somewhere in the mix remember I was still a high-school student. I was sixteen years old and waltzing into bars without any questioning because I was paired with a bearded man and a guitar.

With permission and support from my high-school principal, I left school a year early to study business psychology at Massey University. Around this time I also realised the guy playing music beside me had become more than my best mate; he turned into my boyfriend.

My three years as a university student involved early-morning nannying and late-night social events, fuelled by power naps. I also visited Ireland for five months on study exchange and spent one and a half months travelling around Europe on my way home.

After I graduated in 2016, I moved straight into the role of office culture and marketing coordinator at an IT company in Auckland city. I was the chick who flew into work with a smile and a brightly coloured vintage skirt, with a mission to make the IT nerds work more sustainably. I ran events, turned the storage room into a yoga studio, and thrived on the challenge of making the staff not simply turn up to work, but love their working environment. Even though the two-hours-per-day commute was gruelling, as an extrovert in an office of 120 staff, I flourished.

The beginning of Ethically Kate

While this was all happening, Ethically Kate was emerging.

In August 2015, I made my way to my boyfriend's house (The Rose Garden!) to watch a documentary with friends. A casual evening, nothing unusual. I had no clue that it was the evening that would completely change the trajectory of my life.

I sat, listened and cried as I realised one of my favourite things (fashion) was doing major damage to the planet I adored. When I woke up the next day, I made the decision to purchase only clothes that I knew were made fairly, with sustainable fabrics, and that were a need — not just a want.

Turns out, finding transparency in fashion supply-chains is harder than it sounds, so I went digging. I became a highly conscious and active consumer. I emailed brands, I spent hours on Google (though now I use a more sustainable search engine called Ecosia), I read audits and reports, and I slowly reconstructed my understanding of clothing. No longer did I salivate over bargain bins. My love of second-hand shops grew and my hatred of malls ballooned.

The more I learnt, the more devastated I was that fast fashion wasn't being talked about. Some of the most caring and kind people in my life had no idea of the industry they were endorsing every time they put on their clothes in the morning. It was an injustice. And one I wasn't okay walking away from.

As a constant communicator, I needed a platform to get this information out. Even though I'd only dabbled in social media, I took to Instagram. I tagged the sustainable brands I was beginning to love. I messaged the fast-fashion companies demanding they do better. I spoke about what I was learning, in the hope that others would learn with me too.

And boy they did.

I didn't realise it at the time, but this was the birth of my business, Ethically Kate, and the start of what I do now.

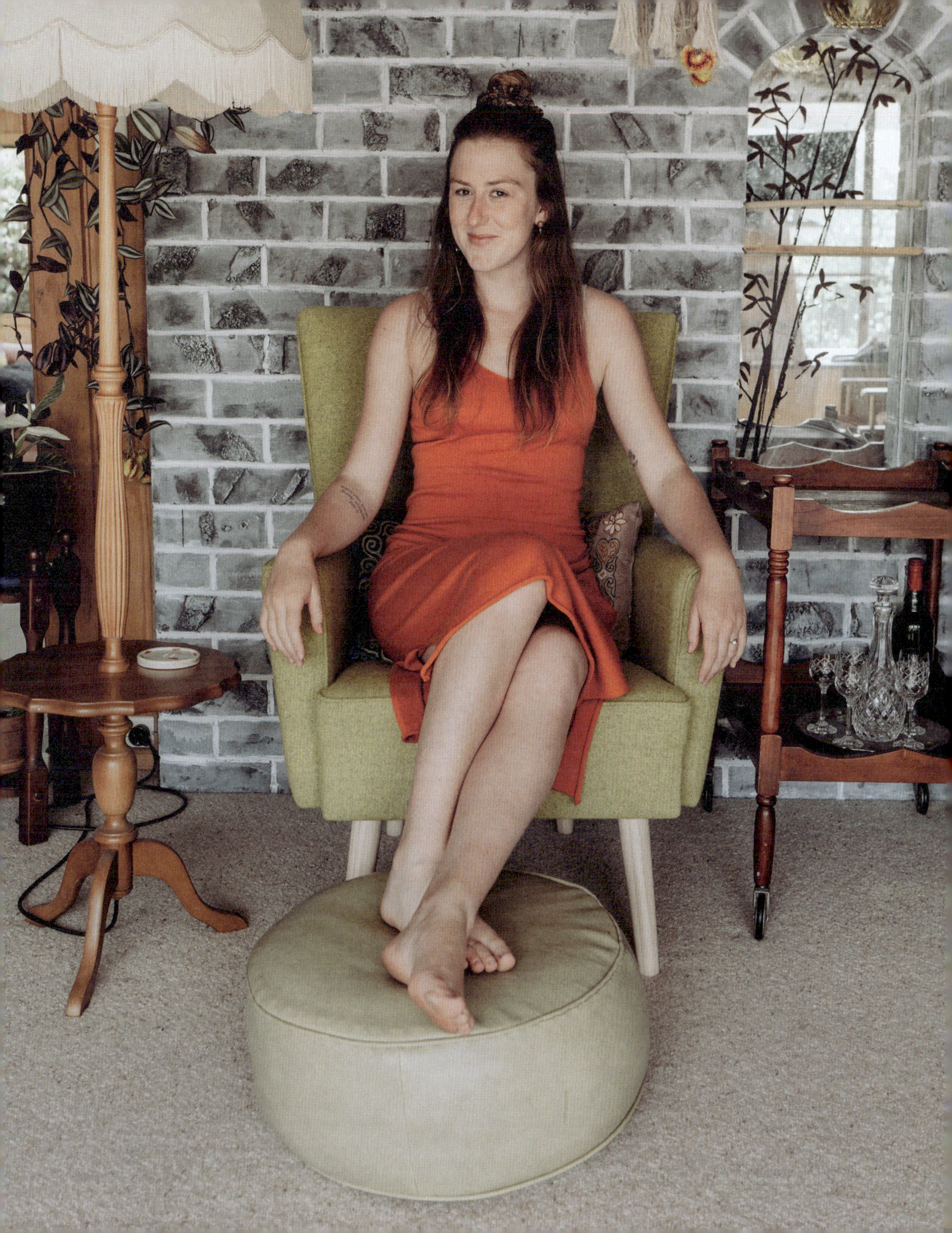

Doing my own thing

In 2017, I committed to working for myself. To date, this was the biggest year of my life. I started two businesses. Got married. Bought a house. Honeymooned in Myanmar. Travelled to India.

I realised that to keep going with what I'd started, something had to quit. So, in September of that year I stopped working for someone else and went out on my own. At the time I had no idea how big this move was. People often ask me 'How do you know when it's the right time to leave a job and work for yourself?' But I can't really answer that question; I just did it.

The business that sucked most out of me at this stage, and one of the main reasons for leaving my office job, was my in-home childcare business. I had around 23 part-time staff who I sent out to babysit in the evenings, nanny during the day, drop off kids at school and everything else in between. I worked 24/7. At any point in time, my friends would know I might leave a party to cover a shift, walk out of the room to take a call (especially on busy Saturday nights when parents wanted to party), or generally stare at my phone while promising I wasn't scrolling Instagram (sometimes I was, if I'm honest).

Pair this responsibility with freelance writing, blogging and running my swiftly growing Instagram account, and you have a hectic life with little capacity for flexibility or anything to break down.

There are times I wish I'd stuck to growing maybe just one business, or stayed at my office job and focused on my friends and family. But I don't regret a thing. The knowledge that came from diving in was phenomenal and could only have been learnt on the job.

Two years later, in 2019, I sold my in-home childcare business for $15,000 and made a profit of $250, which we spent on a celebratory dinner. I launched full time into freelance writing, blogging, Instagramming and running sustainable businesses' social media accounts. I was writing upwards of twenty articles a month for sustainable news hubs and businesses, while trying to develop a website of my own. I began attending events like New Zealand Fashion Week, the likelihood of random people stopping me in the street grew dramatically, the invites to PR events grew and my work as a content creator was organically blossoming.

Taking it to the next level

In 2020, I dropped my social media clients, focused on Ethically Kate and decided I'd get more out and about. As an in-person person, I hated the amount of time I spent on my phone as a social media manager. I needed people! I toured the country in an e-Golf sponsored by Volkswagen, and hosted eleven events around Aotearoa New Zealand to inspire people to live more sustainably. I spent six weeks on the road speaking to over 630 people; planning, hosting, coordinating, catering and running all the events on my own, capturing content along the way, and posting about every single moment of it. It was some of the best weeks of my entire life.

The most special part was meeting people I had known online for years. We hugged, we laughed and we looked at each other funny, having never seen each other without a screen between us.

What struck me most when I talked to people wasn't necessarily the 'Thank you, Kate — you've inspired me to reduce my waste and buy ethical fashion!' comments. It was the 'I feel so much happier living more sustainably', or the 'I constantly giggle when following you online', or the 'You bring me joy'. Ultimately, I want to make people happy. The world lacks laughter and smiles. There is so much to be happy about, but instead we're in robotic jobs, driving to work listening to negative news, ignoring our neighbours, and doing the same thing every freaking day of the week. This way of life is destroying us, and, in turn, our environment.

I want to help people thrive. And I don't just think, I *know* that living more sustainably is the answer to that. Living with values that respect people and the planet. Being aware of our impact on other people and our environment. Understanding that we are part of a global community.

I'm often asked how I respond to climate-crisis deniers. To them, I say 'I hope you're right; I hope the planet is actually okay! But, even if you are right, I will still live this way. Because it's better. In every single way possible.'

So there you have it. That's me in a few pages, and you're about to get to know me and the intimate happenings of my life a whole lot better.

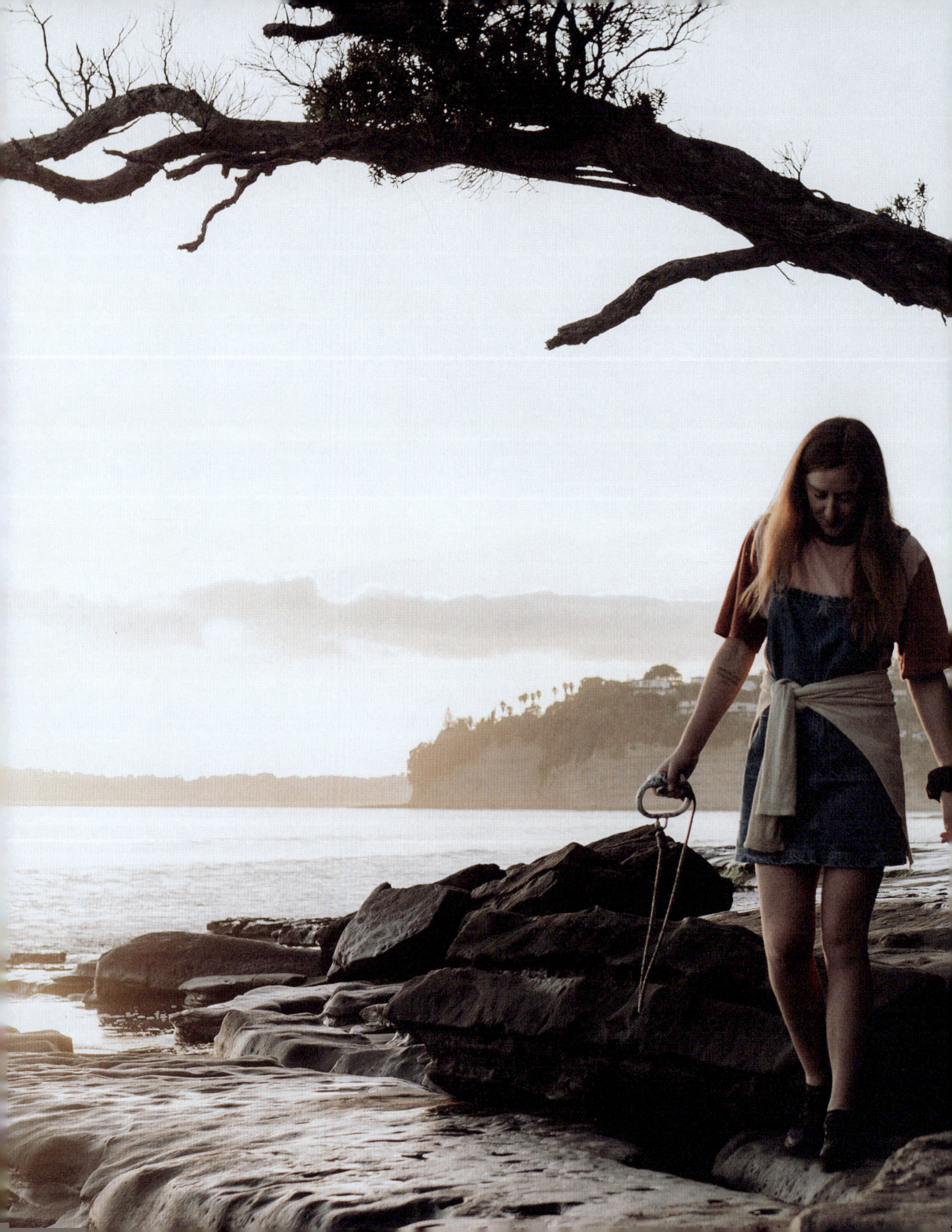

Wellbeing

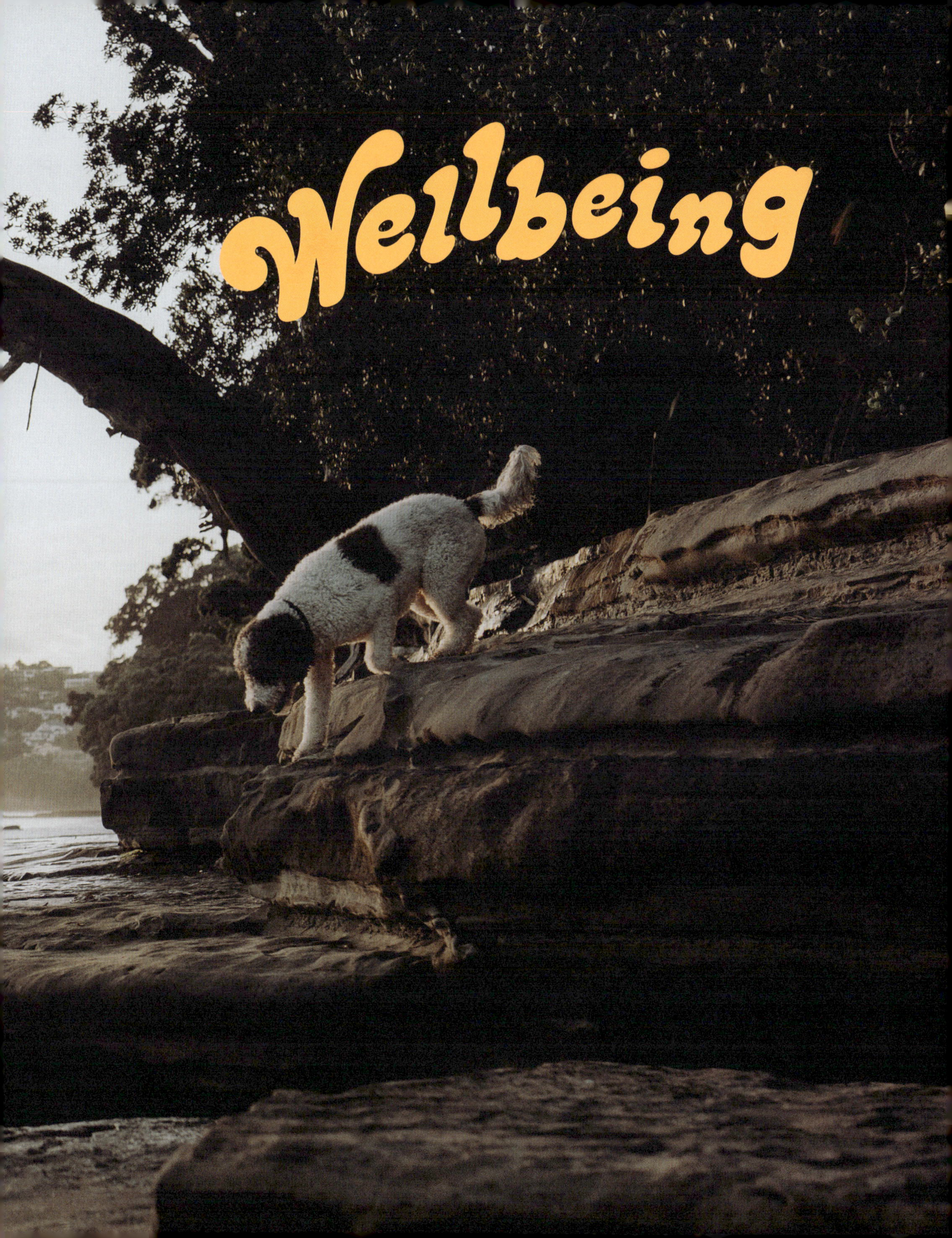

It wasn't until recently that I realised I didn't have to take a bubble bath to care for myself. Screw 'self-care' and what it has become! It's a tainted term that makes me think of Instagram influencers in white robes surrounded by pink-themed platters and a million toxic-smelling nail polishes that will make them run out of the room coughing — only after they've taken the perfect selfie. I love caring for myself, but the self-care movement has boxed itself into a corner filled with waste and unattainable experiences.

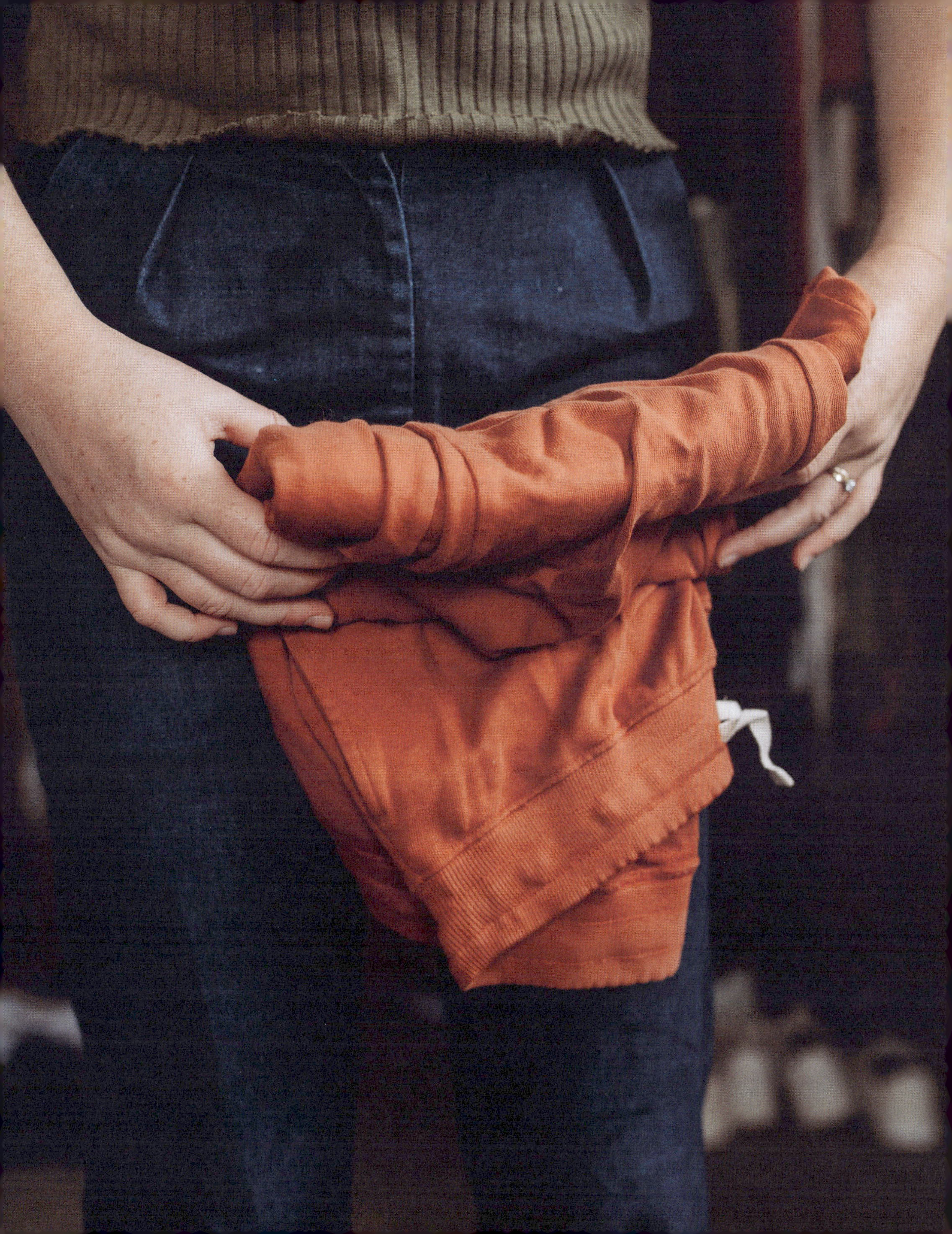

To me, self-care looks like making a meal from scratch, cleaning my house, reading a book, going for a run or doing the washing. Organising my wardrobe, tending to my house plants, deep cleaning the kitchen sink, refilling my hand soaps or washing my hair. With these things in mind, 'self-compassion' sounds better to me. Yet even then, when you're trying to live more sustainably, self-compassion seems like a world away from the 'right thing to do'.

I've watched sustainable-living enthusiasts burn themselves into the ground because they're too focused on 'saving the world' and looking after other people to remember they have to put their own oxygen mask on first. There's not many people I know who have worked in sustainability and not experienced a dramatic burnout. The type of burnout that comes from working 24/7 for the planet and its people, while forgetting they're a person too and they deserve to enjoy the planet they're fighting for. The story we're all told is if you're not being a martyr and giving up everything that brings you joy, you're not doing sustainable living right.

Bullshit.

If all the sustainable companies I've seen collapse in the past few years were run by people who realised the importance of sustaining themselves, those brilliant (and positively world-changing!) organisations may still be alive. If wellbeing was promoted as an essential part of life rather than a sin in the volunteer and charity space, more volunteers would have turned up to that tree-planting day, fewer sustainable entities would go bankrupt, and a greater abundance of people would be attracted to work in a role that benefits the planet and its people.

It's ironic to burn yourself out while fighting for the environment. You are part of the environment, not separate from it.

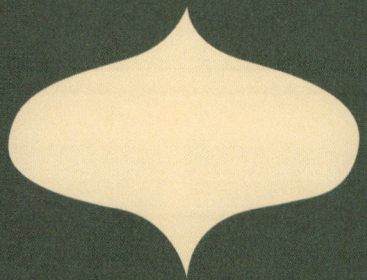

With this in mind, I want to firstly give you permission to be selfish. Living life more sustainably doesn't mean you have to forget who you are, sign a pledge of allegiance to wearing potato sacks, give up your weekends to volunteering, and never have a bath again because it consumes too much water. Looking after your own wellbeing is not only non-negotiable for a joy-filled life; it's fundamental to doing good. After all, a burnt-out person is more likely to take the car instead of walking to their friend's house two kilometres down the road. I say these words as if I am the master of relaxation. On the contrary, I've learnt these lessons the hard way and I continue to relearn their truth.

When I was thirteen I was diagnosed with chronic fatigue syndrome and spent a few years battling overwhelming exhaustion. I'm still advised to monitor my exertion so it doesn't return. As a sixteen-year-old, I was completing high school, house-sitting permanently, working in childcare, playing gigs and falling in love with my now husband. I burnt myself out and developed shingles; a reactivated version of chickenpox that is common in people with weakened immune systems, predominantly found in those aged 65 and above. I never want to repeat those experiences, and I wouldn't want you to go through that either. Every time I feel my wellbeing priorities slip, I'm reminded of the emotional and physical pain.

It's important to realise that to use your power and privilege to support the most vulnerable, you need to prioritise your wellbeing. Too often I see people shut off because it's all too much. It's heavy and it's paralysing because you can't fix it all, so you do nothing.

You can, and you must, prioritise your own wellbeing if you want to live more sustainably. That's why this chapter comes early on, before we get into the nitty gritty of how to make more sustainable choices around things like food and clothes. Following are some habits to sustain wellbeing.

'And, no matter how disturbing the present and future may appear, we have neither the time nor the luxury to shut down emotionally, especially those of us who live in countries where the climate crisis is a daily reality.'
— Vanessa Nakate, climate justice activist, *A Bigger Picture*

Carry out simple things differently

To foster wellbeing and resilience, spark my creativity and 'spice things up', I have a habit of attempting to do everyday things in different ways. Doing this brings laughter, helps with problem-solving in other areas of your life, opens your mind to new ideas, and sometimes means you discover even better ways of living. Some things to try:

- brush your teeth with your opposite hand
- shower in the dark (this helps strengthen your 'touch' sense instead of relying on your sight)
- drink wine in a mug (this idea is from my friend Artur)
- skip somewhere instead of walking
- sleep upside down (more details on page 131)
- change your morning beverage
- swap your knife and fork to different hands
- rearrange the furniture in your home
- take a different route to work
- open doors and cupboards with your non-dominant hand.

Other ways I practise self-compassion include:

- drinking at least 2 litres of water every day
- lying on my Shakti mat before bed
- spending time naked (I've heard that an hour a day is optimum naked time)
- making a meal slowly
- regularly listening to music I love
- taking the stairs instead of the elevator or escalator (unless it's unreasonable, e.g. 25 flights).

Set boundaries around phone usage

When my health is at its worst, either mentally or physically, I know my screen time has contributed. Setting strong phone use perimeters is something I have yet to fully master, but I am proud to say I've put my phone on charge in another room for several years. I don't check it first thing in the morning, and I try my best to put it on charge at least an hour before I hop into bed. It's easy in this digital world to forget about your immediate reality. Less time online means more time for my community.

    A challenge for you: turn your phone off an hour before bed, and charge it in another room. Turn your phone back on after being awake for at least one hour. Social media-free weekends are often relaxing too.

    Additionally, set guidelines for your phone use. Most phones record your usage and allow you to set time limits for different apps. Use these to set healthy boundaries so you don't fall down the rabbit-hole of phone addiction.

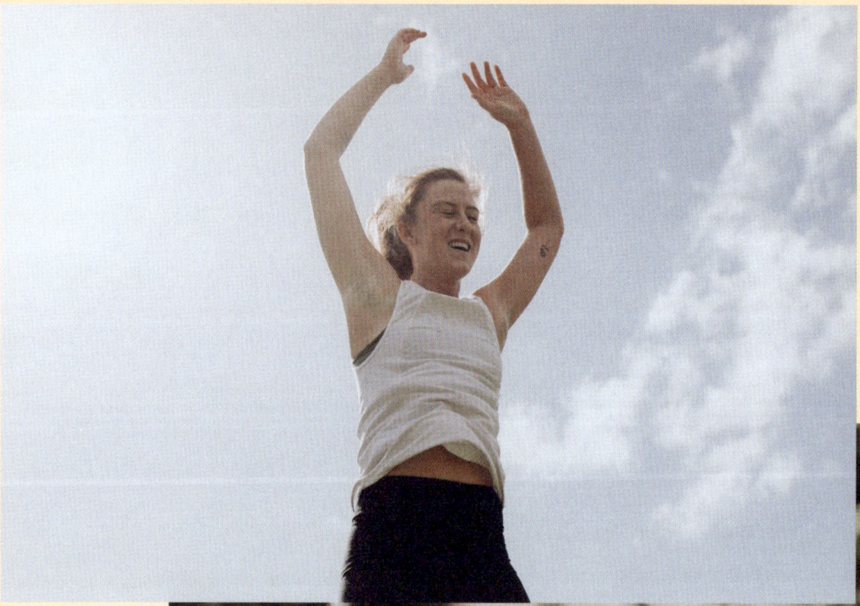
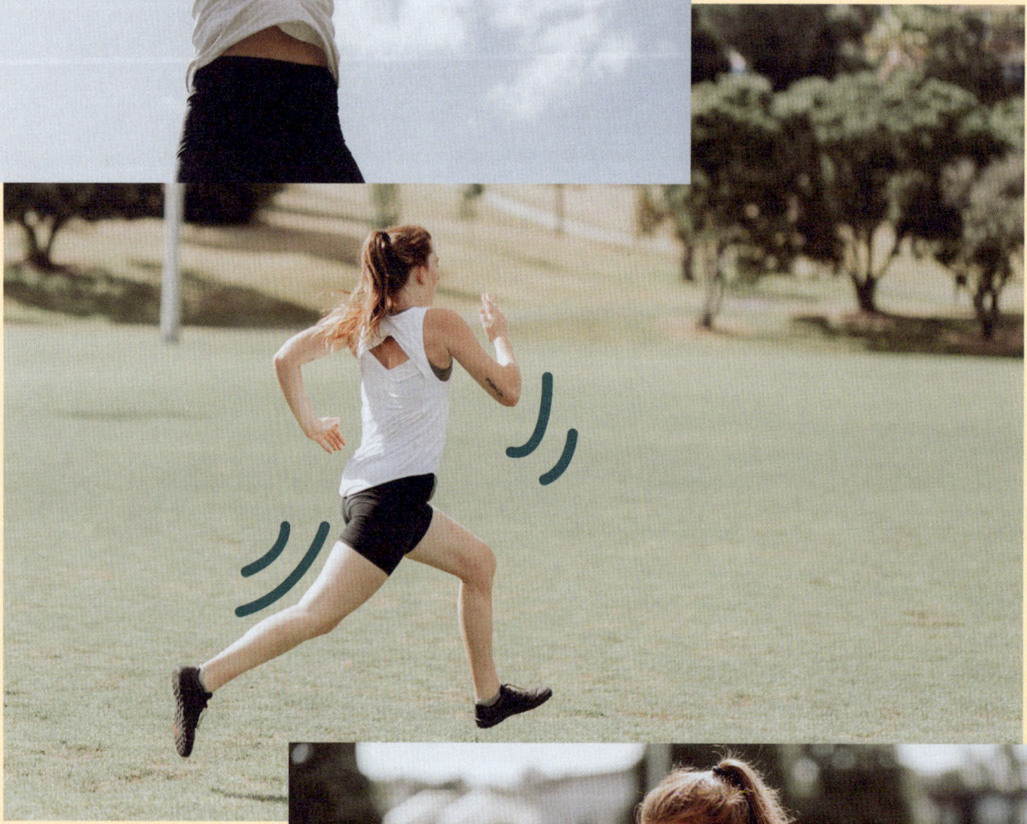
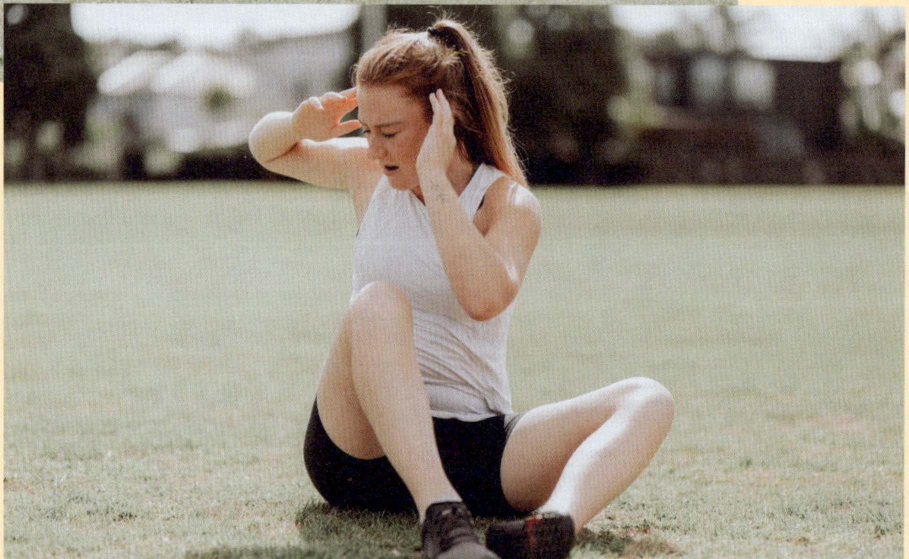

Exercise

Forget that marathon, feel free to laugh at 6am runners while you're still in bed, and don't think you have to do a burpee with me. Exercise is a loaded word, and the way the world goes about promoting it often makes me feel yucky. Let's use a better one.

Exercise. Movement

Movement is my personal favourite way to support my wellbeing. It reinforces my ability to live more sustainably in a world that doesn't always make things like low-waste living easy. When I don't move, I lose physical and mental momentum. I become stagnant. I reach for convenience (which often comes wrapped in waste), and I lose joy.

Over the years, my forms of movement have varied. I ebb and flow between movement styles, but no matter what, I am always moving, even if it's just a little shoulder jiggle when a movie soundtrack is good.

Walking

Every morning, I walk. Mainly because I have a dog, but also because it's a lifesaver. Moving at the same time every morning sets off the day. I have space to think (I never walk with headphones), and I am aware of my natural surroundings.

High Intensity Training (HIT)

Gosh, I love a short and sharp burst of movement. Half an hour of constant movement is addictive. Squats, sit-ups, push-ups, sprints, burpees — any type of movement that I am feeling that day. A common HIT for Tim and I looks like this:

- slow run to warm up
- 50–100 burpees
- 3 sprints around a rugby field (short breathing break in between)
- 15 sit-ups
- 30 side sit-ups (15 right, 15 left)
- 3 one-minute planks.

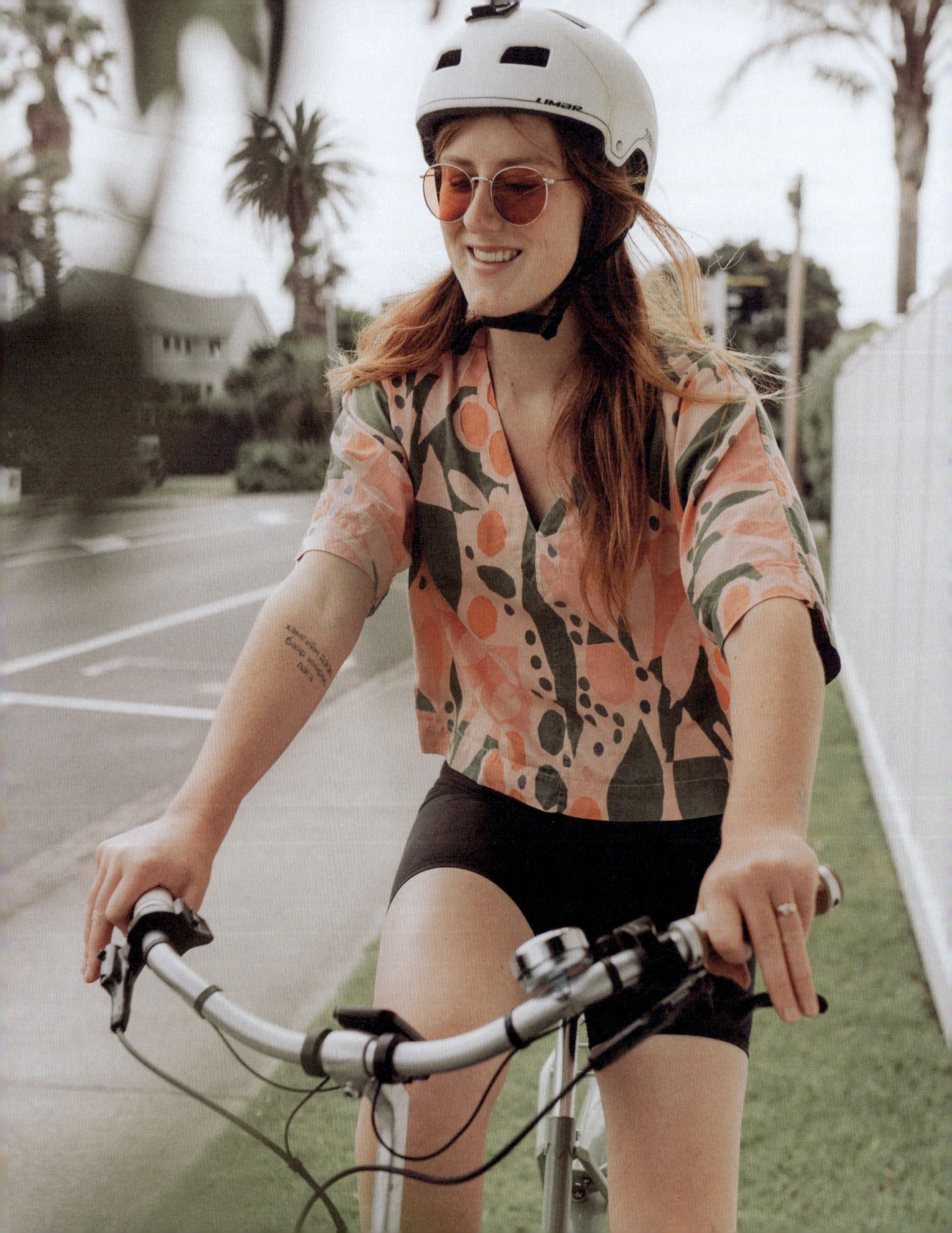
LIMAR

Yoga

Some months I practice yoga daily. Others, twice a month. I ebb and flow as a 'yogi' and feel dramatic differences in my overall health when yoga disappears from my routine. After attending a class for several years and establishing an understanding of the classic movements, I find free YouTube videos helpful guides so my brain doesn't have to think about what's next. When I don't do yoga, things like hanging out the washing and getting up from the floor are more difficult. I don't practise yoga with the intent of doing the splits or learning party tricks; for me, it's a form of movement for the mind and the body that translates into the ease and comfort of everyday life.

Stretching

Stretching can look like lying on the floor and reaching your hands above your head. It could be an attempt to touch your toes every day, or stretching your calves by pushing against your kitchen bench while you wait for dinner to cook.

If you struggle with stretching time or capacity, just do this one stretch (encouraged by my physio friend, Bart): stand with your feet shoulder-width apart with palms gently on your lower back. Slowly, without bending your knees, stretch backward as far as possible, while exhaling for 3 seconds. Repeat this two times whenever you're waiting for a bus, brewing a cup of tea or in line for the toilet.

I stretch constantly throughout the day. This is made possible by my dynamic desk![1] My Limber desk moves up and down and is built on the philosophy of 'the best posture is the next posture'. I sit on the floor, kneel on a stool, stand, squat and stretch during every pose. I haven't had a chair in my office since 2019 and I don't miss it!

Dancing

Dancing is my daily tonic. I dance most mornings in my office, when I am making dinner, and if ever I feel in a funk. It's an inclusive movement that has no rules or boundaries. Dancing can look like *anything*. There's even a class called 'No Lights No Lycra', where participants meet for an hour of dancing in the dark! One day I hope to have the honour of attending one.

Meditating

Often meditating looks like the opposite of movement, but it's still an intentional moment that I include in my wellbeing arsenal. For me, meditating can look like sitting down cross-legged for 15 minutes, but most commonly it is a simple ritual I carry out when I walk or rest between tasks.

This is an easy meditation that inspires me to remember I have five senses. I know I'm not alone in being guilty of overusing one of my senses and paying for it with fatigue or pain.

First, I breathe deeply for a few moments. Four counts in, six counts out. Next, I go through my five senses and focus on each one for approximately 30 seconds. I ask myself these questions:

- What do you smell? Can you name the smells? Do they remind you of anything?
- What do you feel and touch? Be aware of the clothes hanging off you or the wind on your skin. What is beneath your feet or your butt?
- What do you taste? Can you taste a hint of your toothpaste or the last meal you ate? Is it a pleasant or unpleasant taste?
- What do you hear? Listen to noises in the distance, and then identify noises close to you.
- What do you see? Look around and notice what you weren't previously aware of. Find something small and discreet, then look at something large and obvious.

This meditation only takes around three minutes, but it leaves my body refreshed and my mind grounded.

Meditation of the senses

Smell

Touch

Taste

Hear

See

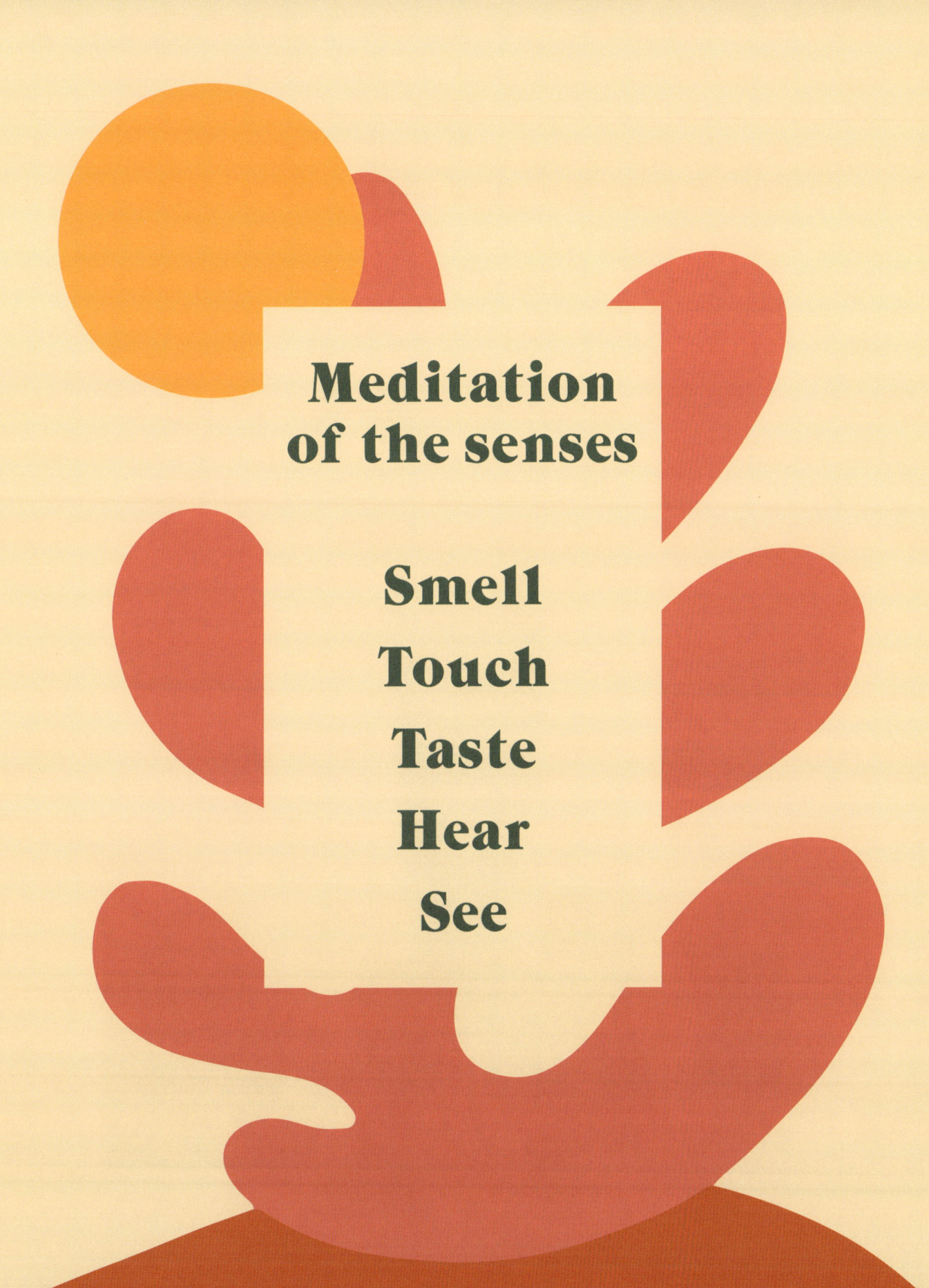

Menstrual cycle

If you menstruate, understanding your cycle and the options for managing your period is a brilliant way of nourishing your wellbeing. If you don't menstruate, it's helpful to understand menstrual cycles to better care for people around you. I began using a menstrual cup because I didn't want to fill up my bathroom rubbish bin with stinky waste, but this sustainable swap turned into one of the best things I've ever done for my wellbeing.

On average, a person who menstruates uses 11,000 single-use period products in their lifetime,[2] filling our landfills and costing people who menstruate *a lot* of money. I'm so happy reusables exist and are flooding into mainstream stores!

When you dive into using a new reusable period product, you learn a lot. I learnt where my cervix is, that everyone has a different shaped and sized cervix, and that my body isn't only part of a cycle once a month when I bleed; the cycle is always happening.

Reading books like Lara Briden's *Period Repair Manual*[3] helped me learn to schedule my life with my cycle in mind and give myself what I need at certain stages. For example, in the past I would get a stunning headache on the first day of my period, but I realised it was the combination of menstruating and strenuous exercise. Now I have a rule: no exercise on the first day of my period. It's not because I'm lazy. It's because I respect myself. The headaches stopped.

Three sustainable options for people who menstruate

	Menstrual cup	Reusable pads/liners	Period underwear
Concept	The cup sits in the vagina just below the cervix, collecting blood	Pads absorb blood in an absorbable fabric	Underwear has a built-in layer of absorbent fabric to absorb blood
How long they last	Medical-grade silicone: 10 years; TPE (thermoplastic elastomer): 3-4 years	Up to 8 years (dependent on care and frequency of use)	Up to 5 years (dependent on care and frequency of use)
How often to change	When full or every 8 hours	When full or every 3-4 hours	When full or every 4-6 hours
Made from	Medical-grade silicone or TPE	Organic cotton, polyester, conventional cotton, often TPU (blend of rubber and plastic) for the waterproof outer layer, hemp or bamboo	Organic cotton, polyester, conventional cotton, nylon, some from hemp or bamboo
How to use	Fold to insert, pinch and pull to remove, then empty, wash and repeat	Pop it on your underwear gusset with the absorbent layer facing up, snap the domes, and put your underwear on	Wear like normal underwear
How to wash	Remove and rinse with cold water during a period. Boil or use a sterilising tablet or tool between periods	Wash out blood with cold water, treat stains with a laundry bar, and put in normal laundry load	Wash out blood with cold water, treat stains with a laundry bar, and put in normal laundry load
My favourite features	Ideal for festivals and hiking. Simply take your drink bottle with you to rinse out your cup, and sterilise it when possible	Cute patterns on the pads to make periods slightly more fun! Also epic for light incontinence, pregnancy and post-partum	Discreet to use, less daunting for new menstruators and helpful if you experience frequent spotting
Money saved over ten years (compared to disposables of the same kind)	$2500	$1930	$2400
Environmental impact over ten years	Only one small cup to landfill (or 3-4 cups if TPE material). Menstrual cups are the most environmentally friendly option	1920 disposable pads saved from landfill!	39.5kg of waste avoided

The four seasons of the menstrual cycle

Winter: menstruation
Slow movements, rest, don't push exercise if you don't feel it, carve out space for yourself, feel empowered to say no to things.

Spring: pre-ovulation
Allow creativity, planning, adventures, new things, schedule that job interview, meet new people, start something new.

Summer: ovulation
Say yes! Host that event, dance heaps, make the most of feeling so alive and use your optimum energy.

Autumn: pre-menstruation
Ride the waves of emotion, set boundaries, change your form of exercise to something more chill, focus on self-care, plan in advance for a lowering of energy.

If someone held me down and said 'You must go back to your old way of living; you can choose only one new habit to keep!' I would answer: 'I'm keeping my menstrual cup.'

Contraception

Sex is amazing, but it also leads to babies, and often that's not the desired outcome. Unlike your high school sex-ed teacher, I won't tell you to *not* have sex or to go on the pill the moment you're old enough. I'd like to think I'm slightly cooler than your sex-ed teacher and I'll tell you to have lots of (safe) sex, but in a way that protects your body and potentially reduces waste too.

I've willingly been a test dummy for many different types of contraceptives. I've tried hormonal implants, I've dabbled with the pill, I've looked into IUDs and I've laughed at abstinence. Just like my menstrual cup experience, I went into contraception research with the purpose of reducing my waste. It turned into a learning experience that made me closer with Tim and more aware of what was going on in my body.

I went off hormonal contraception in early 2019 and I have never looked back. But just because that works for me doesn't mean it works for everyone!

Currently, Tim and I use a mixture of the withdrawal method, condoms and natural family planning. It frustrates me that my favourite thing to do generally involves waste, but I wasn't willing to make a purchase when I found a reusable crystal condom online that made my vagina hurt just looking at it.

Natural family planning

Natural family planning, also known as fertility awareness, has a terrible reputation for not working, though I suggest it's simply misunderstood. I've observed that most people who say 'Yeah, we tried natural family planning and it sucked' while they rock their baby in their arms or wrangle a sticky toddler aren't using the right terminology. That's one of the reasons why it's not used as much.

Natural family planning is a method of birth control that does not involve drugs or internal and external devices. It includes temperature checking, the cervical mucus method and cycle awareness. Natural family planning does not involve having unprotected sex on days when

IUD (copper or hormone)

Rods/implant

Oral contraceptive

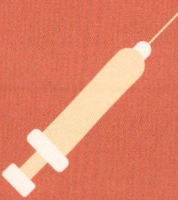

Injection

Hormone patch

Condom

Calendar and thermometer

Diaphragm

a woman is statistically less fertile or when an app tells you it's okay. Natural family planning is taught by a specialist. Having experienced a version of it myself, it's like learning a new language. Every person who has a menstrual cycle has a different one. Mine is different depending on what I've eaten, how stressed I've been, where I am in the world, and how much exercise I've been doing. Natural family planning teaches you to understand your cycle and what is going on every single day, not just the days you bleed. When practised properly and understood by both people in the relationship, it can be as effective as condoms and other contraceptives.[4] Though remember that if you have sex, there is always a chance of conceiving a child, no matter what contraception method you use.

Because we're talking about creating LIFE, I won't pretend I'm an expert and tell you what to do. But I will highlight a few things that I wish I knew when I first started using contraceptives.

- When you're on hormonal contraception, your period isn't your period. It's breakthrough bleeding; you're not actually menstruating.
- The pill can come with all sorts of side effects, including depression and uncontrollable weight gain, so it's definitely worth looking at other options.
- Prioritise your health above your waste-free efforts. Tim and I use condoms that end up in the rubbish bin, but it's better than alternatives and just the way the cookie has to currently crumble!
- Eco condoms generally suck all the fun out of sex and should be used with caution.
- Consider your own health needs before jumping into an option that your friend uses. For example, I have low platelets so I bleed and bruise more easily. I took this into account when considering things like IUDs.
- It takes time to investigate contraception methods, but I promise it's worth it. Knowing all your options and the pros and cons of each provides incredible empowerment and often health benefits in whatever you do choose.

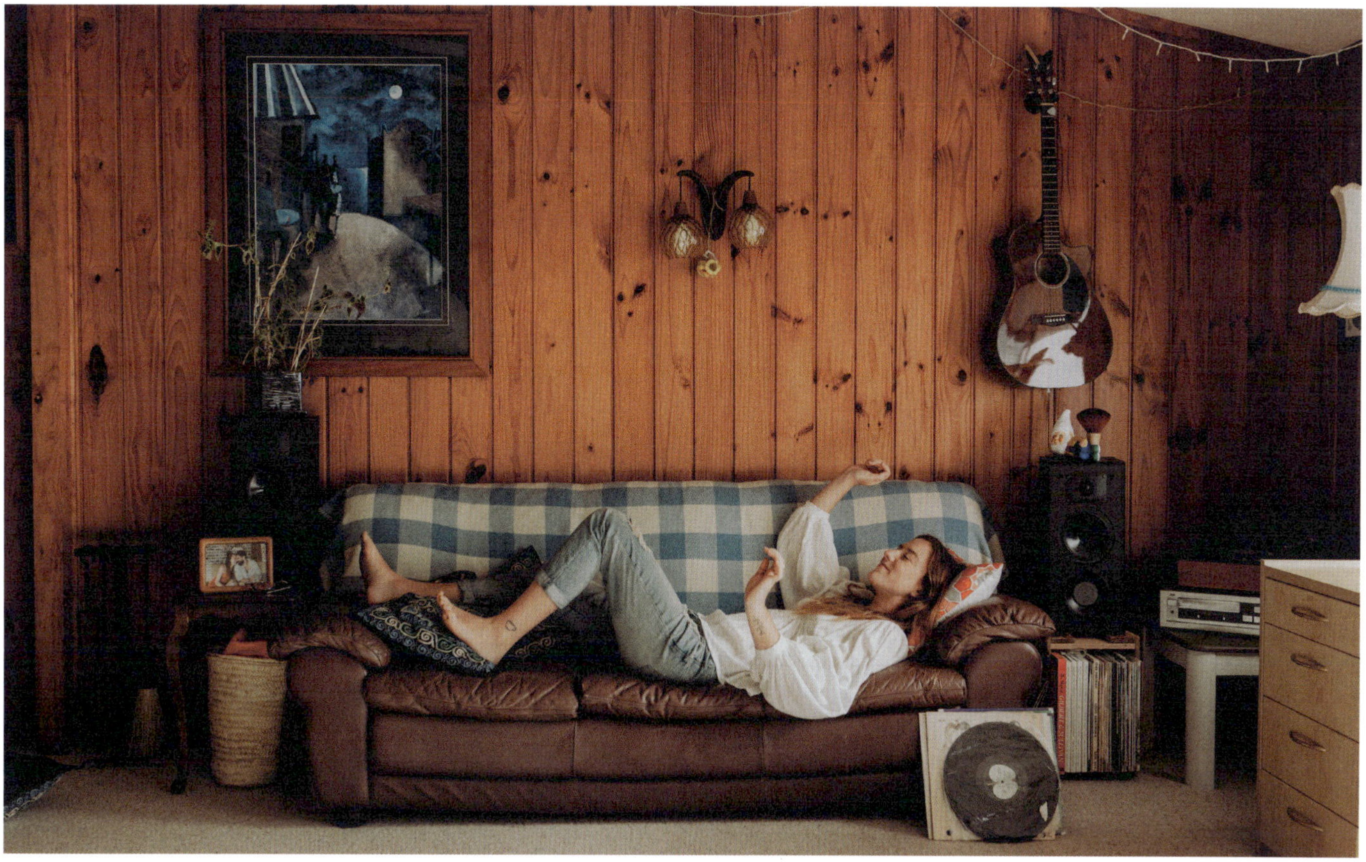

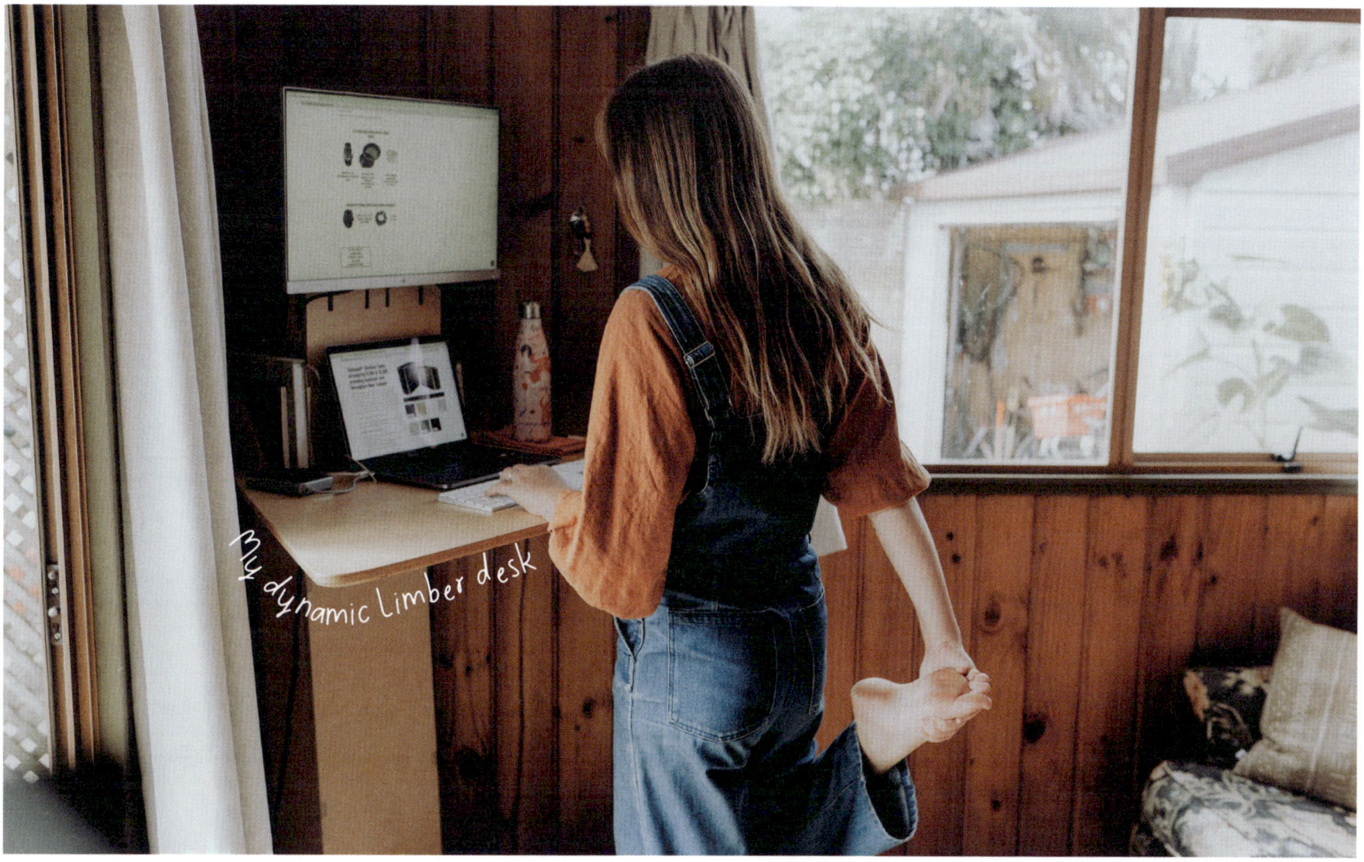
My dynamic Limber desk

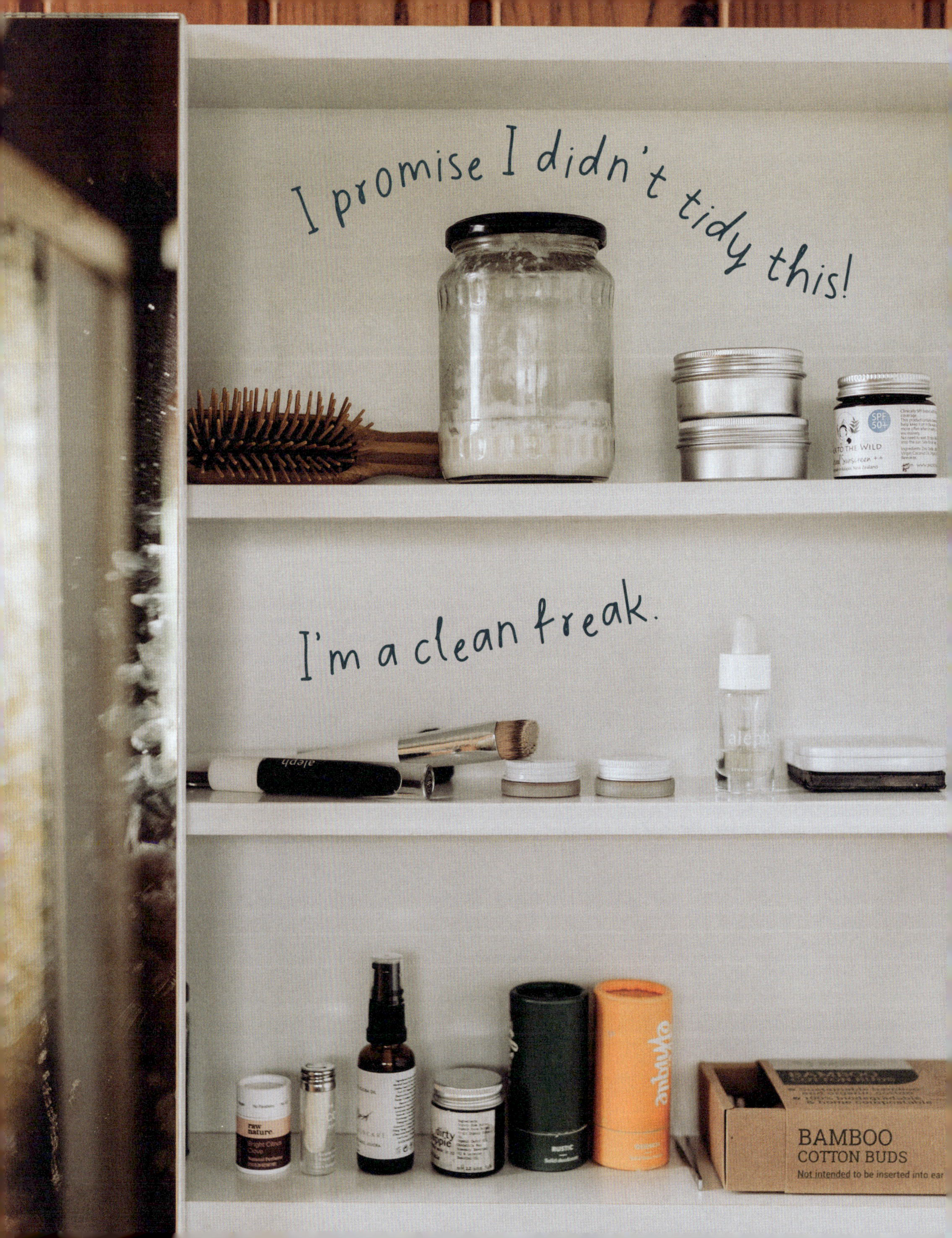
aleph
BAMBOO
COTTON BUDS
Not intended to be inserted into ear

I promise I didn't tidy this!

I'm a clean freak.

My bathroom cabinet

I'm a bathroom minimalist, or at least I try to be. All my essentials can fit in a small toiletry bag when I travel and I screw my face up at any skincare routine that goes beyond a two-step process.

Make-up

Small glass jars with metal lids contain most of my make-up. It's concentrated, so a little goes a long way and they don't clutter my bathroom. The jars can be sent back to where they came from to be reused. I have a dash of eyeshadow in a cardboard slip, and after I've used up my lipsticks that I've had for many years, I'll buy the ones in home compostable tubes.

I tried a sustainably packaged mascara once. It sucked. It took six times longer to apply and I looked like a panda within minutes, so for a long time I used mascara that came in a plastic tube. Now I use a mascara in a glass tube with a plastic lid. I send the packaging back with my jars. Like all rooms in my house, my sustainable bathroom is full of compromise.

If you're keen on making your own make-up, Erin Rhoads has brilliant recipes in her book *Waste Not*.[5] You'll also find a detailed guide to waste-free living in all areas of your life.

Hair

For the majority of my life, my hair was cut in my parents' kitchen by their friend. But over the past few years I've levelled up in the world of beauty and have my long ginger locks cut at a hair salon. Not just any salon, of course! In the southern hemisphere, we're lucky to have Sustainable Salons,[6] a social enterprise that helps its salon members reduce their impact on the planet and invest in local communities. My local salon is part of this group and gives me peace of mind when I visit every six to twelve months that my haircut experience is less wasteful than your average haircut.

At my salon:

- the trimmed hair is turned into hair booms, which soak up oil spills
- when I have lots of long hair cut off, they plait it and cut it into sections to be used for wigs for people who need them
- they have multiple bins for all the different waste streams
- the separated waste is collected by Sustainable Salons and recycled and disposed of responsibly.

Sustainable Salons has a directory where you can find salons in your local area who do these things (and more!) too. I highly recommend jumping onto it, or encouraging your local salon to get involved.

Products (bars)

Everyone knows what a bar of soap looks like, but what if I told you all my beauty products looked like that?

When assessing the waste in my bathroom in 2017, I realised most of it was plastic bottles. I thought these bottles were recycled. Wrong. The global population produces 300 million tonnes of plastic waste annually, and only 9 per cent of plastic is recycled worldwide.[7] Top that off with the amount of water and energy used in creating a bottle, plus the energy needed to transport the bottle and the product from multiple factories to my bathroom, and you've got a huge problem that could be mitigated with a simple, concentrated bar.

My beauty bars are made in Aotearoa New Zealand. They're packaged in home-compostable cardboard boxes, replace up to five bottles of their conventional alternatives and 2% of sales go to amazing charities.

Each bar is:

- palm-oil free
- sustainably made
- made of fair-trade ingredients
- safe for greywater tank systems
- cruelty-free and vegan
- made in a living-wage-certified factory.

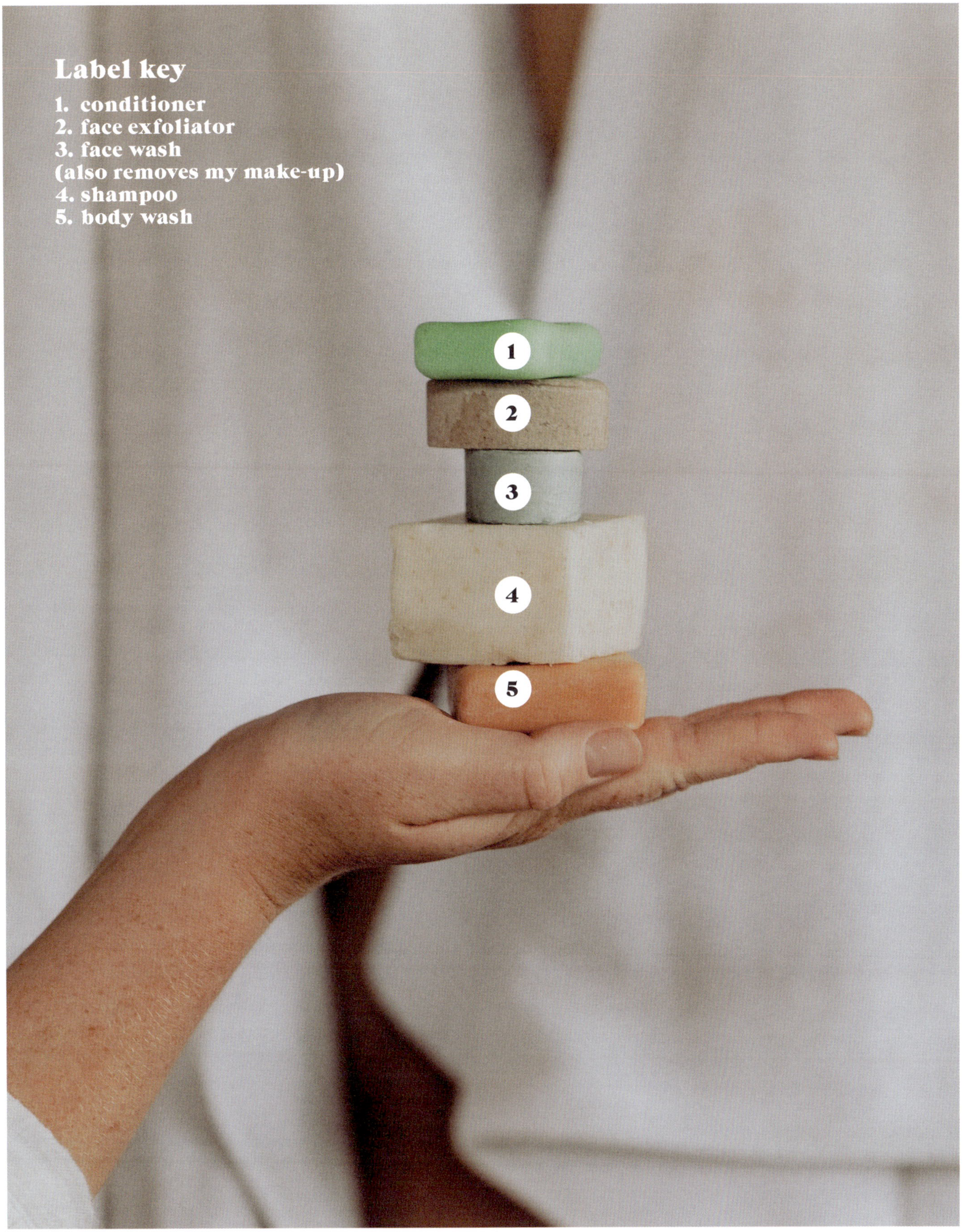
Label key
1. conditioner
2. face exfoliator
3. face wash
(also removes my make-up)
4. shampoo
5. body wash
1
2
3
4
5

We keep a bucket in our shower during summer to water our plants with. Because of the safe ingredients in the bars we use, it's no problem if the product gets into that bucket!

Travelling with bars:

- Dry your bar on a towel after each use.
- Put them in a ventilated and sunny place whenever possible.
- Cut only what you need to take with you.
- Don't leave them in the shower where you're staying (always put them back in your toiletry bag).

Caring for bars:

- If you have a dome shower or your bathroom isn't well ventilated, don't leave them in the shower. Store them on a windowsill or somewhere with airflow, and take them into the shower with you when you need them.
- If storing them in the shower, make sure the shelf they sit on has drainage and isn't directly under the waterstream.
- During summer, keep the bars out of the sunshine and put them in the fridge if they get too soft.

If bars aren't your thing, refilling your beauty products at package-free stores is an option. Or purchase concentrates. Concentrates come in a bar form (so the plastic packaging is still avoided), but you break them up, whisk them with boiling water, and they turn into a liquid.

Medicines

I rarely get headaches, but when I do I lie down and have a fifteen-minute nap (if I can). After a few hours of drinking lots of water and eating good food (give me all the vegetables) I take pain medicine if the headache has not passed. I make kombucha as a tasty drinking option but also to look after my gut. My philosophy of wellbeing is preventative, holistic and includes modern medicine. Here are a few of my favourite medicinal tips that I reach for before grabbing our medicine box:

- Ginger, honey and lemon juice: grate, spoon and squeeze into hot water when your throat is sore. I also drink this regularly in winter to prevent colds.
- Wellness tonics: made by New Zealanders who know their stuff, I drink wellness tonics that are essentially a concentrate of nutritious fruits, vegetables and herbs. They also make for delicious drinks, especially paired with soda water.
- Sleep: the most underrated treatment for any ailment. Before dabbling in other treatments, I sleep.

If you do have unused medicines, make sure you dispose of them properly. Your local pharmacy will usually accept any medications past their expiration date or general medicine packaging.

Dental hygiene

On my bathroom counter you'll find toothpaste and mouthwash in glass jars that I return to the maker for them to reuse, a bamboo toothbrush, a metal tongue scraper (to reduce bad breath) and home-compostable dental floss in a cute glass vial. My dentist has approved these items and the toothpaste and mouthwash are made by an oral health therapist! Of course I don't leave the tap running while I brush my teeth, to conserve water, and I repurpose my old toothbrush sticks as plant labels in the garden or use them as scrubbing brushes to clean the house.

Living sustainably wellness increases

You've probably picked it up by now, but the main way to look after your health is to live more sustainably. I'm a firm believer that when you truly embrace a different, unique and sustainable lifestyle, your health improves dramatically. I've experienced this, and I watch others reap the benefits, too. It doesn't mean I walk this earth like I'm hovering and constantly stay in picture-perfect health, but the link between the two shouldn't be dismissed.

When I make a meal from scratch, mindfully grabbing the ingredients from my garden or laying them out while thinking of the people I purchase them from, my mental health is supported. When I eat that meal of seasonal produce, my physical health is restored.

Using reusable period products means people who menstruate don't have plastic rubbing against their skin or in their bodies (tampons and pads contain plastic).

I consciously slow down consumption and work hard to understand that I have more than enough. I talk to my neighbours and swap food or skills with them. I bike instead of taking the car. These are all positive actions for my physical and mental wellbeing.

I've said it before, and this won't be the last time I say it: regardless of the state of our planet, living more sustainably leads to a prosperous life.

In a nutshell:

- Move regularly, in a way that suits you.
- Dance lots.
- Stretch whenever you can.
- Consider reusable period products.
- Have safe, healthy sex for you and the planet.
- Reduce waste in your bathroom.
- Opt for sustainable ingredients in all bathroom products.

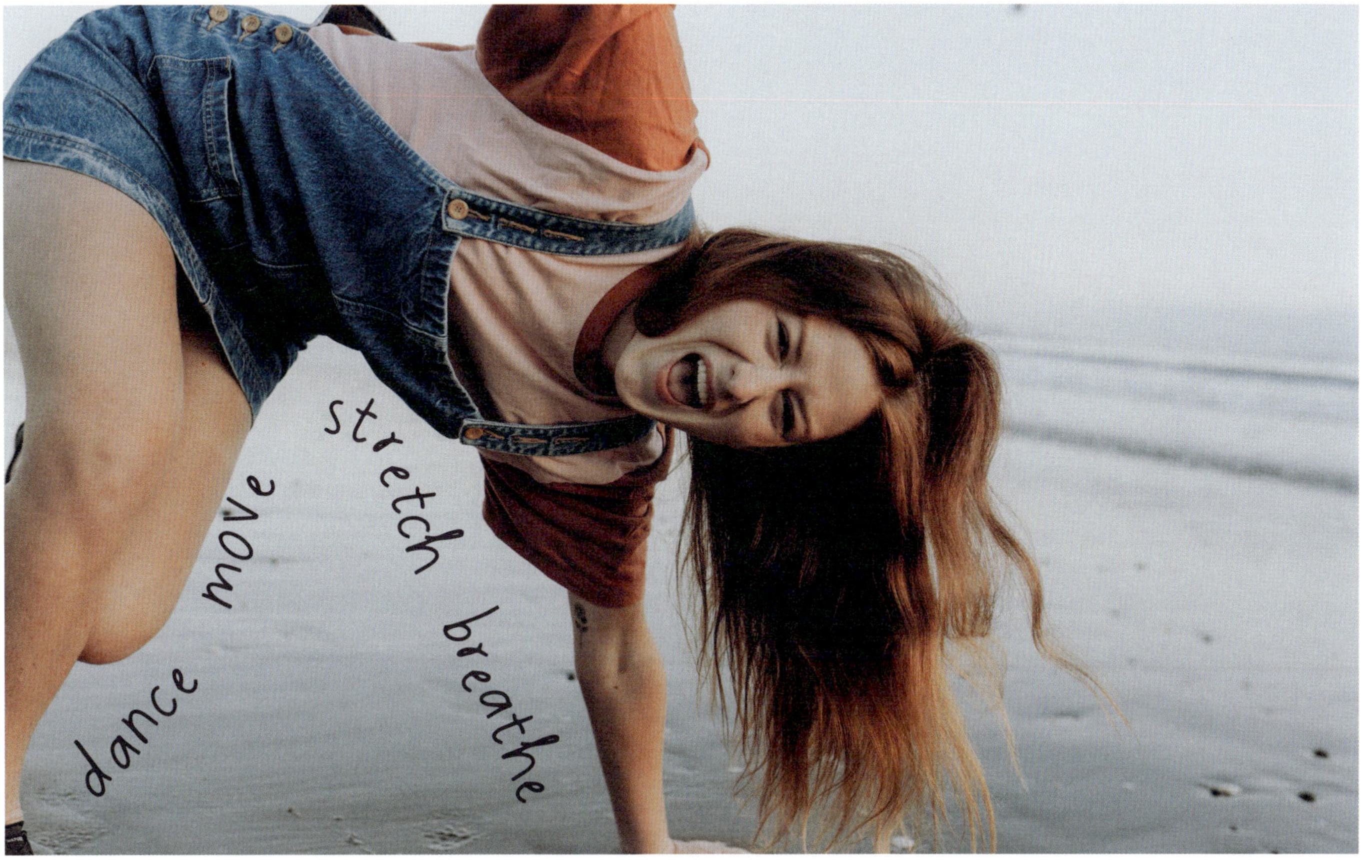
dance
move
stretch
breathe

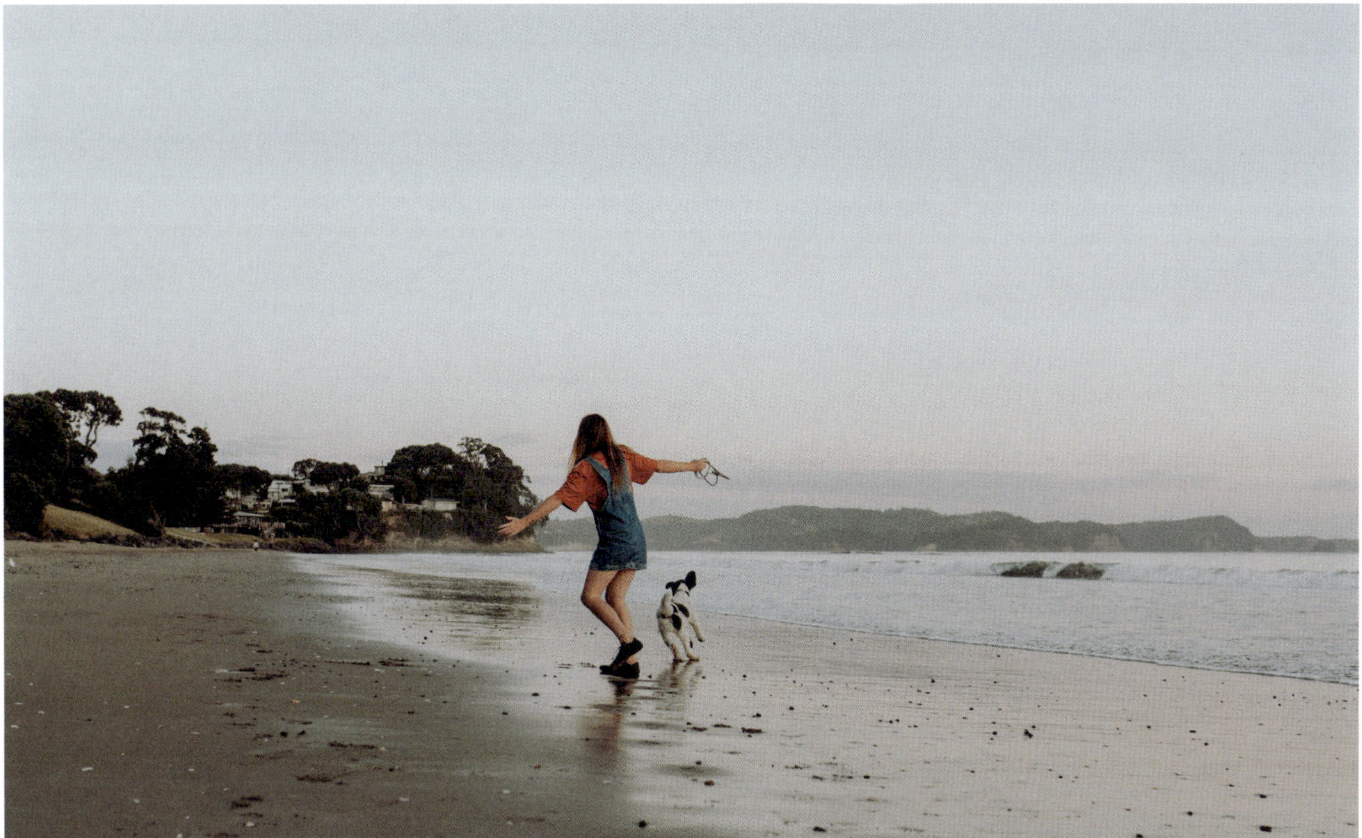

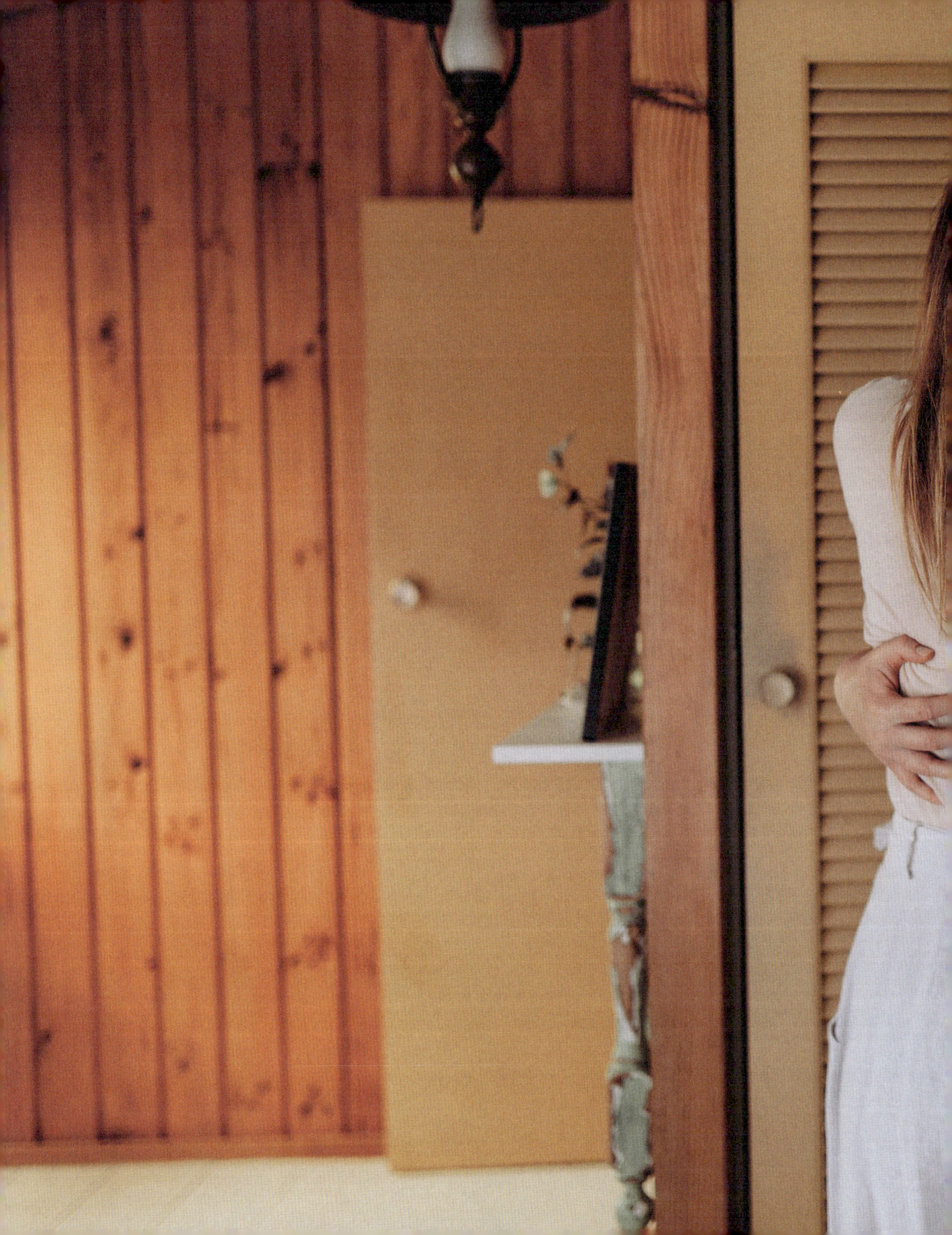

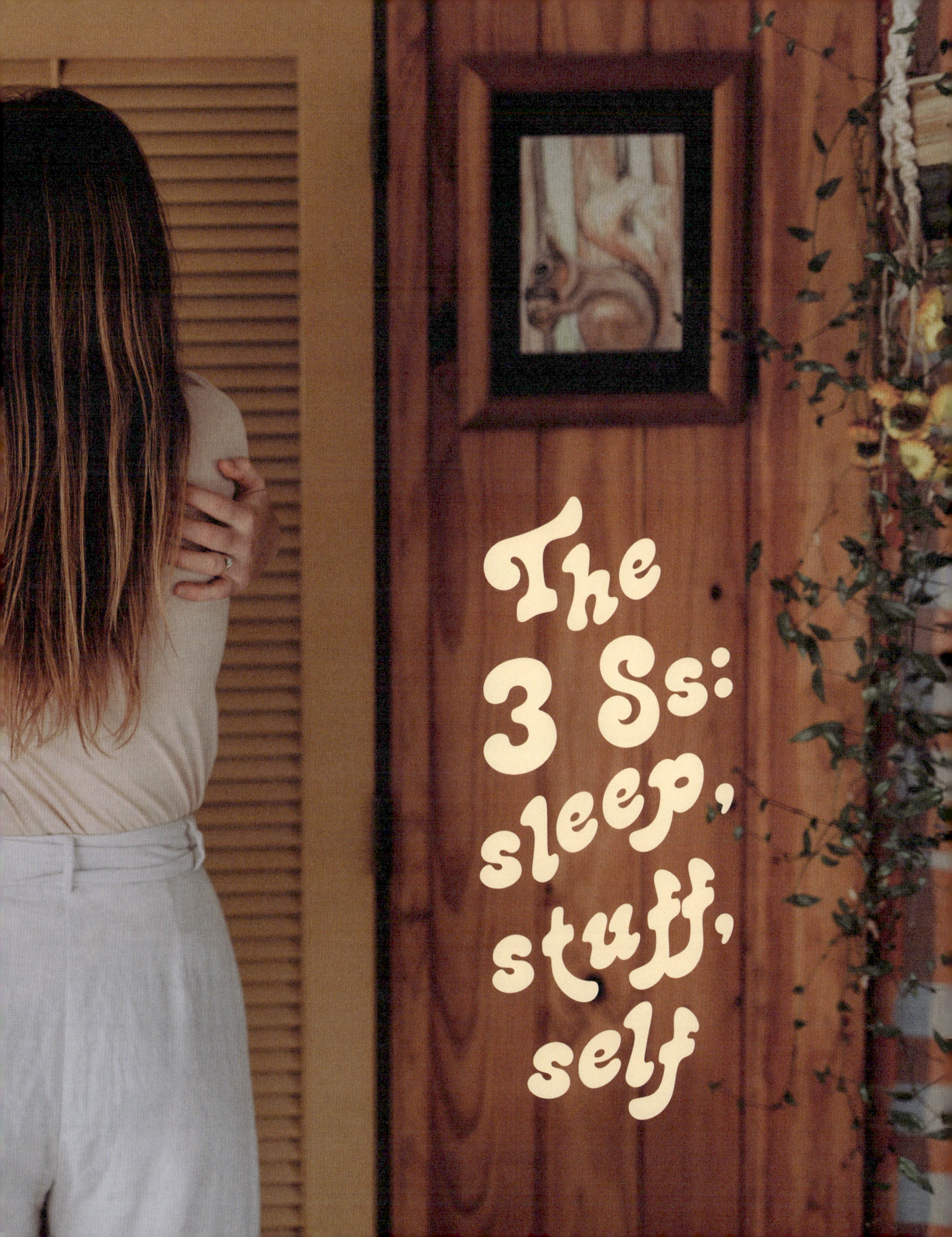

The 3 Ss: sleep, stuff, self

I'm convinced that my strong values and understanding of sleep are what allow me to do everything I've mentioned in this book. I believe stuff is robbing us of contentment, and without a sense of self, life looks like aimless meandering.

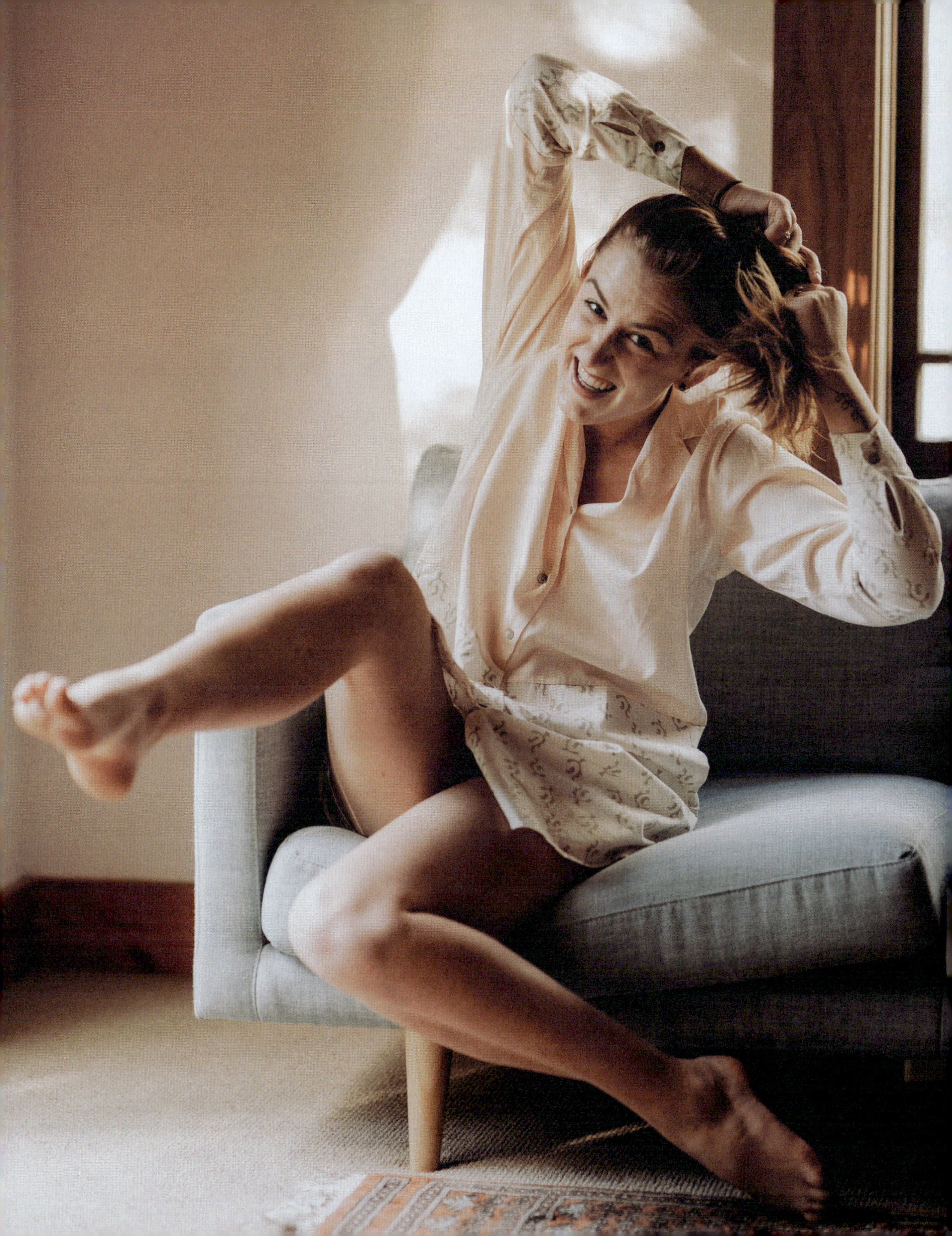

Sleep

Humans are the only species on earth who purposefully deprive themselves of sleep.[1] We socialise, we party, we 'get down' and we work, all prioritised before sleep. It's usually not until someone loses sleep without intent that they realise how important it is. Significant moments like having children, starting shift work or travelling to a new time zone are instigators for a person to go *Aha, sleep is really important!* Yet still, it's low on the priority list for most, regardless of their situation.

In this achievement-praising world, sleep is shunned. If you were to mention you slept for 8–10 hours last night, the people around you may gasp and exclaim 'Lucky for some', while internally thinking you're lazy and a burden to society. I know that sounds extreme, but it's true. In general, sleep is cast aside as something for people with laziness or privilege. Our sleep culture is toxic and it's literally killing us.

'The shorter you sleep, the shorter your life.'[2] Matthew Walker is a renowned sleep researcher and doctor who, like many others, can confirm that sleep is fundamental to happiness and health. The saying 'I can sleep when I'm dead' is incorrect, but overused as a humourous excuse. We can never get back lost sleep. After a long week with little sleep, I used to say 'I need to catch up on sleep.' But after learning more about this luscious activity, I understand that you can never catch up on sleep. Sleep doesn't work that way; it's not accumulative.

If we're going to live sustainably, we need healthy sleep philosophies.
I can sleep when I'm dead = I'll be dead if I don't sleep.

As someone who's owned two businesses and worked a full-time job while settling into her first year of marriage, I can tell you that sleep is the only way I can live the life I do. The amount of times people go 'Oh wow Kate, how do you do it all? You must never sleep!' is hilarious. The reason why I can do everything is mainly the result of regular, regimented and prioritised sleep.

Picture this. It's 10pm on a Saturday night. We are hosting a gathering of twenty people. The vibes are lively, some people are still arriving, the wine is flowing and the outdoor fireplace cradles the perfect mellow embers for marshmallow roasting. Guests are grabbing

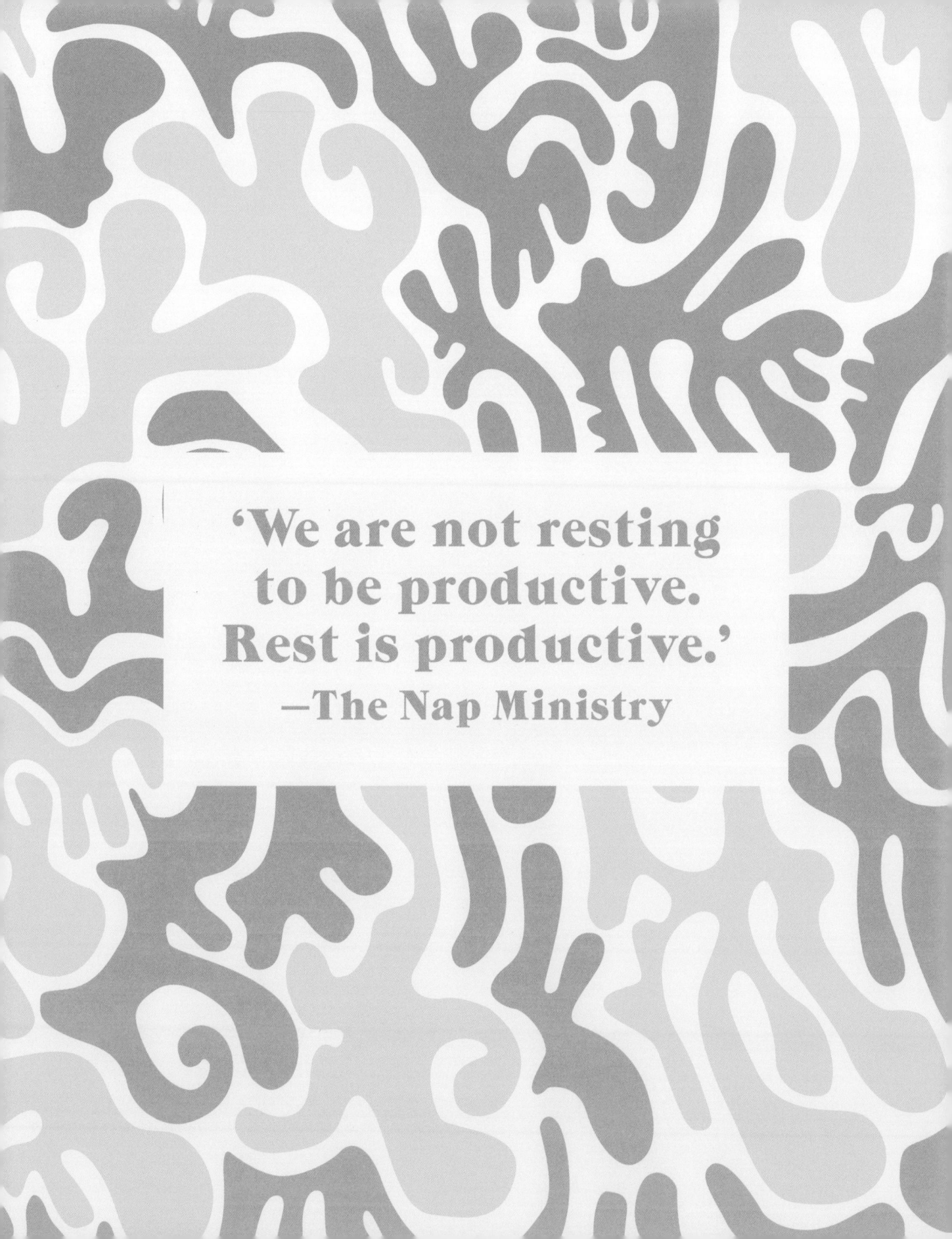

'We are not resting to be productive. Rest is productive.'
—The Nap Ministry

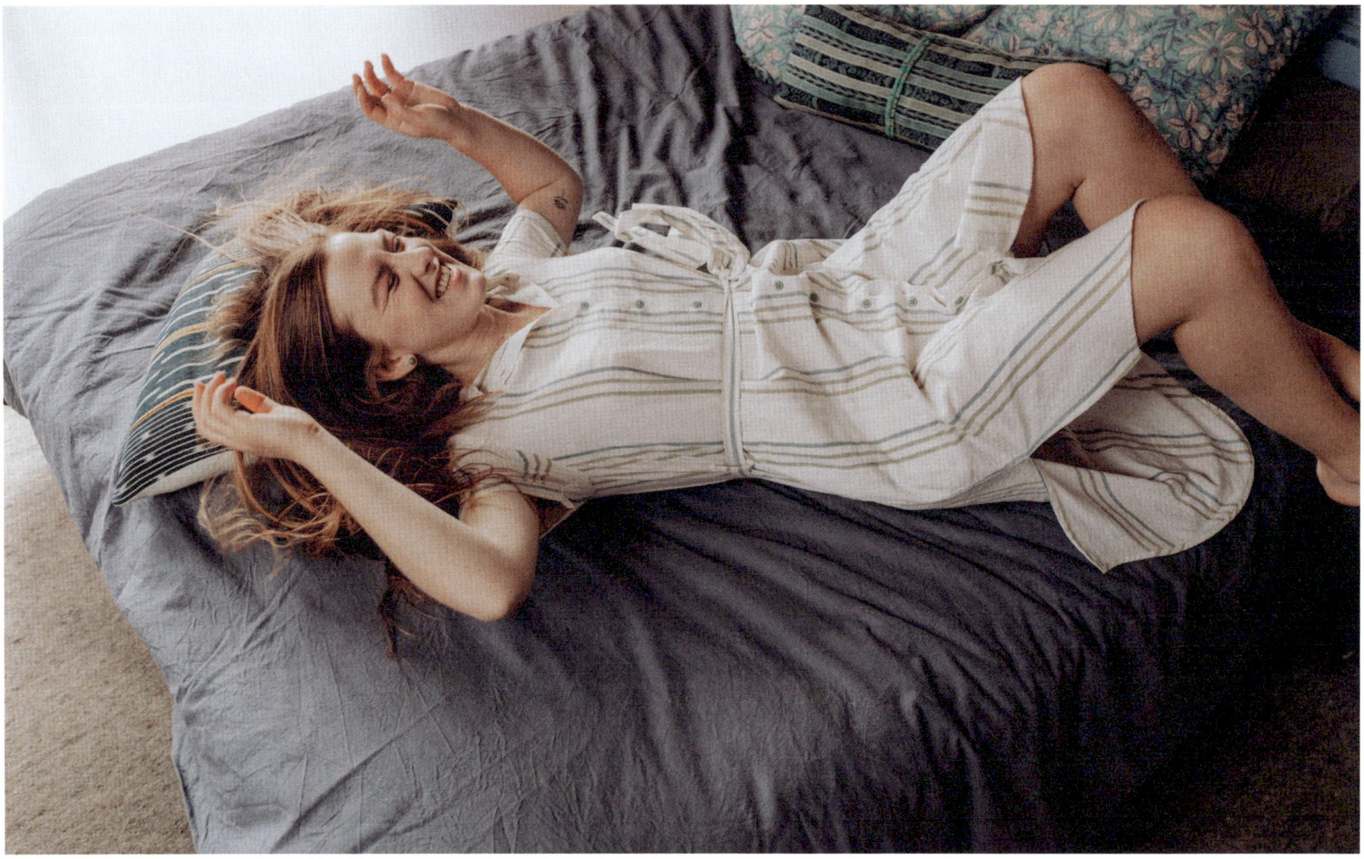

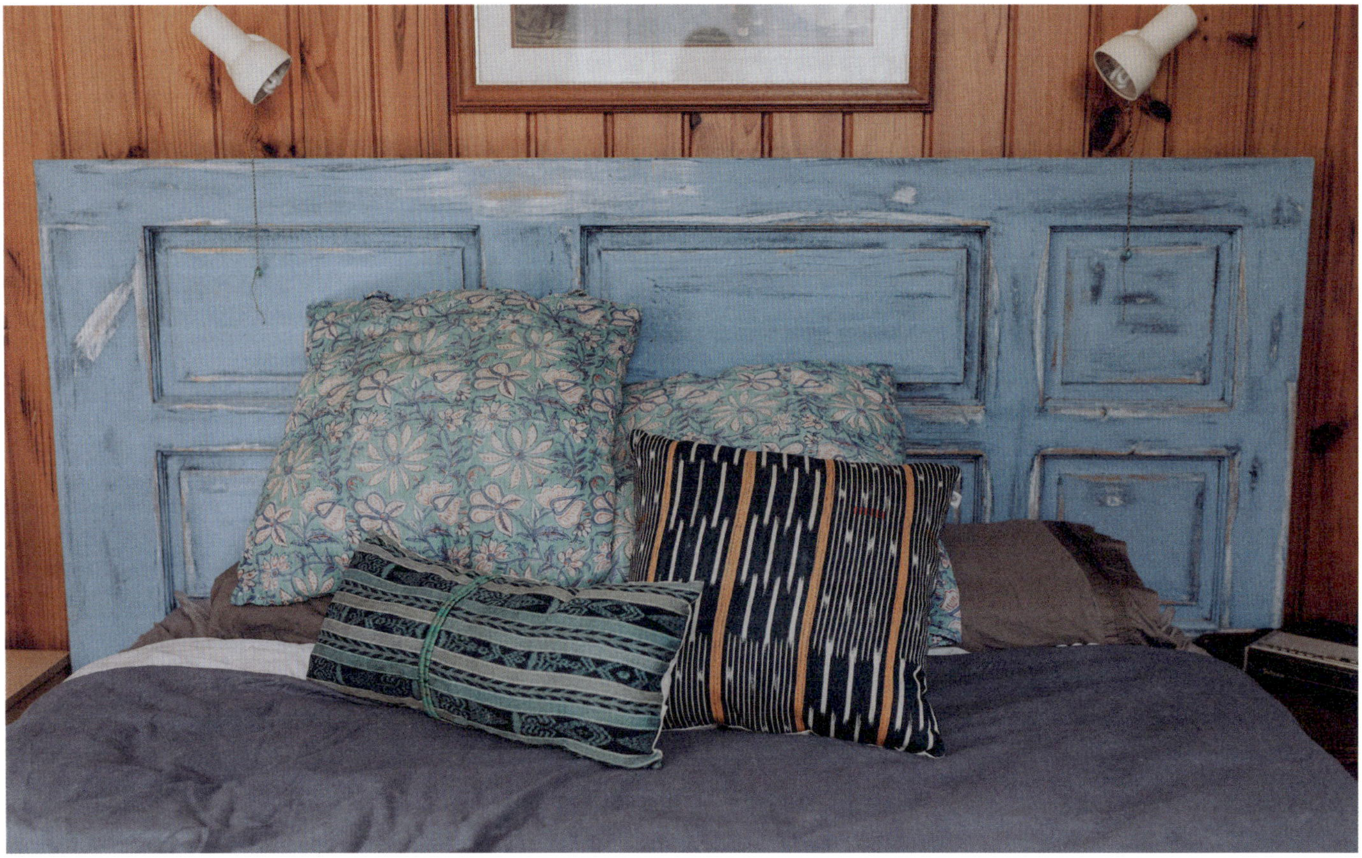

roasting sticks repurposed from metal clothes hangers, and there's a game of beer pong happening a safe distance away. Kate's asleep on the couch. A blanket has been laid over her. The loud conversations and expanding dance floor don't wake her. Nothing will. Her routine bedtime is scarcely disturbed. In a while, she'll gather herself up, bid her farewells to whoever is in the room, and waltz into bed.

As I've already explained, I'm often the youngest in a room. However, I am always the first to leave the party and go to sleep. Usually the parties are at my house, which is very convenient because I can just toddle off to bed! My nickname is 'Reclining Kate' and my friends have tactics for keeping me awake when I'm with them, like encouraging me into an upright chair or poking me with a piece of wood. It never works: sleep is a crucial ingredient to my happy, sustainable, different and joyful life. Few things come before it.

First, let's look at why sleep is important. Then, I will tell you what prioritising sleep looks like for me.

I acknowledge good sleeping habits and sleep itself is incredibly hard when you have children, stressful jobs or other life responsibilities that inhibit your ability to lay your sweet head on a pillow. Yet changing your mentality around sleep, no matter your situation or how easily you can implement changes in your sleep routine, is helpful for all of us. My neighbour, Cory, has two lovely little ones and recently adopted my power nap routine. She's loving it!

Sleep wards off sickness by supporting your immune system, reduces your likelihood of developing cancer or Alzheimer's disease, aids the reproductive system, lengthens lifespan and is generally one of the most underrated treatments for most ailments.[3] When daylight savings time changes and one hour of sleep is lost, heart attacks spike in frequency. When the clocks move back and an hour is gained, heart attack rates decline dramatically. Studies conclusively demonstrate the importance of sleep, yet we still ignore it!

Every one of us will know someone who survives off just a few hours of sleep a night; the ultimate night owl combined with the early-morning gym junkie, or the med student who works two jobs. They say they're totally fine and thrive off it. That's nonsense.

A person can only stay awake for approximately 24 hours without entering an altered state of consciousness. When someone has experienced regular nights with just 7 hours or less sleep, they start to enter microsleep (the brain cannot register the world for brief moments and control of motor actions is compromised[4]). We all know that feeling of sleep deprivation, when it's harder to control your rational mind, your words, your emotions or your appetite. But yet, we hero the person who sleeps just four hours a night in order to achieve as much as possible.

My parents instilled a strong napping culture in me from an early age. On weekends, at around 2pm, you would find my parents curled up for a 20-minute doze. You'd find me and my siblings on our beds reading a book or napping too. I have continued this into my adult life whenever possible, and it was the only way I could work nearly full-time while achieving my degree. I'd be nannying by 5:30am most mornings, then I'd head to university after dropping the children at school, in the afternoon I studied at home, before picking up another group of children from school, work until dinner time, then head out to maintain my raging social life. The only way I could keep this up was my fifteen-minute power naps in the afternoon. A fifteen-minute nap was the difference between an hour of effective study or an hour wasted going over the same thing again and again and not absorbing it. A fifteen-minute nap also determined my ability to be present and helpful as the seven-year-old explained their school worries and concerns, or recall my Year 10 science knowledge as I helped little Johnny with his homework after school.

How to sleep

Sleep is a complex phenomenon and a superpower too many of us miss out on. If you're persuaded you need to sleep more (I hope by now you all are!) but you struggle to sleep, I recommend seeing a specialist.

There are books upon books on sleep (my favourite is the previously mentioned *Why We Sleep* by Matthew Walker) and specialists who've studied it for decades. I personally won't be able to solve your sleep problems in one chapter of a book, but I can offer you my best sleeping habits:

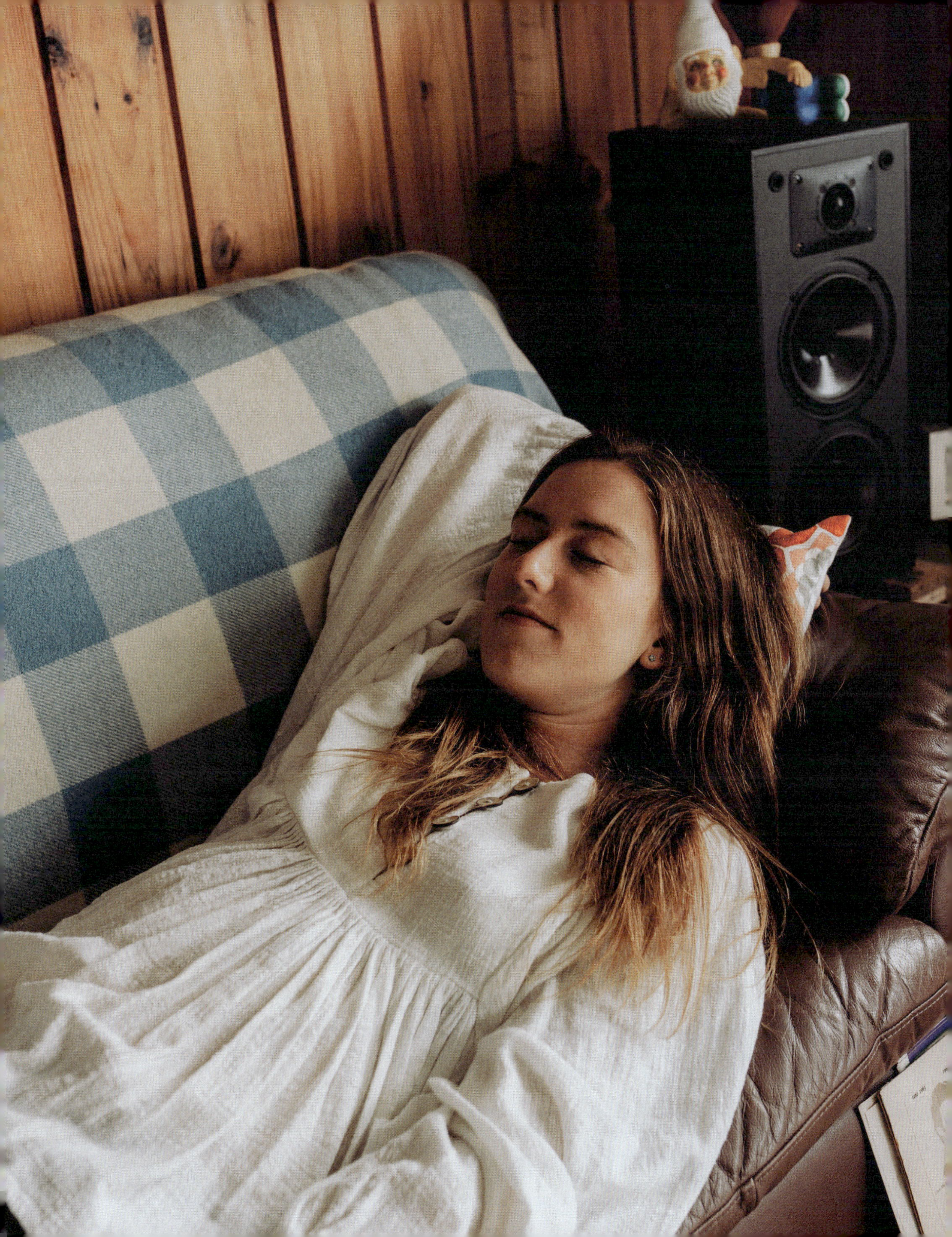

- Turn off screens at least an hour before bed.
- Try your best to avoid hanging out on your bed when it's not time to sleep.
- Restrict your caffeine intake, especially after midday.
- Incorporate rituals into your routine that signal to your brain and body it's time to go to sleep (e.g. I lie on a Shakti mat most nights before bed).
- If you get hooked on books and have low self-control, don't read before bed.
- Get out of bed as soon as your alarm goes off or as soon as you wake up.
- Attempt power naps in the day, but never nap for longer than 20 minutes.
- Have a bath or do something relaxing before bed.
- Get outside as much as possible during the daytime.
- Aim to wake and sleep at the same time every day.
- Lower your light exposure in the evenings (e.g. our lounge and bedroom lights are a low, warm colour).
- Finish eating one to two hours before bed.
- Make sure your bedroom isn't too hot.
- Go to the toilet before you get into bed.
- Use an eyemask or pillow (to block out light, plus I find the weight calming).

Another key tip, passed onto me by my grandmother, is this: 'Don't be afraid to spend a lot of money on your bed and your shoes. If you're not in one, you're in the other.'

Investing in a comfortable mattress, pillow, blanket and sheets can help dramatically with your sleep quality. When you're purchasing these things, use the list on pages 200–202 to ask the store questions before purchasing so you're confident the items are made sustainably too. Although you may have concerns about second-hand bedding hygienically, don't rule out that option either. Ask around! We scored an amazing bed base and mattress for our spare room from a couple who had separated and needed to split up their house and downsize. We also found some high-quality bed sheets at a second-hand shop for $2.

You cannot live sustainably if you do not have a strong understanding of the benefits and power of sleep.

I'll leave the rest of the sleep advice to the experts and leave you with this. You may think it's strange to include sleep in a book about sustainable living and living differently, but without sleep, how can someone live differently? Sleep allows me to have novel ideas. To challenge the status quo, to have the energy to question things I know are not okay, to be confident doing life differently even when people are looking at me strangely. Sleep is the most underrated phenomenon I know and I won't sit back and let you miss out on it.

In a nutshell:

- Prioritise sleep.
- If you haven't already, seek more information to help you understand how powerful sleep is.
- Visit a sleep specialist if you struggle with sleeping.

 Stuff

Where's your 'stuff' drawer? Is it in the kitchen? The garage? The spare room?

Do you know what's in the back of your laundry cupboard? How many times do you actually open that overflowing wardrobe in the spare room?

We have too much stuff. Full garages, teeming pantries, jammed drawers, stuffy storage units and brimming attics. We spend springtime sorting through our junk, only to repeat the sorting every year while wondering *How did this happen AGAIN? How did this get here?* To use a concept borrowed from a great book, *Stuffocation* by James Wallman, most of us are 'stuffocated'.[5] And no, that doesn't mean the feeling you get after you've eaten one too many burgers and regret going back for that second helping of fries. Stuffocation describes the overwhelm of having too much stuff.

When you walk into a room, open a cupboard or fling open the garage door, see too many things and immediately close it again, you're experiencing stuffocation.

When your kitchen bench keeps on piling up, no matter how much you sort it, you're being stuffocated.

When you sort through your wardrobe and lay everything out on your bed, only to realise the mass is too much for your brain to handle so you back away, that's the result of stuffocation.

Stuffocation is a complex feeling, one that comes from the privilege of having the means to have more than you need. It's almost as though we're still instinctively hoarding items like our survival relies on it, without realising we already have enough. I have yet to find someone who enjoys how a chaotic cupboard makes them feel.

The Minimalist Game

In April 2018, Tim and I completed a challenge called the Minimalist Game. This challenge was one of the best things I've ever done for reducing the feeling of stuffocation. The Minimalist Game pushed me to positively reframe my understanding of stuff and reduce the amount of things I own. Tim and I ended up on national news in both Australia and Aotearoa New Zealand because of the Minimalist Game, and we still have people asking us about it online.

We started the Minimalist Game because of my work as a freelance writer. I was writing about twenty articles a month for sustainable brands and media platforms, and was asked to write one about minimalism. Having never dived into it myself, this involved a lot of research. Once the article was complete, I read it aloud to Tim. After I'd finished reading it, Tim gave his approval, but then turned to me and said, 'If you can talk the talk, could you walk the walk? I challenge you to the Minimalist Game.'

The Minimalist Game was created by world-renowned minimalists, Joshua Fields Millburn and Ryan Nicodemus.[6] The purpose of their strategic challenge is to help people minimise their belongings while reducing the chances of opening a messy cupboard and feeling paralysed. The challenge starts slow and warms you up.

For the month of April, Tim and I gave away the amount of things that corresponded to the date. On 1 April, one thing; on 5 April, five things; on 17 April, seventeen things. You get the picture. We did this for the whole month, separately. For example, on 24 April, 48 things disappeared from our home. We also chose not to stick to their rule of having things out of the house by midnight, as that would have meant throwing things in the rubbish bin — which obviously we were not into!

By the end of the month, we had gotten rid of 930 items from our home. With a few extras thrown in at the end of our clear-out, the number was close to 1000. As conscious consumers already, our friends and family were scared that we would end up without pillows or underwear. Fortunately, we still have those essentials, along with a new-found understanding of stuff.

We quickly realised how many items we had in our home that looked good, worked well, were sometimes used, but didn't serve a big enough

A chaotic
home full
of stuff
fosters a
chaotic mind.

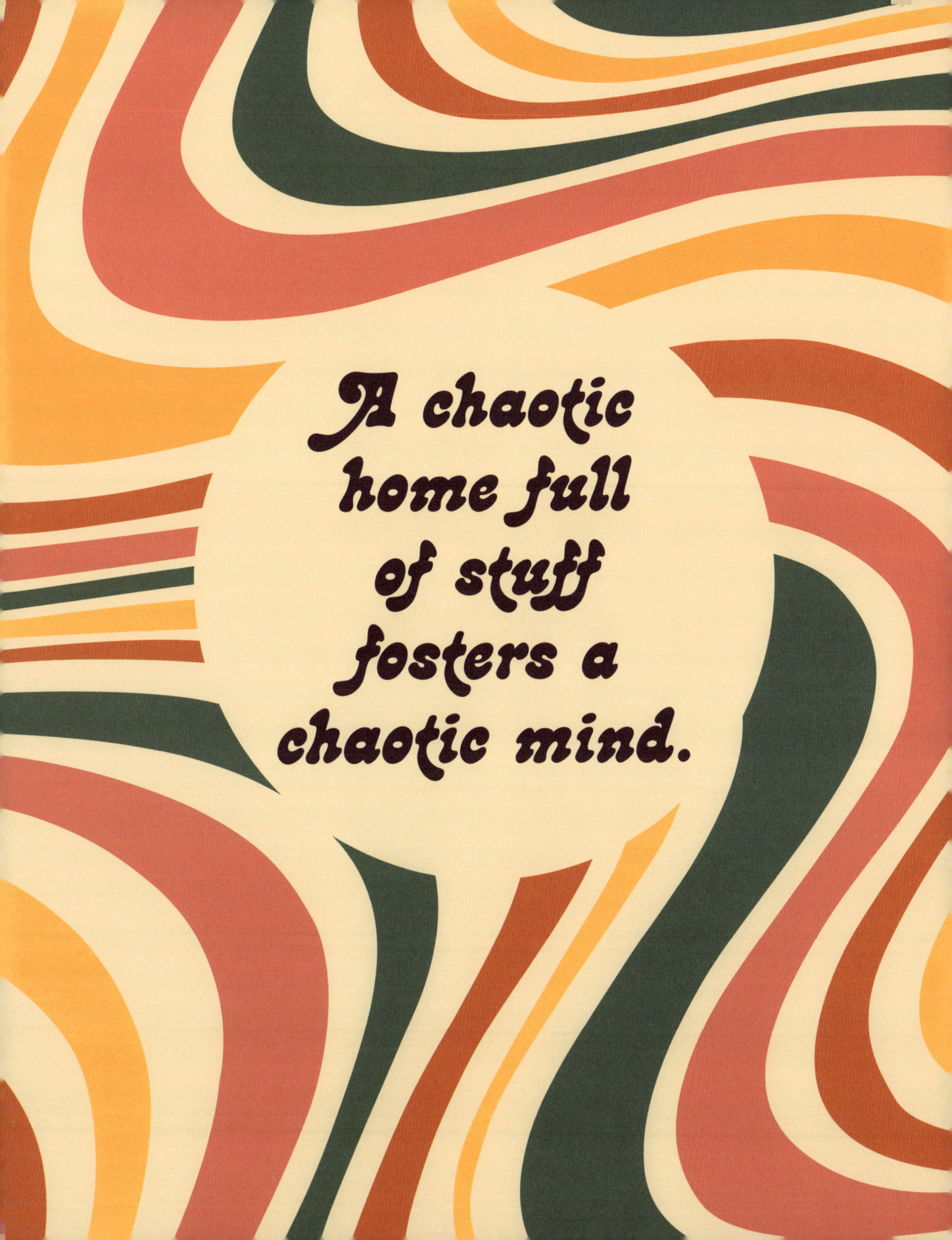

purpose in our lives to warrant keeping, storing and managing. As the challenge went on and the dates grew higher, we even started picking at each other's wardrobes and asking the hard questions. We let go of the things that should have been out of our lives years ago but had stayed simply because we'd spent a lot of money or time on them, and we dug deep into every crevice of our house. Even our childhood heirlooms.

Honestly, that month was hectic. It was emotionally draining and time-consuming. Having to work out how to get rid of gifts, what memories to keep, and what we may need in the future became a full-time job.

Luckily the purpose of it was to never have to do it again. Now, we have strict rules about what comes into our home. We think about things in depth before purchasing or even accepting free things to understand if it's truly missing from our lives, and we discuss everything together.

Completing the Minimalist Game felt incredible. I felt free, cleansed and lighter. We aren't minimalists and never intended to be but having less stuff is fiercely rewarding.

I know where everything in my house is, so I spend less time hunting for things.

I know that I'm using all the resources I have, rather than storing unnecessary things that could be used by others or exchanged for money and used in a different way.

I spend less time dusting, cleaning and repairing things.

Wherever I look, I see items that have been placed with intent. I feel at home and at peace.

Now, even if something is free, I don't immediately take it. It may not take from my wallet, but it takes from my capacity, my mental health and my time that could be spent enjoying experiences instead of maintaining stuff.

The Minimalist Game was a pivotal moment in my life. I understand the responsibility of stuff, have a strategy for keeping our home decluttered and know how to thoughtfully rehome things if we don't need them.

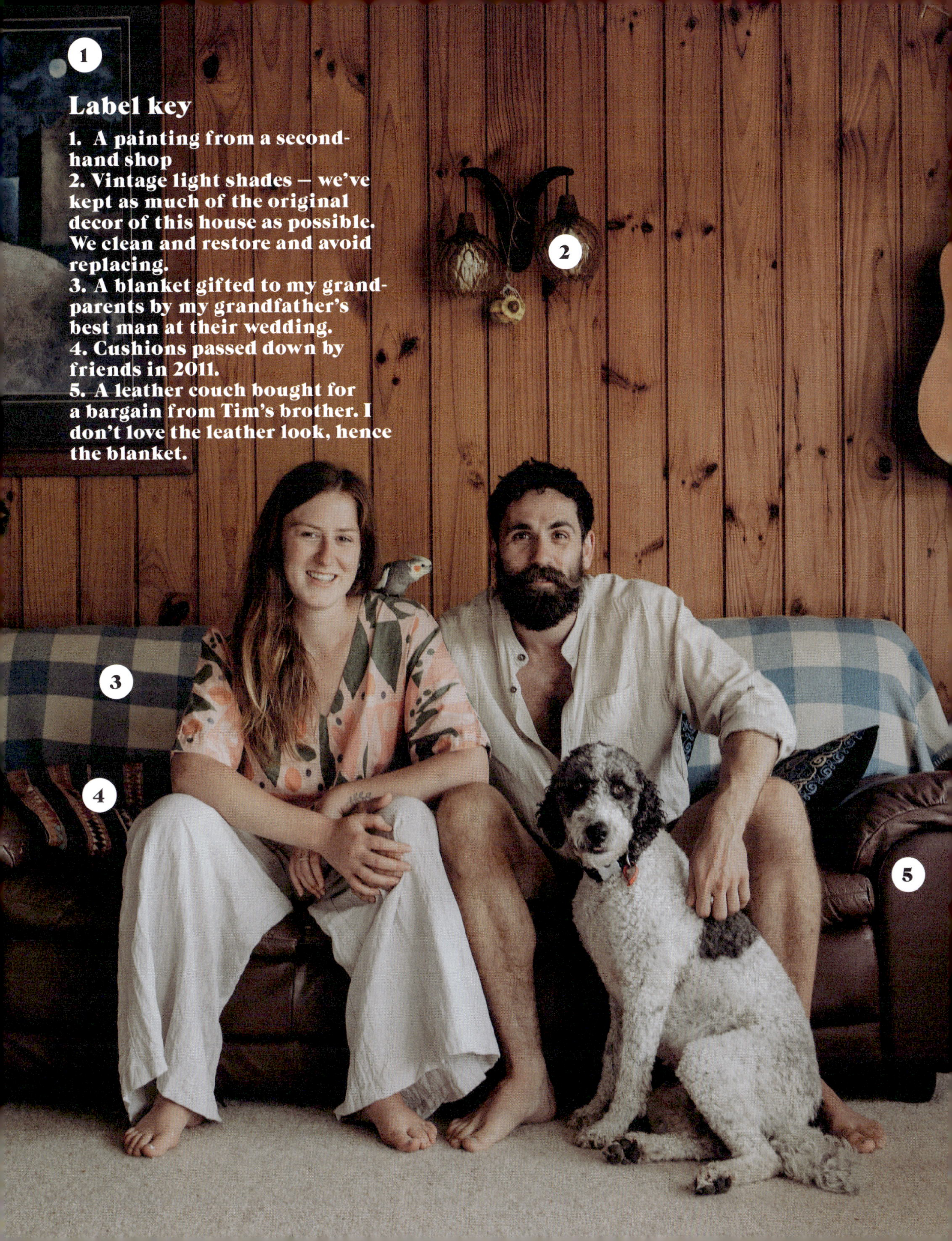
1
2
3
4
5

Label key

1. A painting from a second-hand shop
2. Vintage light shades – we've kept as much of the original decor of this house as possible. We clean and restore and avoid replacing.
3. A blanket gifted to my grand-parents by my grandfather's best man at their wedding.
4. Cushions passed down by friends in 2011.
5. A leather couch bought for a bargain from Tim's brother. I don't love the leather look, hence the blanket.

Why we all want more stuff

The Minimalist Game taught me the huge responsibility that comes with owning something. The maintenance, the emotional weight, the physical space needed for storage and the responsibility of rehoming or disposing it when it's no longer needed. I also began to understand, and get incredibly frustrated by, how things are made and how marketing has steered our desperation for owning things we don't need.

As I carried out the Minimalist Game, the amount of things I owned began to feel embarrassing. I was baffled. As someone who consumed a lot less than the average person, I struggled to wrap my head around how this overload of stuff had happened. When I talked to people who were older than me, I realised that this 'stuffocation' feeling is a new phenomenon and not totally my fault.

A few decades ago, stuff wasn't an issue. Disposable incomes were rare, there wasn't as much stuff available to purchase, and items were created to last longer so they cost a lot more upfront. My mother-in-law made Tim's clothes when he was a child (in the 1990s) because it was more cost-effective. Now, you could buy around ten readymade T-shirts for the same price as the fabric to make just one.

Put this together with two toxic phenomena called perceived and planned obsolescence, and you've got people who JUST WANT MORE STUFF without realising why they want it.

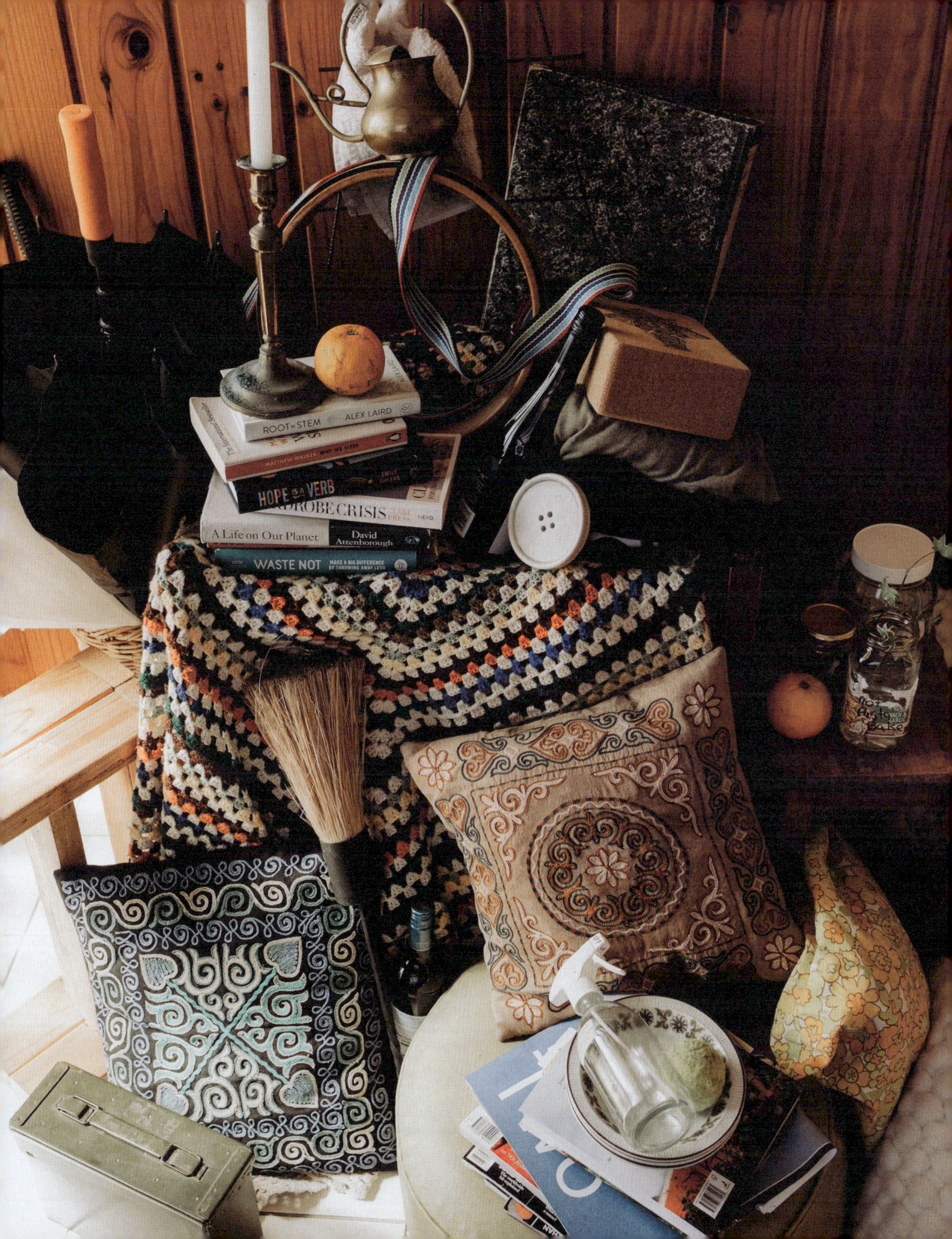
ROOT to STEM
ALEX LAIRD
MATTHEW WALKER WHY WE SLEEP
HOPE IS A VERB
CLARE PRESS
A Life on Our Planet
David Attenborough
WASTE NOT
MAKE A BIG DIFFERENCE BY THROWING AWAY LESS

Perceived obsolescence

This describes the feeling you get when a brand tells you they have a new colour of the same dress you bought last year. It's a fresh colour, totally on trend, your friend bought this new one, and your life would be so much better if you had it too!

We pretend we're immune to perceived obsolescence, but we've all been there. Humans are vain, whether we admit it or not. There isn't much we wouldn't do to be accepted by the majority, and owning new stuff is believed to lead to acceptance. There's nothing wrong with a desire to be accepted, but we can avoid being sucked into perceived obsolescence by asking ourselves why we actually want the item. What need does it fill? Also, focus on spending time with groups of people who value you instead of materialistic things.

Planned obsolescence

'They don't make 'em like they used to!' This saying may sound annoying when your great aunt says it yet again at your Christmas dinner as the potato peeler breaks, but she's actually right. Planned obsolescence is when a company makes something with the intent for it to last a short amount of time, so they can take more money from you sooner. T-shirts are made to last only ten wears! And what about your phone? You'd think with the incredible technology advancements we have, someone would be able to make a phone that lasts longer than just a year or two, but nope. How else would the company be able to make more cold hard cash from you?

No one is exempt from experiencing these two phenomena and unfortunately they're only getting worse. Our society follows a make, take, throwaway culture, and we're falling further and further into it.

Clever consumption

To live more fulfilling lives and escape these sneaky marketing tactics, we must rethink our consumer-driven values and sort our priorities.

When I talk about the Minimalist Game, some people screw up their noses at the idea of not buying any more stuff. They think we must only spend money on bills and food, but that's not true in the slightest.

Tim and I still buy stuff. I love stuff. New stuff comes with excitement and rejuvenation. So I'm not suggesting you stop buying, full stop. I'm simply nudging us all to consider what stuff we need and find ways to consume items that avoid negatively impacting our health and the planet.

Use the guide overleaf to help you avoid perceived and planned obsolescence, save money and reduce the amount you send to landfill.

We're only human. So while you may try these things, marketing experts literally spend years at university studying how to prey on human qualities to lure you in to make a purchase. Don't beat yourself up if you fall into a trap and make an unneeded purchase. Simply go back to the chart, reflect and reset.

All of these tips are great to read in a book, but they won't work if you don't take action. So:

- Write out the clever consumption tips overleaf (in your own words) and stick it to your fridge.
- Make a list on your phone of things you need when you think of them. When you go to the shops, follow the list instead of your impulses and flashy sales.
- Challenge yourself to visit a mall without any intent to spend, and write down a list of all the things you were going to buy. Mull over this list when you're home — away from the bright lights, alluring marketing and environment that is set up to make you buy things you do not need.
- Find an accountability partner or get your household on board. Show them this chart and work out a strategy for how you and your home will evade stuffocation.

Clever consumption tips

Tip	Why?	Example
Move your furniture around	Reimagining your space and changing the layout can make you feel like your home is new without making a purchase. The floorspace you can see is novel, the colour arrangements are fresh; newness is attained without consumption.	We move around our cushions regularly to mix up the patterns and colours in each space. Artwork is switched from hooks, and our couches are constantly on the move.
Put seasonal clothes away	When you get them out in the right season, they feel new to you. This avoids you seeing the same clothes all year round and getting bored of them even though you haven't worn them recently.	I have a vintage suitcase under my bed where I store seasonal clothes. At a change of season, I move the appropriate seasonal clothes to easier-to-reach places in my wardrobe. E.g. summer dresses hang at the back during winter.
Replace mall time with restoration and/or cleaning time	Finding pride in restoring what you already have can replace the feeling of needing something new. A good spring clean goes a long way!	When Tim and I feel a desire to have something new in the home, we will paint a bookshelf, deep-clean a room, or repair something that needs a little TLC (e.g. adjust the wobbly legs on a stool).
Visit a second-hand store or browse local online sharing/swapping pages	Preloved items are generally more meaningful and more fulfilling than something new. They come with stories and memories. Plus older items are usually made to last — they won't fall apart after a few uses so the store can sell it to you again next spring.	Most of our furniture is second-hand. We make a 'need' list and browse for those things online or look out for them when we visit second-hand stores.
Buy plants instead	Fill the itch for something new with a plant.	Plants, both indoor and outdoor, are a common gift in our household.
Buy someone else something	If you desperately want to spend money, spend it on someone else! You'll still get the rush of using your hard-earned coin, but the item will be used and treasured a lot more by someone who actually needs it.	I get thrills from buying people presents. Sometimes the presents aren't even tangible things, but I love the opportunity to pick someone a thoughtful gift and spend my money — especially when it's not even their birthday.
Swap household items with other people	You'll get the benefits of having something new in your space, without having to spend any money. Plus you don't have to say goodbye to anything in the long term — you can always swap it back.	Swap your coffee tables with a neighbour, swap your ornaments with your sister — go wild.
Think creatively	Just because something has a label, doesn't mean you can't use it for a million different things! Thinking of items as materials or resources that fill a wide range of purposes will help you utilise what you have and throw away less.	I had a jar labelled 'pantry jar'. I thought creatively and used it to brew my kombucha in. When it cracked, I turned it into a cacti garden.

Ask friends and family before you buy	Your mate may have what you need sitting redundant in their storage room! Second-hand shopping doesn't have to happen in an official store.	We needed a garlic crusher and an electric mixer. I had been searching for them in second-hand stores for weeks. When I happened to mention this in a conversation with my in-laws, they said they had both of these things and that we could have them!
Make it yourself	Putting your own time and energy into creating something: - is rewarding - is usually more cost-effective - provides autonomy over the design and functionality - is an enjoyable pastime	We needed a bedhead for our new bed when we were married in February 2017. Instead of buying one, we bought a second-hand door and antiqued it together. It's now a statement art piece and everyone loves it.
Just don't buy it	You probably don't need it. Like my friend Heidi asks herself, 'Would I still buy this if it wasn't on sale?'	There are many things I've loved and let slip away. I enjoy window shopping and looking at all the beautiful things in this world, but I've realised I don't need to own them to enjoy them.
Support local and ethical production	Avoiding mass-produced and unsustainably made products is a great way to vote with your wallet. Often locally and sustainably made things last longer too.	Our green-yellow chairs are one of the only new pieces of furniture we own. They're made in Aotearoa by a company with sustainable values.

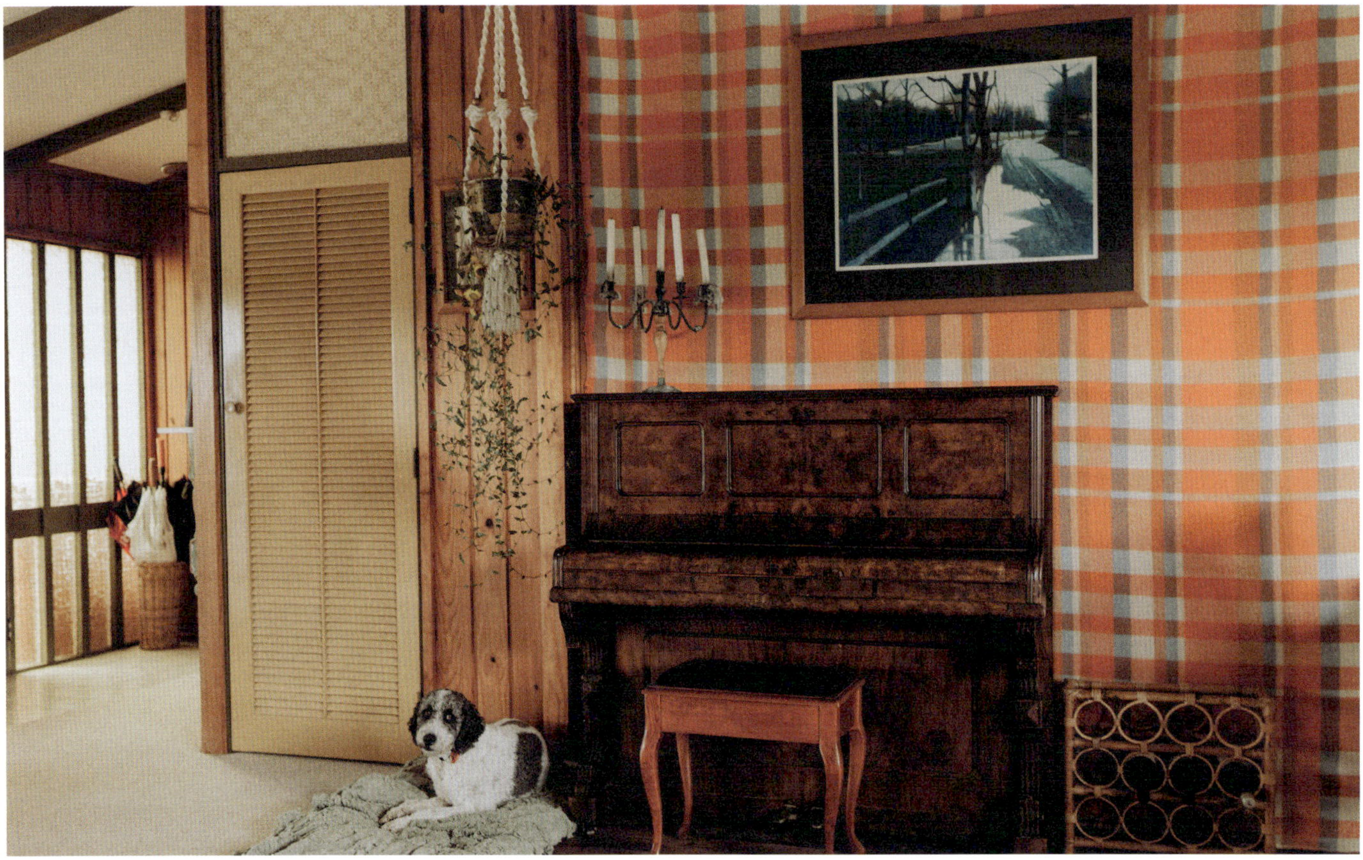

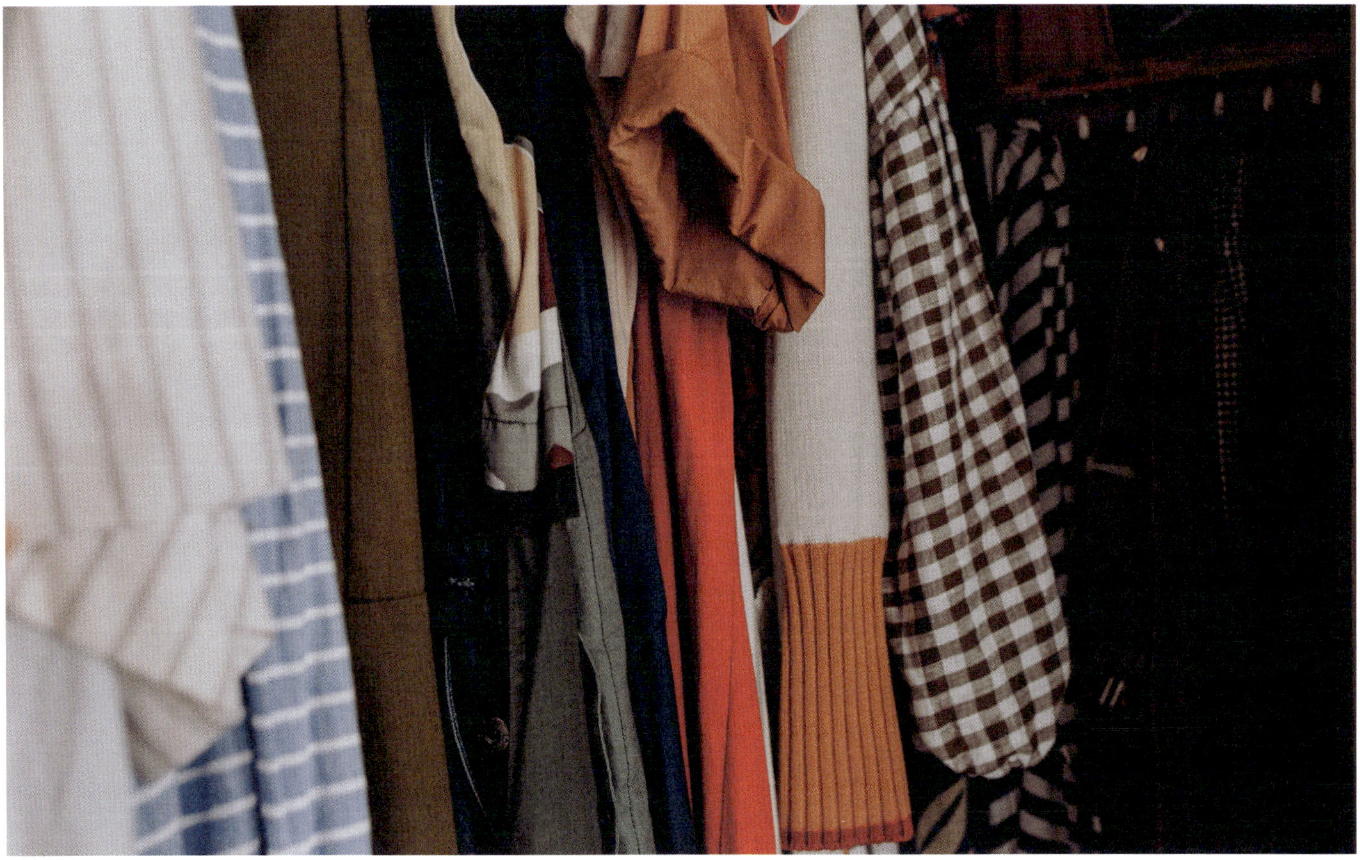

Thoughtful decluttering

Unlike most spring cleans that end up with large black rubbish sacks destined for landfill, after the Minimalist Game we rehomed and disposed of everything as cleverly and sustainably as possible.

Step 1: We passed items on to our friends and family.
After the Challenge, we invited friends and family over to raid our 'goodbye' pile. We thoughtfully rehomed items to particular people who had shown interest in them, too. For example, when I was debating whether to give away a blue shirt with lace sleeves, I wore it for a day to see if I liked it enough. During the day, I bumped into my friend Anna. She said 'Nice top, I love it!' A few days later I decided I didn't love the top enough, so I gave it to her. I bought the top from a second-hand shop, so it must be at least third-hand now!

Step 2: We sold items online.
When an item was worth money, we sold it on our national second-hand online marketplace, TradeMe. This was incredibly rewarding because we made money from all our hard work and many hours spent doing the Minimalist Game! The money paid for my travel costs to attend Eco Fashion Week Australia.

Step 3: We held a garage sale.
This was brilliant because we were able to see who was rehoming our beloved items. Tim had an obsession with orca whales when he was younger, and had held onto around twelve orca whale toys. He kept one of them for memories and to pass down to our potential future offspring; the others were picked up by excited children at the garage sale on a beautiful sunny Saturday morning. Although it was hard for him to say goodbye, seeing them loved and cherished by others, instead of sitting in our attic, was a wonderful feeling.

Step 4: We donated to second-hand shops.
Before anything was donated, we made sure everything was clean, repaired and in working condition. We also asked the lovely volunteers if our full trailer-load was needed (sometimes second-hand stores are

overwhelmed with donations and cannot process or store extra stuff). As the items we were donating were in great condition and not just our junk, people were already buying things off the trailer as we unloaded it! The second-hand shop, run by a charity, was so grateful.

Op-shop etiquette

I have a confession to make. I was once the type of person who'd drop things off at the second-hand shop and run away. I didn't read the signs that specified what they were not accepting (e.g. no winter clothes accepted in summer because they don't have the space to store them), because I love a good clear-out and when I have things to get rid of I want them gone as soon as possible. These days, I know how selfish it is to leave the responsibility of sorting my junk to a lovely second-hand-shop volunteer. I'm a changed person. My op-shop etiquette has dramatically improved after learning second-hand shops spend so much money on landfill fees every year. That's money the second-hand store cannot use to support the charity they often exist to serve, or to grow their store, implement easier systems for shoppers or pay their staff more.

As the second-hand market grows, so does the cost of disposing of everyone's junk. The 'Oh, I'm such a good person, I donate to second-hand shops' mentality doesn't work when it's done irresponsibly. Globally, our op-shop etiquette is horrific.

Circulating items that already exist is one of the best ways to live a sustainable lifestyle. But in order for the second-hand market to continue growing, we need to improve how we engage in it.

Here are my op-shop etiquette guidelines:

- Does it need repairing? Repair it yourself or find someone (perhaps a seamstress or local handyperson) who can.
- Does it need a wash? Read the care instructions carefully. If it's an object, make sure to get in all the cracks and crevices. Polish that puppy up!
- Ask yourself: would you give this item to a friend or would you happily pick this up from a second-hand store if you needed it? Make

sure it's in great condition before donating. Second-hand stores generally don't have access to washing machines or repair services. If something is broken or stained, it's often thrown away.
- Is your item clearly labelled, paired and ordered? For example, if you have a puzzle that is missing one piece, write that on the box. If you have a pair of shoes, tie a piece of string around them so they don't lose each other. If you have an obscure item, label it (with a label that's easy to remove, perhaps attached with string) so the volunteers know exactly what it is. Things like jewellery also need some attention and are best donated in jewellery boxes or bags so necklaces don't get tangled and earrings don't separate from their pairs.
- Does the second-hand shop need the item? Read the sign at the front of the store. Generally second-hand shops have a list of things they need or are not accepting at the time. If there is no sign, kindly ask the volunteers at the store if what you have in your bags will be helpful to them.

In a nutshell:

- Attempt a stuffocation reset and try the Minimalist Game.
- Write lists of what you actually need.
- Avoid malls; opt for second-hand shops (online and physical).
- View an item as a resource with many purposes.
- Improve your op-shop etiquette.
- Find places and people to help you repair and restore your stuff.
- Fill purchasing urges with cleaning, experiences or something else you enjoy.

Self

Just a few months into our relationship, Tim and I were sitting down flicking through one of his old photo albums. I vividly remember a picture of him dressed as Captain Jack Sparrow from *Pirates of the Caribbean* at his school ball in high school. Tim was dressed head to toe in costume. The whole shebang. He looked like he could have been part of the cast! As the conversation went on and I saw more pictures of him and his friends at the ball, I noticed something was out of place. I asked, 'What was the theme of the ball?'

Tim: '*Midnight in Paris*'.

Some people have a fearless confidence to be nothing but themselves, in all contexts. It can seem endearing, unusual or weird to some. This kind of 'carefree' attitude can even be perceived as obnoxious, but most commonly the underlying, and often unconscious, feeling from those looking from the outside is envy.

So, when it comes to living differently, thinking sustainably and being open to a way of living that is alternative to the mainstream, it's important to attempt to both find out who you are and match yourself (your values) with your actions.

I feel like I'm one of the lucky ones. I've known who I am from a very early age and I am constantly, unapologetically me. Sometimes it feels like a curse, because some situations would be easier if I was able to tone myself down for a moment, but in general, it's liberating. Recently, when sitting around a campsite with friends and family, I overheard someone ask my dad a question. 'What do you think it is about Kate that has led her to what she does today?' He answered 'She's just so comfortable being herself. She literally cannot be anybody else.'

I struggle with those quotes that are sprinkled throughout the internet reminding everyone to 'be yourself'. I don't connect to them; I have never had difficulty being myself and perhaps that's why people like listening to what I have to say and observing how I live. Being myself also means I avoid most of the online hate and trolls that many public figures experience regularly. I still experience it, but far less than most because I have already pointed out all my flaws and faults well

**Know yourself.
Let who you
are show up in
everything you do.
I dare you.**

before any troll can get to them.

To help you find the same freedom, I'll discuss ways to establish values and understand yourself, touch on the weird, sustainable things I do that make me *me*, and talk about some of the things I've changed that align who I am with how I live, and ultimately benefit others too.

How the heck do I find my values?

You may be reading this book and already bubbling with a new enthusiasm and intention to put many of the things I've suggested into action, and a fresh outlook on how you live your life. Brilliant! But if we all lived the same way, if everyone who read this book began living exactly like I do, we'd be robots. Plus that would be weird — we'd be living parallel lives. I'm not keen on that.

Our values will not all align. Some will be identical, others similar, but it would be wrong and untrue to live by someone else's code of conduct. So, find yours.

Note: A value is something important to you. It could be as broad as trust, or as specific as a cup of tea in the morning. A value is something you prioritise and stand up for, and ultimately your values make you *you*.

Ways to identify your values:

1 **Actively tune into other people's values.**
    When you're in a conversation, listening to a lecture or chatting with colleagues, pick up on the values that others are putting out. Ask them further questions. Learn from those immediately around you and more importantly, learn from those with different cultures and life perspectives to you.

2 **See a counsellor or therapist.**
    Visiting a counsellor was a huge help for me. Establishing values wasn't the intended goal of my initial session, but simply talking to someone else (specifically an expert who's literally trained in talking) about my most private thoughts and feelings helped me understand more about who I am.

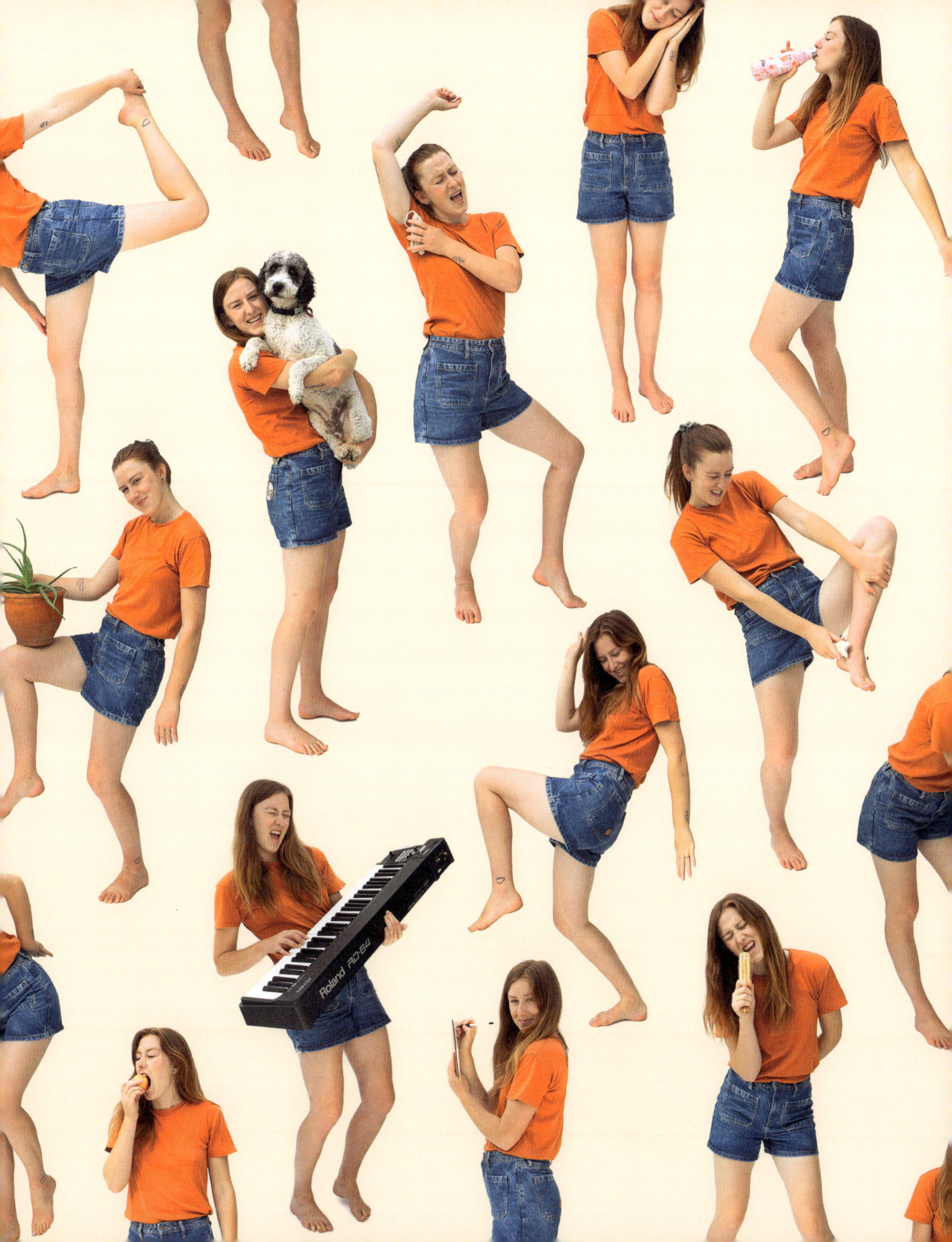
Roland RD-64

A few of my values

Contribution — volunteering, planting trees, giving back.

Authenticity — giving #nolovetolitter on social media (no likes, shares, comments on single-use cups). I don't engage with social media posts that have disposable, single-use litter in them. This movement was started by my friend Laura from uyo.co.nz

Self-respect — weekly check-ins, work-time boundaries, self-care practices.

Play — spending time with kids, playing with my dog, playing board games with Tim every week.

Learning — constantly reading, watching documentaries, listening and being inquisitive. Particularly being open to learning from people in different parts of the world, who share contrasting opinions, and have diverse world views.

3. **Absorb information.**
Whether you're a podcast addict, a movie buff, a documentary enthusiast, a music fanatic or a book lover, absorb what you can by listening to what others have to say about life on earth. All these forms of media I just mentioned are examples of ways humans communicate their values and philosophies with other people.

4. **Notice the little things.**
If you are conscious of the small actions that make up your life, you'll be able to put a finger on your values. Write a list of the things you do every day. Document the things you hate other people doing, the things you could not live without (tangible and intangible), and the things you want to do more of. Dig deeper into them. Understand why you felt so strongly about them that you wrote them down.

For example, I value sitting down in the morning and drinking a cup of tea thoughtfully. I value the taste of tea, yes, but I also value slowing down and acknowledging my existence. To me, that's what slowly having a hot drink at the start of the day symbolises. In our fast-paced society 'slow' is a value that is getting more and more difficult to hold on to. I'm sure if you analyse the actions you do regularly, e.g. picking up rubbish when you walk to the bus stop, visiting your grandmother every week for dinner, or saving your gift-wrapping to reuse, you'll be able to pinpoint values that you didn't realise were so important to you.

Once you've identified your values, it's easier to live a happier life and know what activities you'd like to prioritise. Your values guide your actions and can help you make decisions.

Three key values that help me live life differently and navigate sustainable living are :

1. Reject busy.

2. Your reaction is your responsibility.

3. Joy first.

Weird stuff I do that show the values I have and that make me ME:

- Hang my dog's fur on the washing line for birds to use for their nests.

- Use the least amount of toilet paper squares possible.

- Water my plants with the water I used to boil eggs or sterilise my menstrual cup.

- Pick hair ties up off the ground because the ground is one huge hairtie store.

- Freeze overripe/rotting fruit to use in baking and smoothies.

- Wash and reuse things usually classified as rubbish.

- Use vegetable scraps to make stock.

- Keep a large bucket in the kitchen sink during summer to water the veggie garden.

The zero waste hierarchy

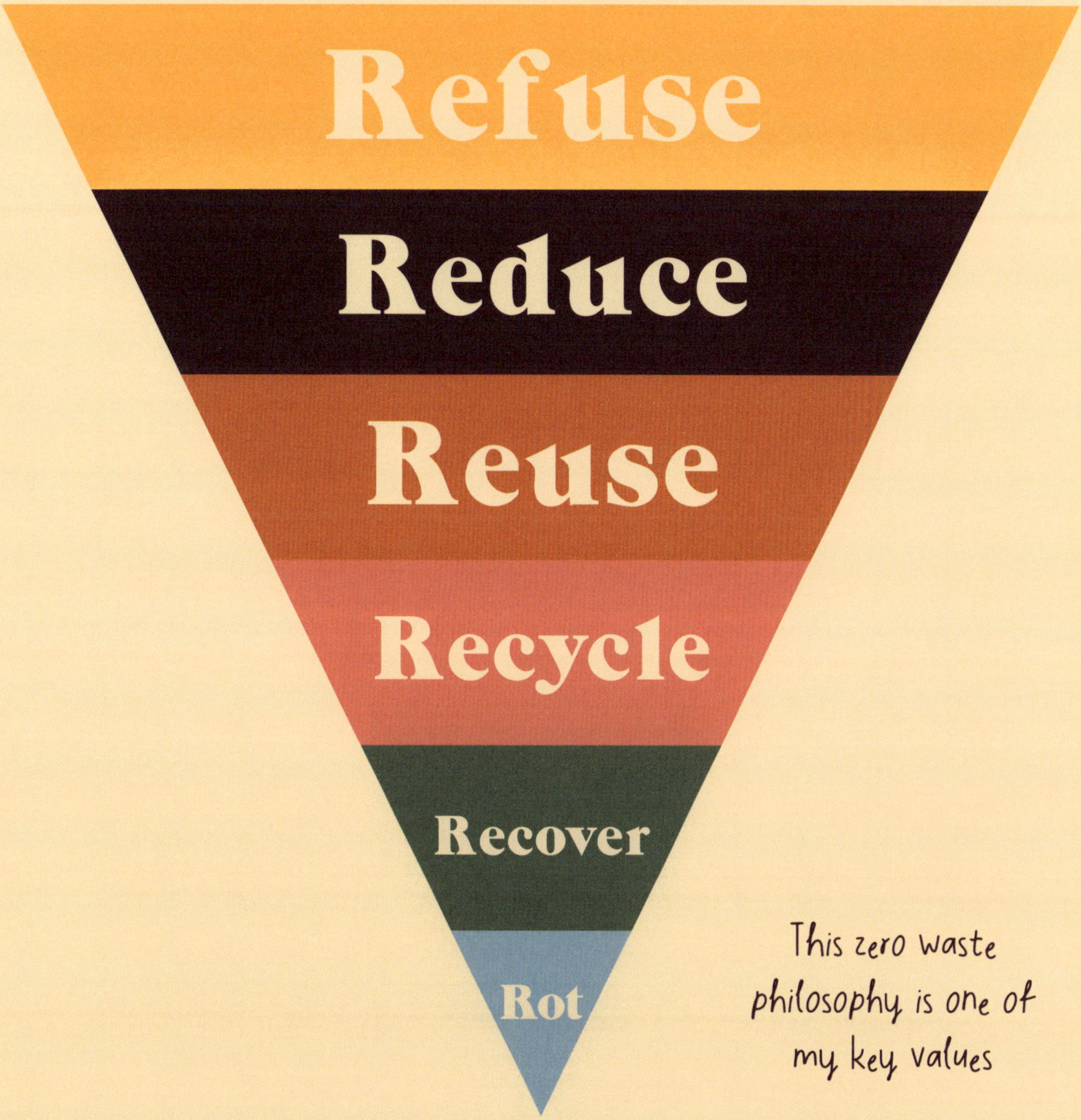
Refuse
Reduce
Reuse
Recycle
Recover
Rot

This zero waste philosophy is one of my key values

Storytime

One of the best days of my life happened in Mongolia. I was with Dad on a vet trip in the countryside. We travelled through vast, desert-like land and visited a few villages where help was needed. I would entertain myself while Dad worked. On this particular day, we were stationed at one family's home for the day and joined by a Mongolian vet. She brought along her daughter, the same age as me. For an entire day, we occupied our ten-year-old selves.

We communicated with each other in signs and emotions. We pushed tyres up hills and stared at the goats. We balanced along dodgy fenceposts and ran around the sheep pens. Most of our communication happened through laughter or weird eyebrow movements and we didn't need anything else apart from each other to have the best time of our lives.

I often think back to that day. As time goes on I forget the exact details but I still remember the feeling. The feeling of simply being. Being together with no form of entertainment aside from random pieces of junk around us and the hilarity of communicating in different ways. That day constantly reminds me that life doesn't have to be busy. I don't have to always be achieving in order to be fulfilled.

Reject busy

When someone asks 'How are you?', it seems that 90 per cent of the time, the reply is 'Busy'. This is a pet peeve of mine because 'busy' doesn't usually tell someone how you are. 'Busy' is basically replying 'I'm doing lots of things and filling my time to make myself valuable to society at the cost of my health.' Sure, I've overanalysed this common conversation, but most often it's true.

Everyone's thirst for busyness is unhelpful. Most people who are 'busy' could have avoided this busyness. We're all running around being 'busy' even though we've advanced in technology to make things like washing machines and toasters so we can spend less time surviving . . . yet we're arguably the busiest (and most unfulfilled) we've ever been.

This classic conversation isn't only a personal dislike of mine, but I believe it's also one of the reasons why we have such a huge mental health and climate crisis on our hands.

If we're not busy, we are useless.

If we're not stressed, we are not contributing enough to society.

If we're not tired, we're selfish.

The world as we know it doesn't allow us to simply be — and shouldn't that be our main focus?

I'd like to propose that the reason we're in this environmental mess (or whatever you want to call it) is because we don't spend enough time making our food, healing our bodies, breathing and loving. We've become too caught up in our own success and the pressure of society to perform to remember how to 'be'.

To live life differently and sustainably, the best thing you can do is *slow down*.

Spend time sitting. Learn how to make your own food. Stop and chat. Say 'no' more often. Breathe. Look around you. Touch a tree. Watch someone laugh. Turn your brain off. Enjoy someone's company. Change something in your life to benefit your body. Smile. Declutter the week of events you're dreading and don't feel obliged to tell anyone why you're cancelling. Unfollow those who don't fill your cup on social media. Uninstall apps that drain your time. Dedicate a space (even if it's just 30 minutes) to doing something selfish.

I've banned 'busy' from my vocabulary in efforts to try to stop 'busy' culture and replace it with values of wellness and joy. I see 'busy' as a state of mind and a state of being. The truth is, most people have a full life and always have something to do. We're all 'busy'. But you can go about those tasks and activities with a 'busy' state of mind and a busy presence, or you can achieve them one by one with a strategic and grounded mindset.

I'm constantly re-learning how to avoid being 'busy'. When I reflect, I realise it's less about cutting things out of my life, and more about how I conduct myself. My life will always be full, I'll always have something to do, but I will always have the choice to be 'busy' in this full life, or to go about my tasks with joy, gratefulness and mindfulness.

Your reaction is your responsibility

Tim has taught me many things — like pairing your socks on the washing line saves time and avoids lost socks — but my favourite so far has been this: 'Your reaction is your responsibility.'

I've taken this philosophy, this glorious advice, and woven it through my life. It's why I cannot hold a grudge or hold hateful feelings towards someone for longer than a second. It's why when huge, stressful situations happen at work, I can usually manage them without breaking down.

When I owned my childcare company one of my employees brought her dog with her to her usual family that she nannied for. This was not an uncommon occurrence and she had the family's permission.

I remember exactly where I was in the house when I received a phone call from her, telling me that her dog had killed the family cat. I could have broken down on the spot, I could have yelled at her, I could have given up my business altogether — I could have done many things. But 'your reaction is your responsibility' whispers in my ear in moments of stress and chaos and it didn't fail me this time either.

'My reaction is my responsibility. It's my responsibility to manage my feelings and emotions, to choose the best way to react in this situation.'

So, I calmly made sure she was okay. I made sure the family was okay, too. I did what I needed to do. I processed the loss and fear of what the situation could have grown into if the family weren't so darn lovely, and welcomed my emotions after dealing with the practicalities.

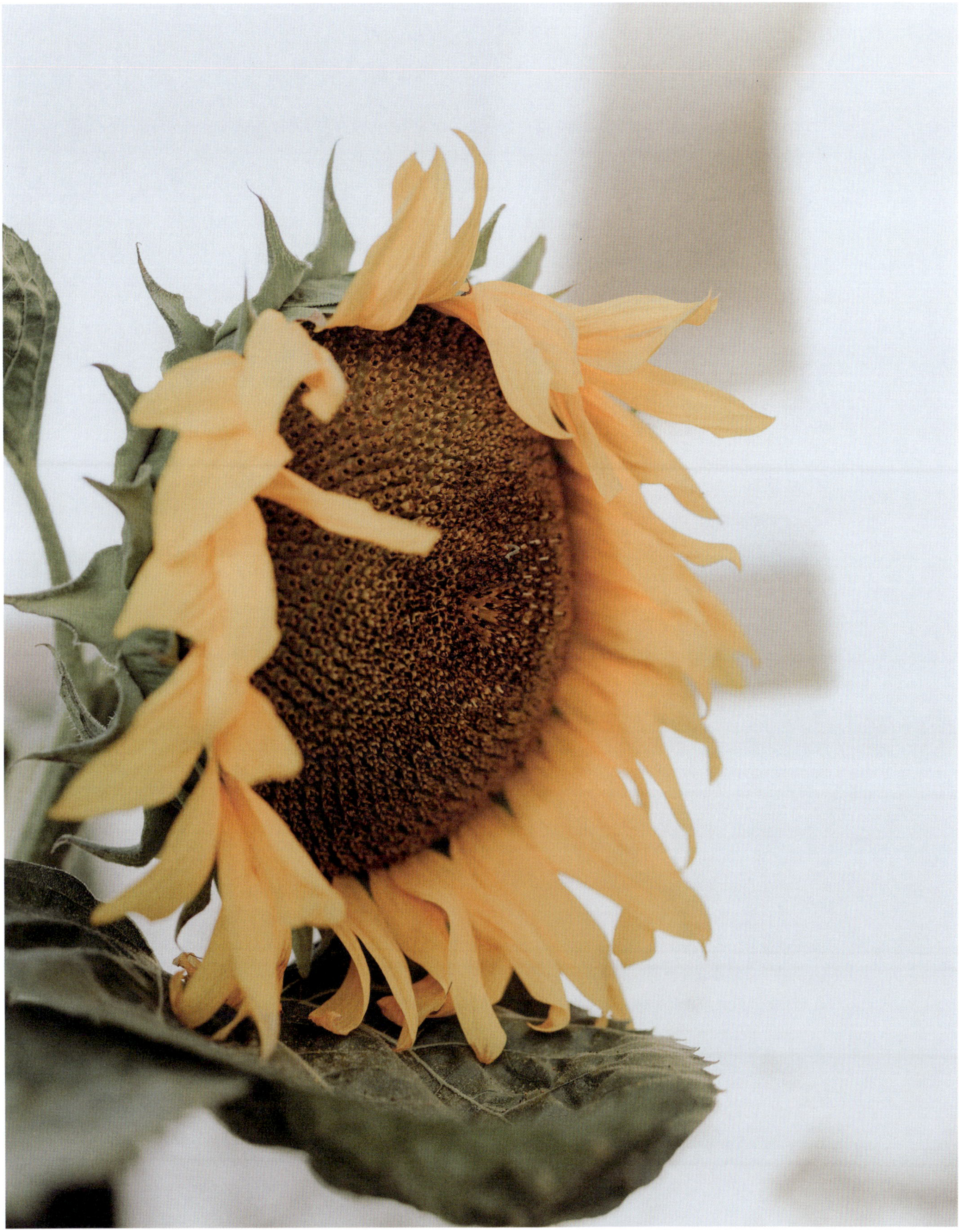

I still think back to this moment. I cannot believe that I handled it that way. I am one of those 'wear your feelings on your sleeve' kind of people and could easily have melted into the floor right there and then. This is just one example of how 'your reaction is your responsibility' has helped me. I use it to guide myself in times where I could be offended, I could judge or I could run away. My reaction is my responsibility so I can choose to make it a healthy one, leaning into the situation and attempting to understand every part rationally, or I can choose to react in an unhelpful way that may hurt myself or others. Of course I am human, so it doesn't mean I respond excellently to all situations, but keeping this value close increases the chances of major moments turning out better for everyone.

Joy first

Our world is heavy, always. Toxic people, natural disasters, corruption and discrimination are found everywhere you look. At any point in time, I could search for a recent headline and let the weight of the world drown me.

But I choose joy first.

Not in an ignorant way (I do my best to stay up to date with what is happening in the world) but in a helpful way that doesn't rob me of living. For example, take this common question 'How do you deal with climate anxiety and grief?' This is how I deal with it and how I recommend others do, too:

- Don't deny climate anxiety. Honour it, respect those feelings, let them unfold. Understand that they are valid.
- Acknowledge you have a short life on earth. Think rationally: Would this short life be more helpful to others and the planet if you lived in despair or joy?
- Spend time in nature and observe its resilience, systems, strength and beauty. If you don't have an outdoor space close by, watch documentaries (David Attenborough is your man), turn on soundtracks and close your eyes.
- Seek out positive news! There is so much goodness in the world — it just doesn't always make the headlines.

It's a privilege to live within your values.

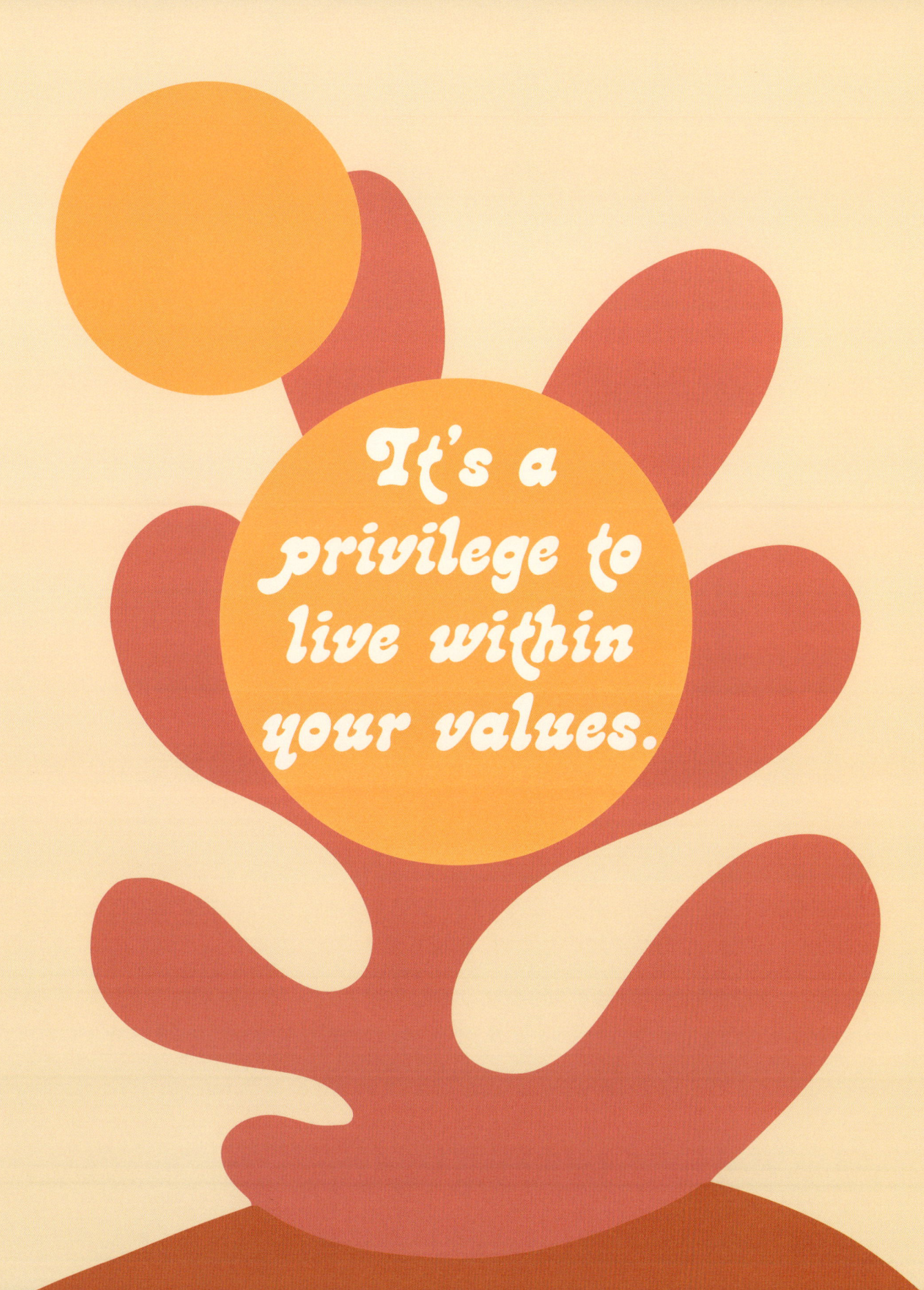

- Fill your life with positive and resilience-building habits (like the ones mentioned in the Wellbeing chapter).
- Talk to people about it. Open up, because it's highly likely they're feeling it too.
- Make small goals. Instead of 'solve our climate crisis', work on reducing your plastic consumption or sign a waste reduction petition. Think of one action to take to work towards your goal every day.

Every day I make a list of three core tasks to complete at work. But every single day of the week my list is always this: evading busyness, taking ownership of my reactions and finding joy. To me, these values *are* sustainable living. They may not be the classic 'BYO reusable cup to get a coffee', yet without them I couldn't live a low-waste lifestyle, connect and share with my community, or have the capacity to look for fair-trade certifications on my food at the grocery store. Sustainable living starts with your values — they are the building blocks.

Routines

I've always wanted to shadow my close friends and family at their work and on the weekends. Even though I know what they all do for a job and their hobbies, without watching them in action and witnessing their everyday routines and habits, I'll never truly know them. It's why moving in with someone is a huge step in a relationship (you witness their most mundane habits), and why most people say travelling with someone is the best test for any type of relationship.

This is what a classic morning looks like in my world:

1. Wake up between 6 and 7am, without an alarm.
2. Grab the dog and head out the door (usually a long walk through the streets, ending at the beach).
3. Sometimes yoga or meditation.
4. Breakfast with a book, while managing my bird's and dog's needs.
5. Reflect on calendar and daily to-do list.

Even in this list, you didn't see the way I took my shoes off at the door. The little piece of rubbish I picked up on the beach. The conscious deep breaths I took while I walked. The thousands of thoughts I processed at the park. The reusable tea-leaf strainer I used to make my tea. To understand yourself, to align your values with your actions, to live a different and more fulfilling life, watch what you do.

Take note of all the little things you do. Write them down, or simply schedule a day where you're incredibly conscious of your habits. Reflect on what actions make you feel happy and what habits you were surprised about or may need to change.

Moving on to the bigger things I do that align who I am with how I inhabit this planet, you may be surprised to find some boring adulting tasks listed. But over the last few years I've been learning that every decision I make affects people and the planet. Bills, banks and savings are big decisions.

The more I've reflected on where I spend my money, where I store my money and the service providers I support, the stronger my sense of self has become. Though I continue to remember the quote on page 103 — 'it's a privilege to live within your values'. I try my best to live to mine and be an ally for those who can't.

Here are some of the bigger parts of my life I've aligned with my values and self:

Savings

In Aotearoa New Zealand, we have a scheme called KiwiSaver. Some people know this as a retirement fund or superannuation. It's retirement savings that can also be used to buy your first home. Most New Zealanders have a KiwiSaver that they contribute to, as well as their employer contributing. Essentially, it means that instead of putting away savings every week to ensure you have a cushion at the end of your life or can afford your first home, you put it in KiwiSaver instead. This means your money supports other projects and businesses rather than staying stagnant, and it generally makes higher returns than if it was held in a bank. Additionally, you cannot retrieve your KiwiSaver money on a whim!

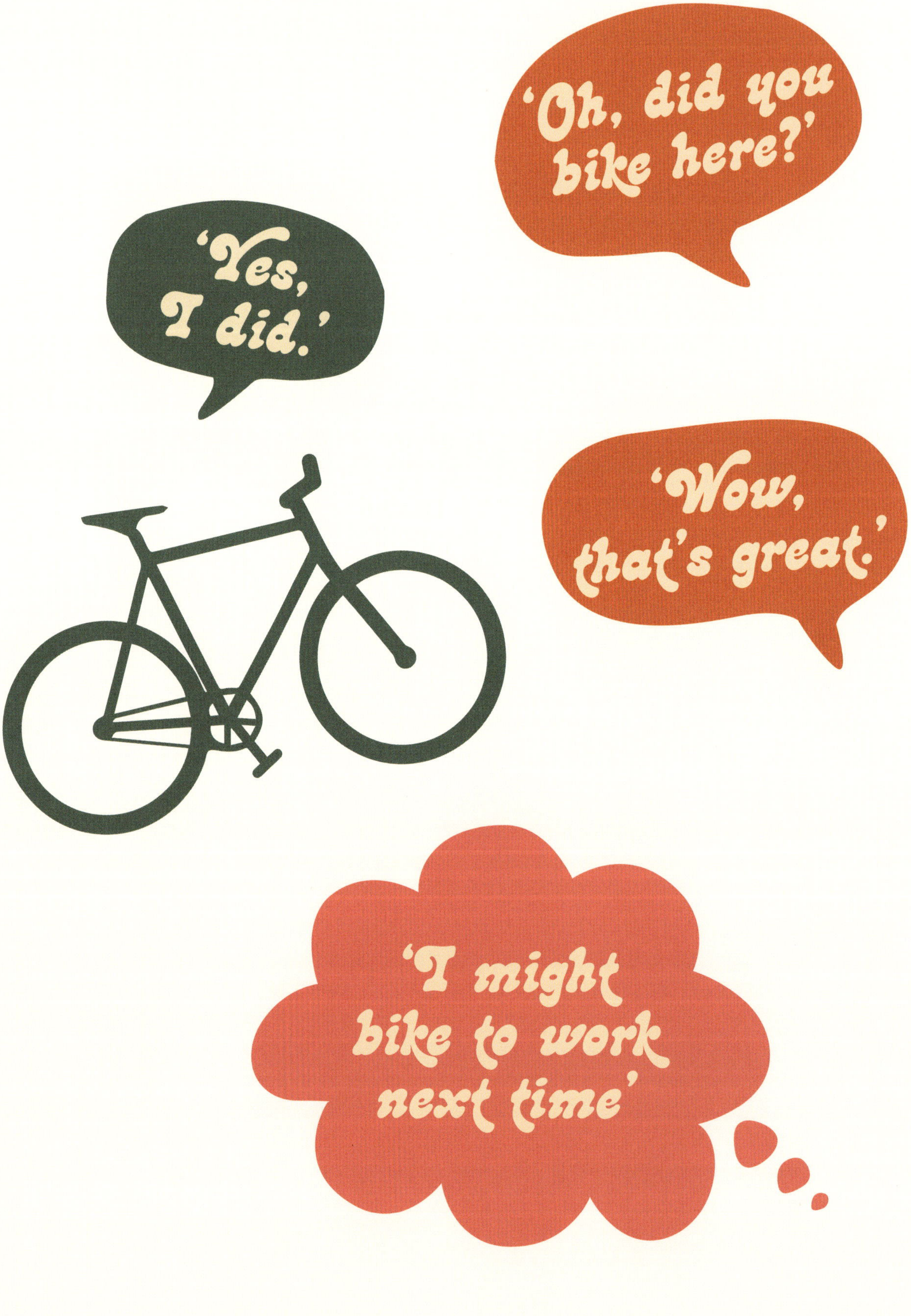
'Oh, did you bike here?'
'Yes, I did.'
'Wow, that's great.'
'I might bike to work next time'

There are hundreds of different KiwiSaver schemes, each with different values and projects that they invest in. Unfortunately, most of them invest in things like fossil fuels, alcohol, gambling, animal testing and weapons. Personally, these things do not align with my values, but for the first few years of having a KiwiSaver this is where my money was going!

Luckily, Aotearoa New Zealand now has several ethical KiwiSaver funds available. Switching to an ethical KiwiSaver scheme took me literally seven minutes, and felt like a massive relief.

Speaking of money, who do you bank with? The 'vote with your dollar' message is hard to escape in the media these days but it's easy to forget that the biggest way we can vote with our pockets is by choosing a sustainable bank. To be honest, most banks suck. It's almost like choosing the best of the worst when it comes to who to bank with.

Tim and I chose our bank because they are locally owned, lend $0 to fossil fuels, withhold business banking services from fossil-fuel companies, and have full corporate exclusion of fossil-fuel projects and/or companies. They also push for customers to opt out of receiving paper statements etc., and have strong values around inclusion in their team. They are a B Corp as well! B Corp certification means they make all their decisions with environmental and social values in mind.

Our insurance company is also a locally operated company and publicly celebrates the diversity of staff and customers. Whenever we employ someone to do a job for us or consider a new service provider, we ask questions instead of solely considering the cost.

By now, I think it's clear what I'm getting at. Living to your values includes all decision making. It covers your bills, your bank and all services you require. Because every time you sign a contract, spend money or associate with a service provider, you're saying 'yes' to the way they do business. As soon as you align yourself with a provider who shares the same values as you do, your sense of self will flourish. Making these decisions has helped me feel more like me. I also feel more in control and aware of my impact and surroundings. It's empowering.

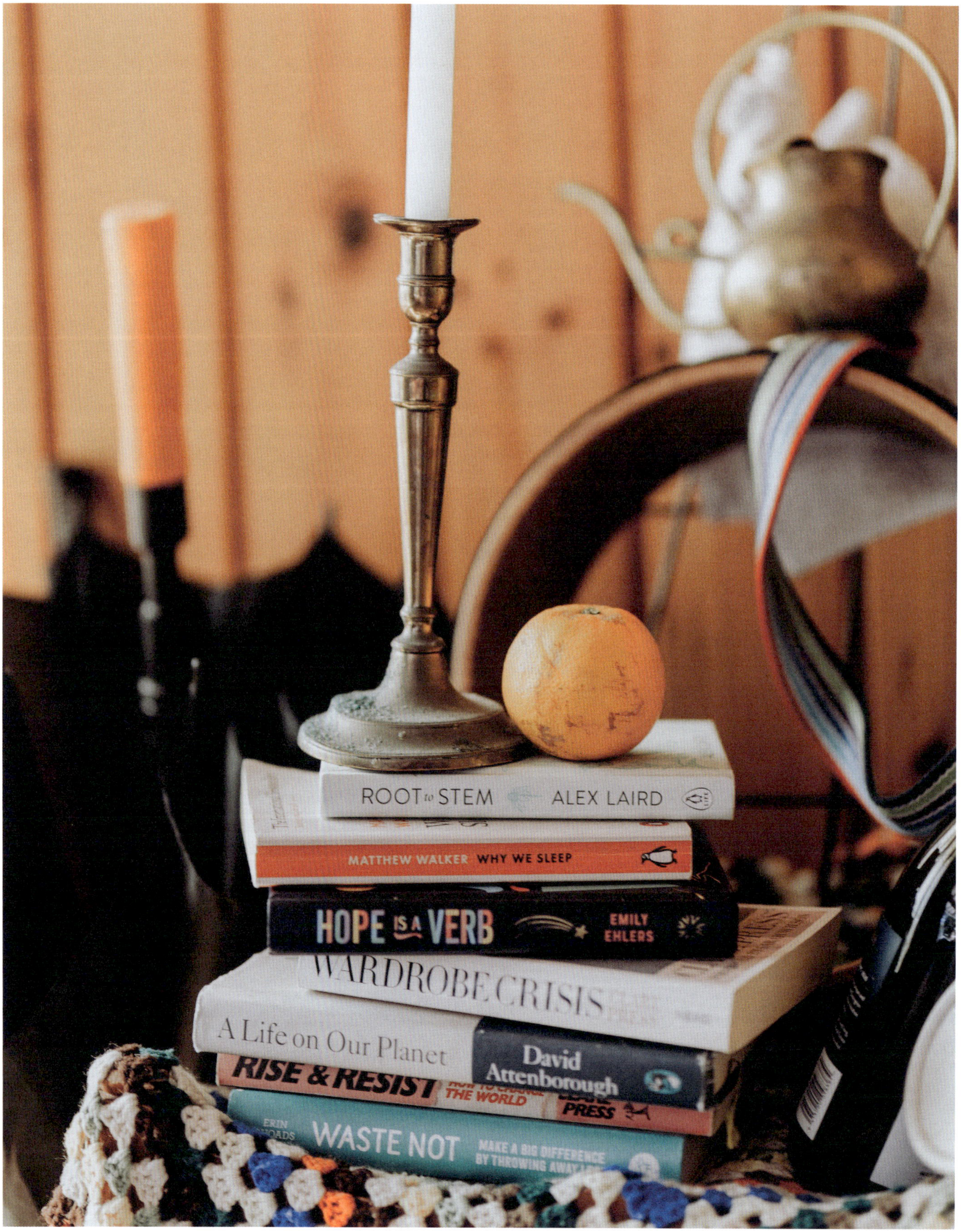
ROOT to STEM
ALEX LAIRD
MATTHEW WALKER
WHY WE SLEEP
HOPE IS A VERB
EMILY EHLERS
WARDROBE CRISIS
A Life on Our Planet
David Attenborough
RISE & RESIST
THE WORLD
PRESS
ERIN
WASTE NOT
MAKE A BIG DIFFERENCE

Car-free

Another part of growing my self-identity has come from my car-free life. In February 2021, I went carless. That doesn't mean I haven't been in a car since then! But I haven't owned a car since then.

This started as a short trial. My intention was to understand what life was like without a car so I could comprehend this uncommon (in Aotearoa New Zealand) way of living and have actual experience to draw upon when I encouraged people to avoid using their cars. No one would listen to me shout 'Use your car less' from my car window.

The trial turned into three months, then six months, and then after seven months I made the decision to purchase an electric bike instead of replacing my car. I went all in!

My commitment to having no car doesn't mean it is easy. In the early days, I felt incredibly claustrophobic and restricted. The extra time required to organise my transport to each meeting or event was taxing, and when the cold weather set in, it became even more of an inconvenience. But slowly, having no car became normal. Factoring in bus timetables or bike routes is now second nature. I make time, and I welcome the physical and mental benefits of strategic travel and being outdoors more often.

Throughout this change to a no-car lifestyle, I also learnt that how you transport yourself from A to B reflects a big part of who you are. It's exactly why car culture is such a huge phenomenon.

People obsess over their cars, even if they aren't 'car people'. We remember people's cars and know it's them when they're coming. The type of car a person owns generally tells us a lot about them. For me, going car-free had a greater impact on my sense of self than I could have ever expected.

Now, there is no car to associate me with. It's a beautiful vintage-looking bike or a tatty bus card and some hand sanitiser. Surprisingly, I find freedom in living life without a car. No parking hassles, no 'clean the car' task on my weekend to-do list. No service bills or WOF appointments. How I transport myself tells the world a lot about me; that I am different, that I don't want to use dinosaur juice to power my mode of transportation and that life can be done differently.

Knowing yourself, identifying what's important to you, and determining what small habits make you *you* is one of the first steps to a sustainable lifestyle. How the heck can we expect to live more sustainably without first acknowledging who we are and how we want to live? Without authenticity and self-awareness, sustainable habits won't be sustainable.

In a nutshell:

- Find your values before you start to make sustainable changes to your life.
- Acknowledge no one has exactly the same values as you.
- Avoid being 'busy'.
- Understand your reaction is your responsibility.
- Choose joy first.
- Self-assess your routine and make changes if needed.

To do list

Friendly reminder to be kind today.

Enrol to vote.

Drink lots of water.

Do your best.

Be empathetic but don't weigh yourself down irrationally.

Listen.

Give yourself a pat on the back at the little wins.

Take at least five conscious deep belly breaths.

Smile.

Relax your jaw.

Do something for someone else.

Do something selfish.

Ask someone for help.

Smile.

Make a tiny habit change for papatūānuku (land).

Watch a one-minute video about a topic you know nothing about.

Stop for 30 seconds to hear+smell+touch+see+taste your surroundings.

Move your body.

Smile.

Eat your vegetables.

Ask someone how they are doing.

Smile.

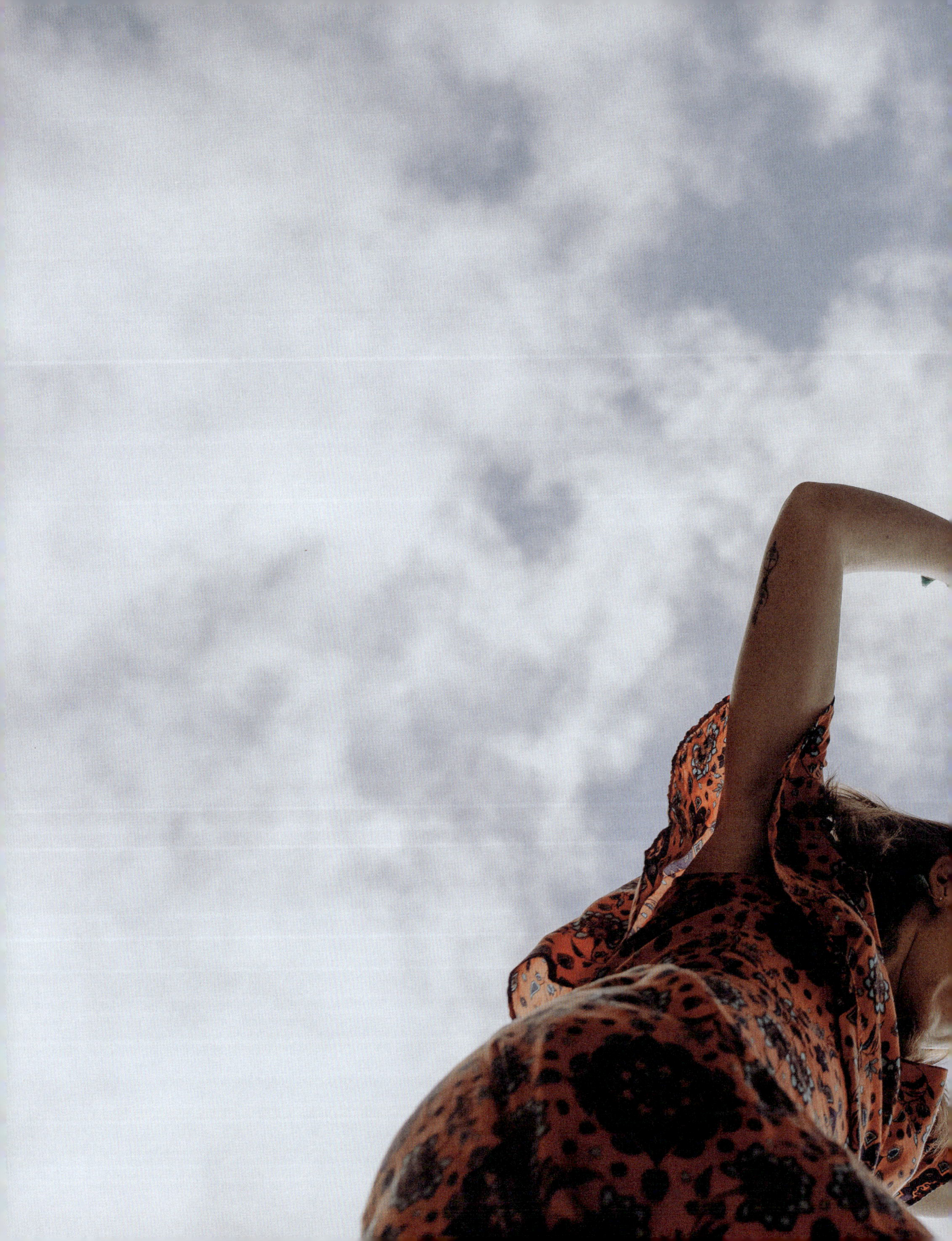

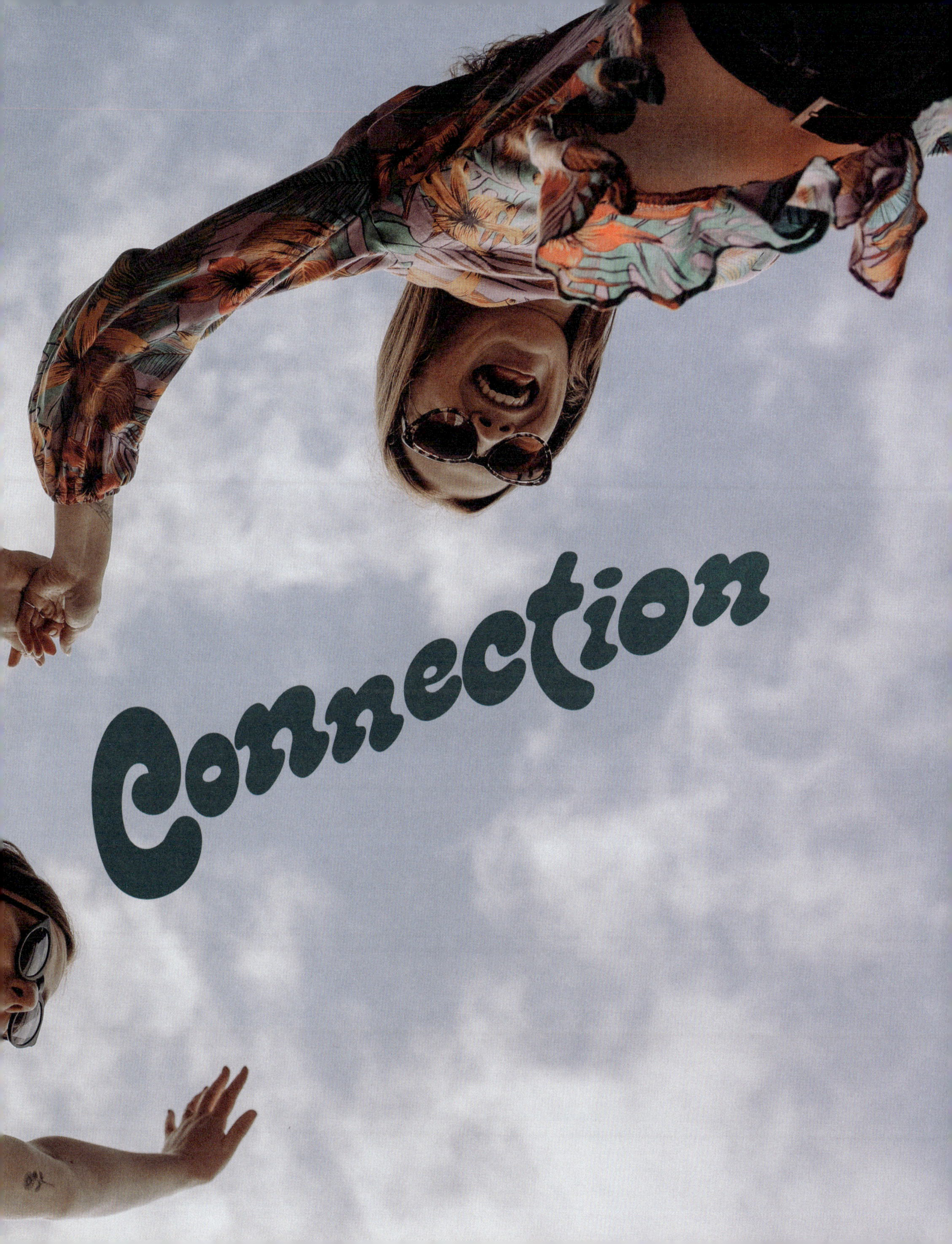

Connection

If it didn't sound too clichéd, this section would be called 'Relationships' — but then you'd think I was about to give you relationship advice for you and your partner and tell you to 'live laugh love' and never go to bed angry. Or if you're single you'd tell me to piss off. This section is way more than that. If we're breaking down the key aspects of life and considering how we can live them better, bolder and differently, then **connection** needs to be right up there.

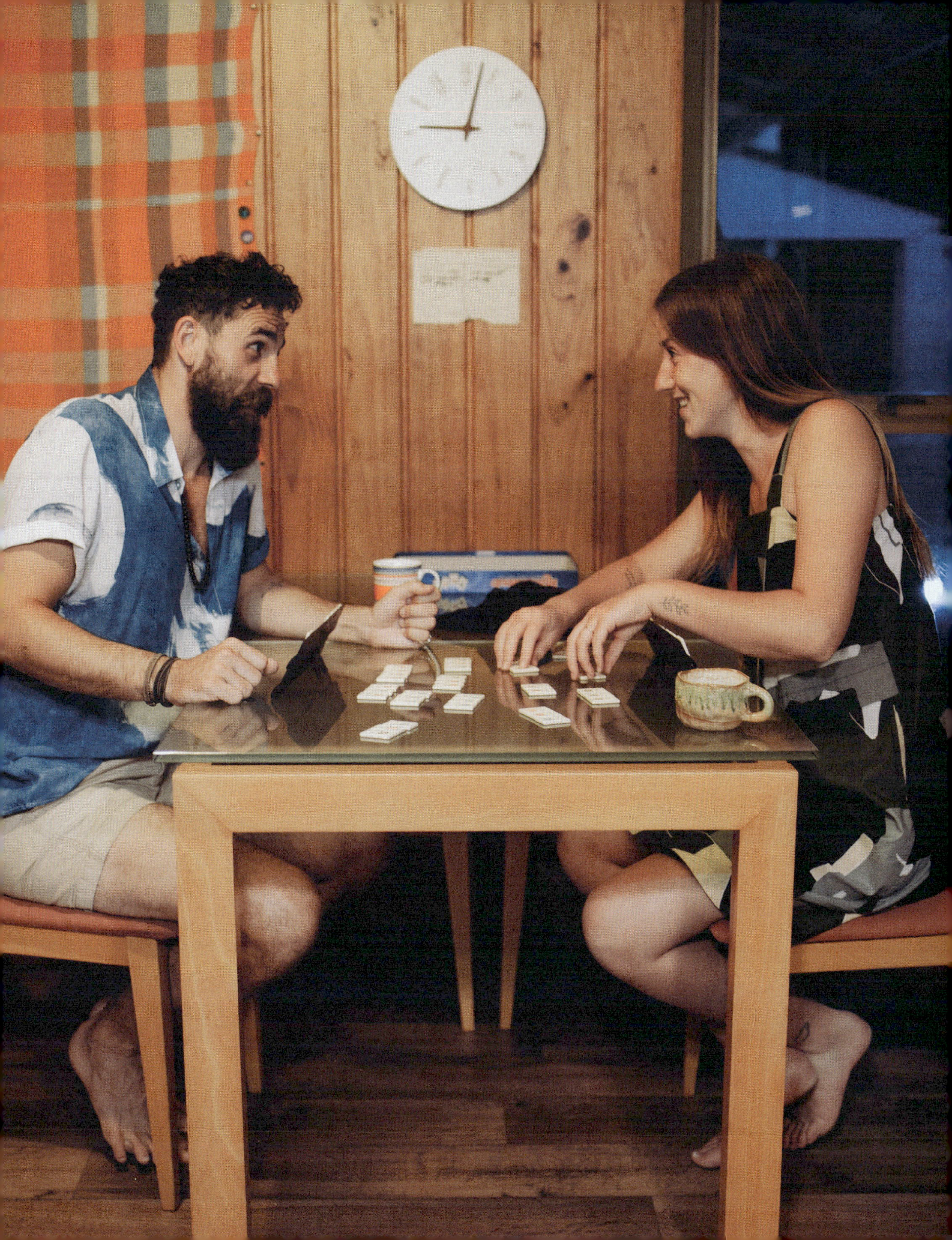

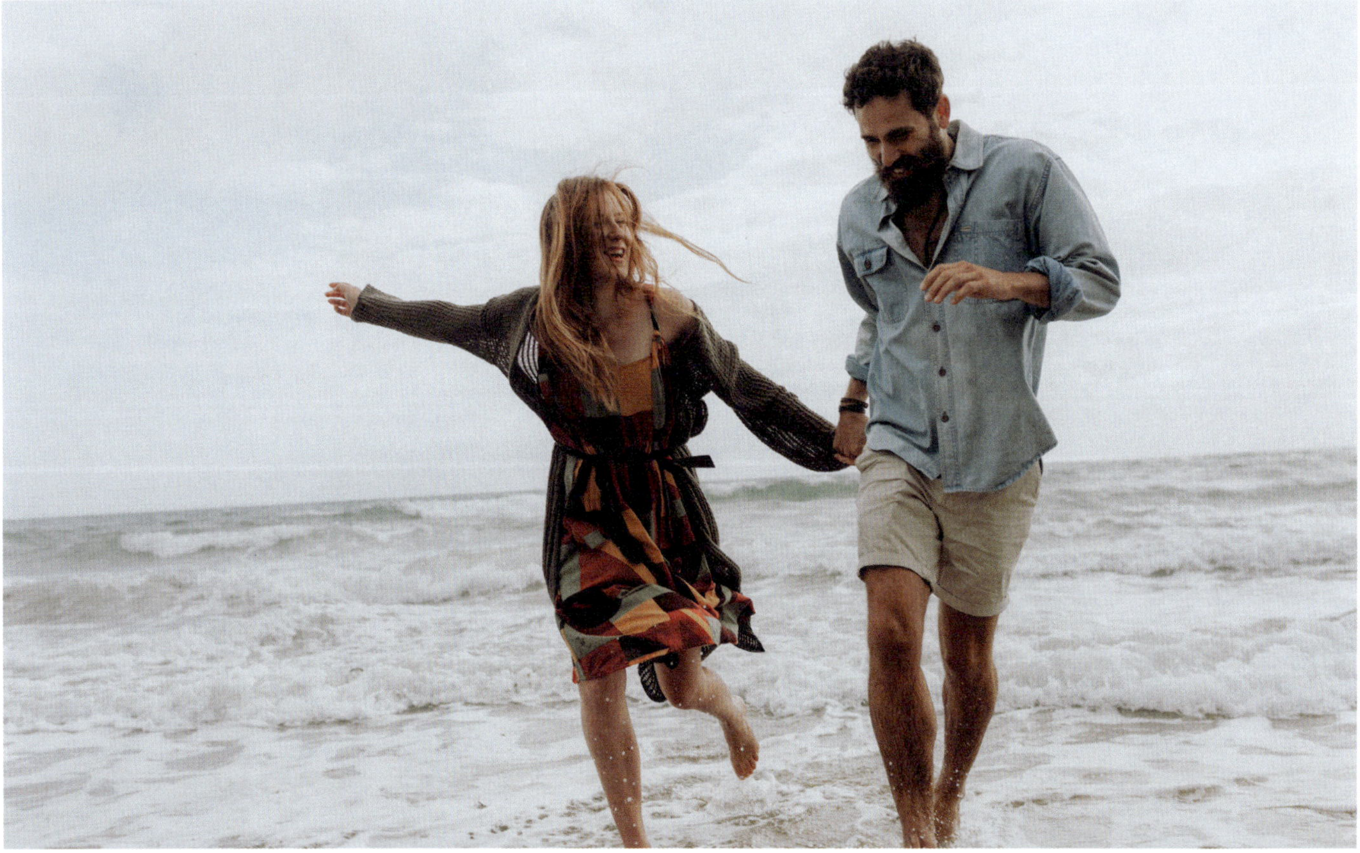

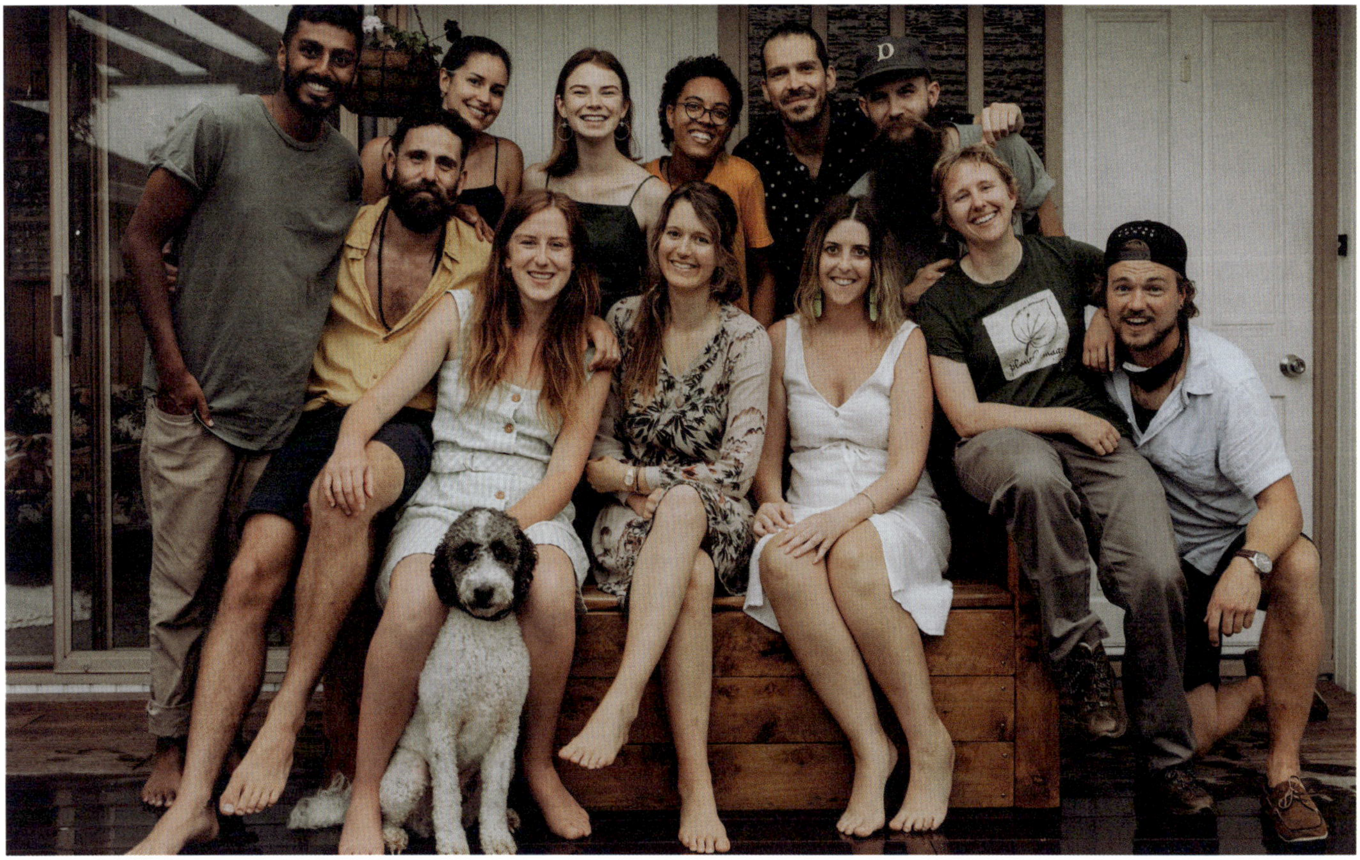

Connection is a well-researched and academically recognised essential need.[1] Without relationships with other human beings, we crumble. Humans are designed to live in community. I don't care if you're the biggest introvert in the entire world; you need people (neighbours, family, friends, colleagues) in order to survive and understanding this leads to a more sustainable life.

I'm ashamed to admit I didn't value connection with my neighbours until several years of living in The Rose Garden (our current home). Although I grew up knowing my neighbours like family, when I moved to my own house, I was too 'busy' to think about the value in connection with the people living right beside me. I was also shy and nervous to knock on their door. Now that Tim and I have reached out to our neighbours, life is better. We swap food, firewood, collaborate on making shared areas look tidier and check in on each other. I feel so much safer knowing who lives around me. This is just one example of how connection and community champion better living.

Unfortunately, society rewards individual success and makes us think ownership of things is the key to living. If instead we see items as shared resources, view actions as collective responsibilities, and strive for our impact to be a positive one made as a group, we'll see a world far more satisfied than the silos of loneliness we see today.

To convince you that you should talk to your neighbours, put more energy into your relationships, use resources more efficiently and value your family, I'll touch on sharing, romantic relationships and how to do things differently amongst your family. I'll even dive slightly off topic and share about our sustainable wedding.

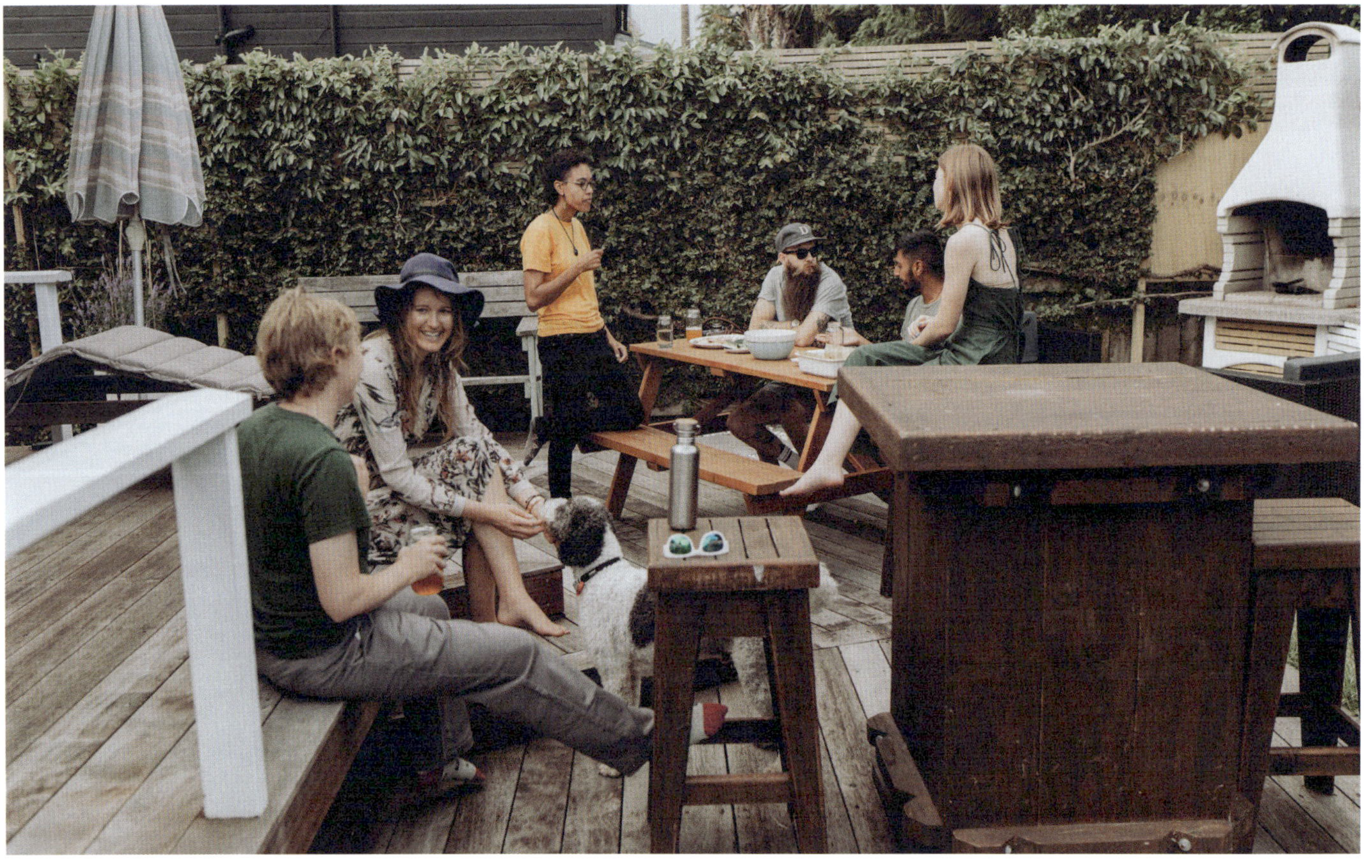

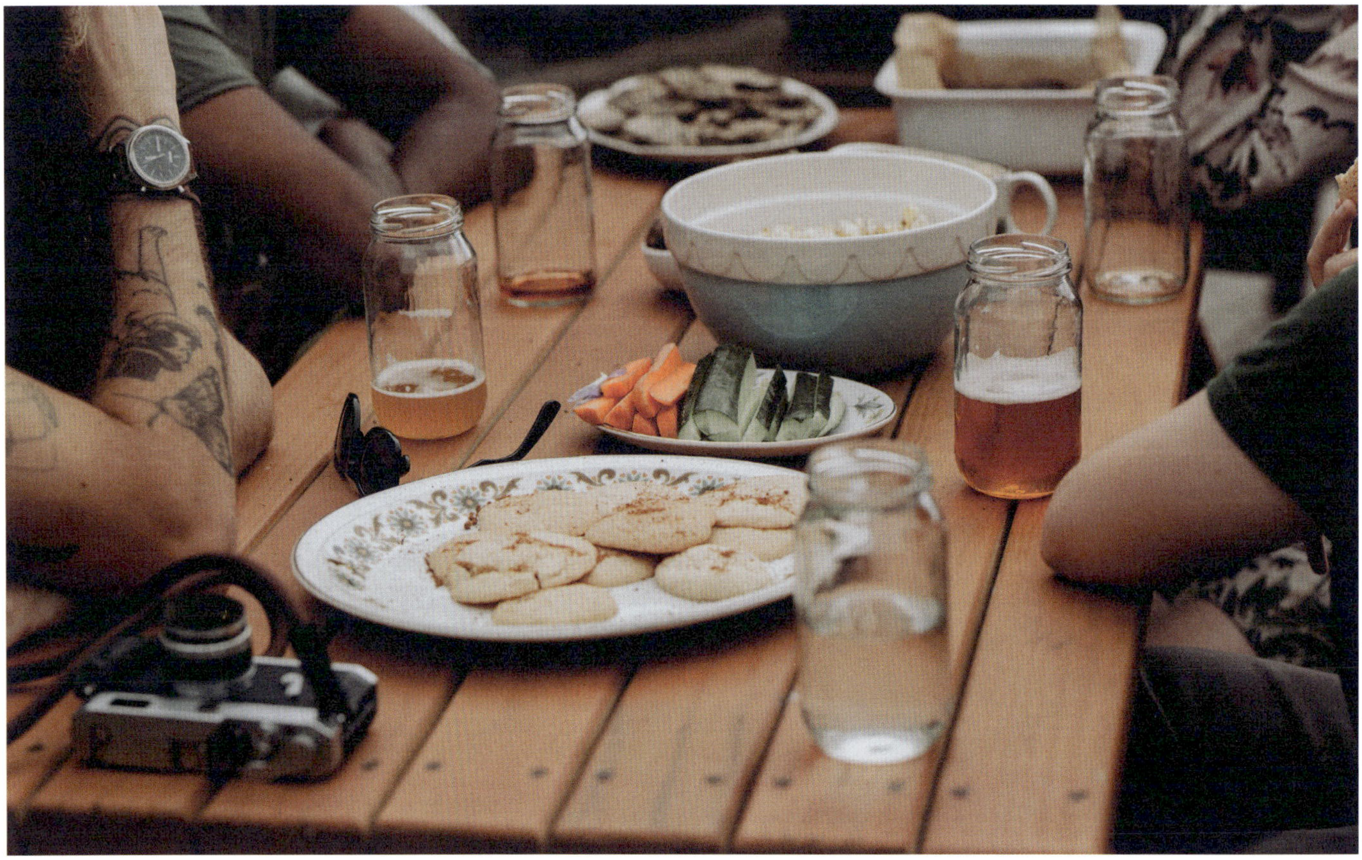

Sharing

As I walked along the street last week, I counted five people mowing their lawns in the space of 500 metres. But what happens next? The lawns are mown, the grass clippings are put in the rubbish (hopefully the compost, but I was doubtful) and the lawn mower goes back into the garden shed to rest for several weeks. I thought of all the surface area the dormant lawn mowers in my neighbourhood took up, the maintenance required and the admin needed, only to be used for just two hours of each month. I then compared this with the relationships that could be developed, the chats that could be had and the community vibe that could be shared if one street owned one lawn mower!

The sharing economy is a crucial part of sustainable living, but oh my goodness it is a different way to live.

Imagine suggesting to the proud owner of a sports car that they should share their car with others when they don't need it. Picture asking your friend with the new expensive dress if you could borrow it. Envisage co-owning an electric beater with your neighbour. Bold, right? Engaging in the sharing economy requires bravery and leadership, but this doesn't stop any of us from starting.

Children are taught 'sharing is caring' from a young age, and I'd like to suggest that this phrase should extend well beyond preschoolers.

Sharing is caring for the environment: less finite resources needed to make objects that are redundant for most of their lives.

Sharing is caring for your community: more interaction with your neighbours, families and friends. More opportunity to connect, to build them up and offer support through relationship with them.

Sharing is caring for your bank account: less cost, dispersed responsibility and lower ongoing maintenance fees.

Sharing is caring for yourself: the benefits of everything I've mentioned above will nurture resilience, joy and connection. No one can deny those are wonderful feelings!

Society has made it normal to share some things, like supermarket trolleys and waiting-room chairs, but there's still a stigma attached to sharing. When you share, people assume you don't have the money to buy your own, when really they should simply be impressed with your wisdom!

To show you that the sharing economy is already alive and well and just needs you to take a leap, I asked a few hundred people what they share with their neighbours, friends and family. This list shows the most common answers.

One of my personal sharing stories involves my reusable kit of cutlery, cups, bowls and plates. Over time I gathered cheap second-hand items and developed a set of serviceware items for around 50 people. Whenever we have a family gathering or picnic or someone throws a birthday party, I offer up my set. It's much more practical than single-use cups that snap in one squeeze, looks more sophisticated (once it was used for a post-wedding picnic) and results in zero waste.

I'm not suggesting you start sharing your underwear or borrow your friend's toothbrush, but next time you need something, why not borrow it?

Things people share:

- tools
- car
- bike pump
- kitchen appliances
- chickens
- compost
- trailer
- newspaper
- baby clothes and toys
- tractor
- lawn mower
- kids' bikes
- washing line
- label maker
- hot water bottle
- ladder
- broom
- sewing skills
- worm farm
- house washer
- paint brushes
- a cat
- a dog
- waffle maker
- baking
- vegetables
- digital skills
- music
- food
- fruit trees
- honey
- seedlings
- beer
- playground set
- apples
- aloe vera plants
- table
- kombucha
- kombucha scoby
- camping gear
- eggs
- books
- jars
- shed space
- firewood
- cake tins
- extra bedding
- board games
- lemons — SO MANY LEMONS!

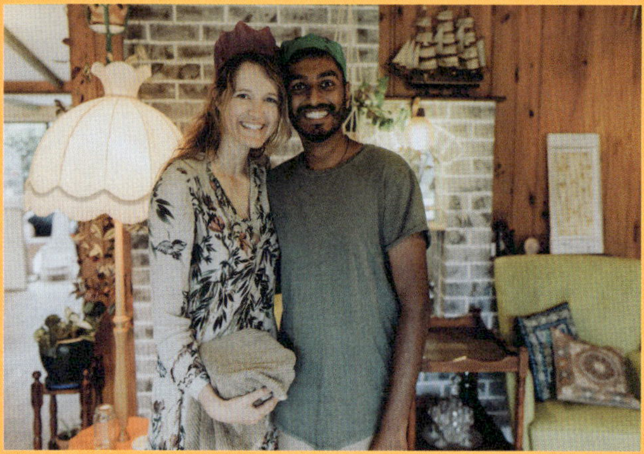

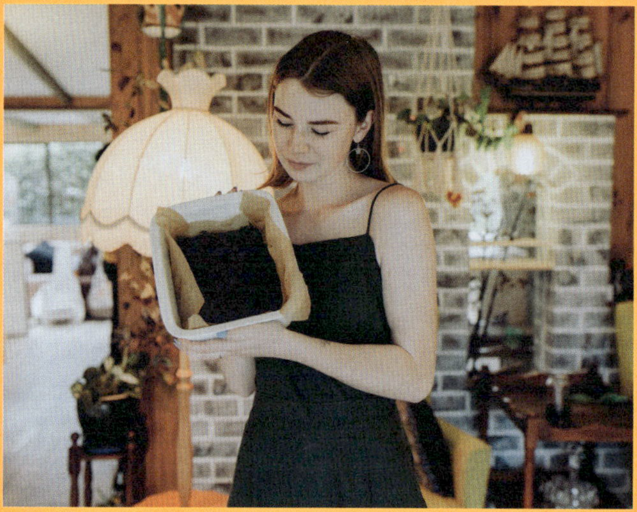

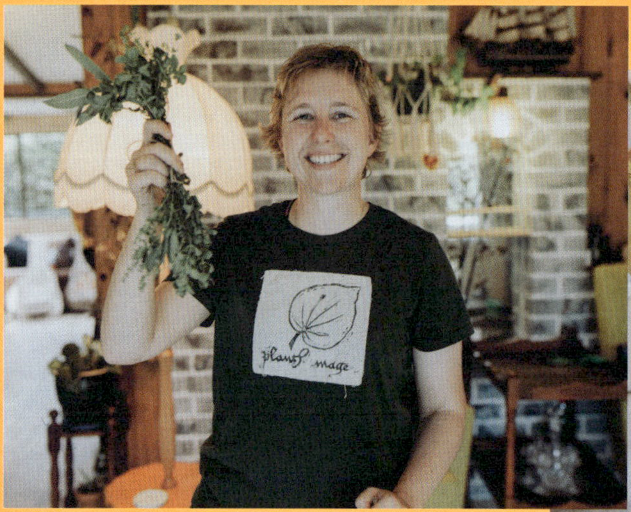

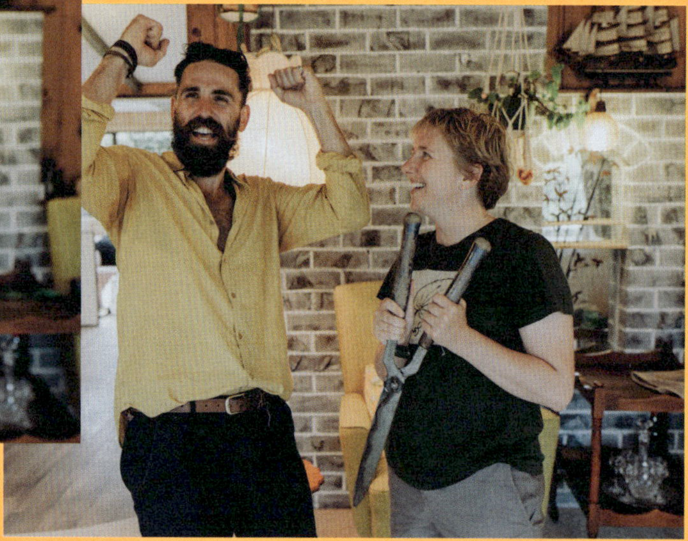

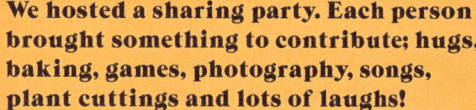

We hosted a sharing party. Each person brought something to contribute; hugs, baking, games, photography, songs, plant cuttings and lots of laughs!

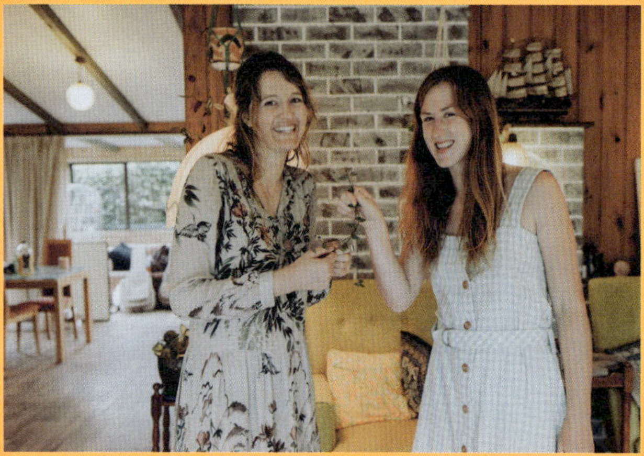

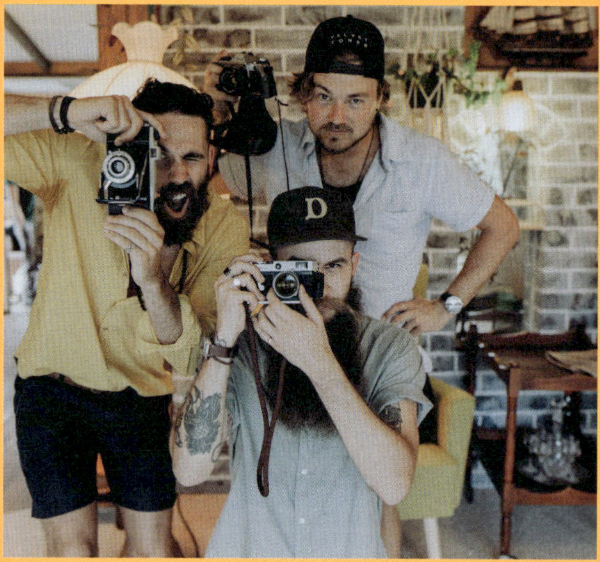

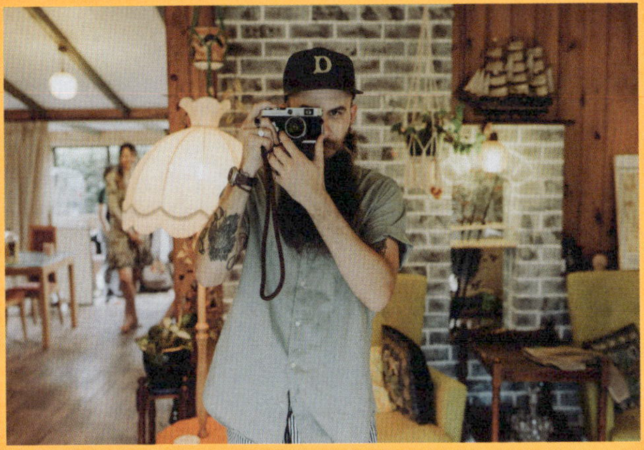
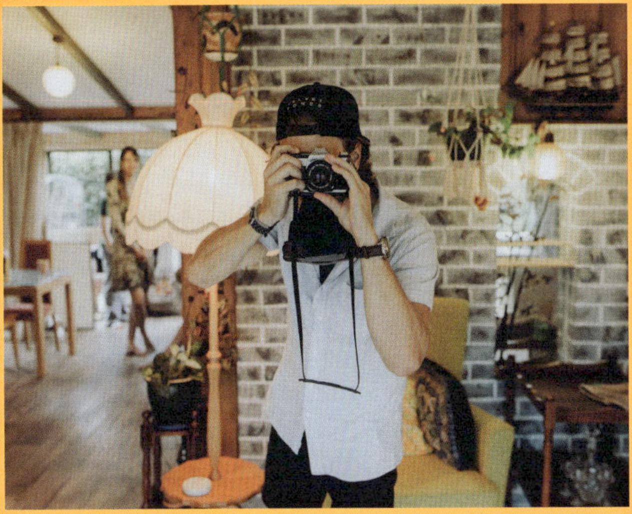
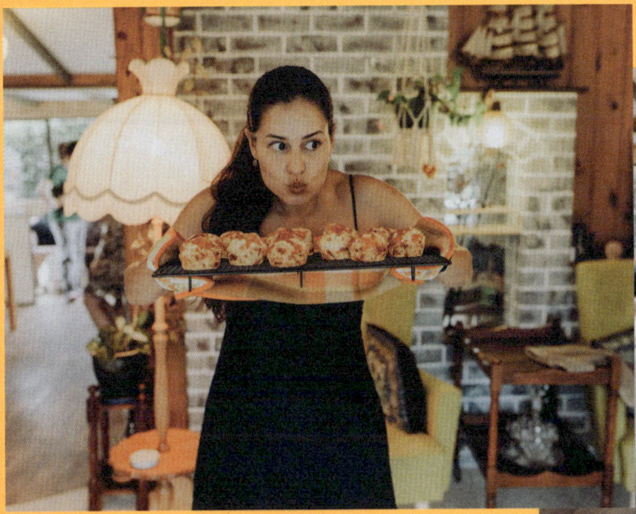
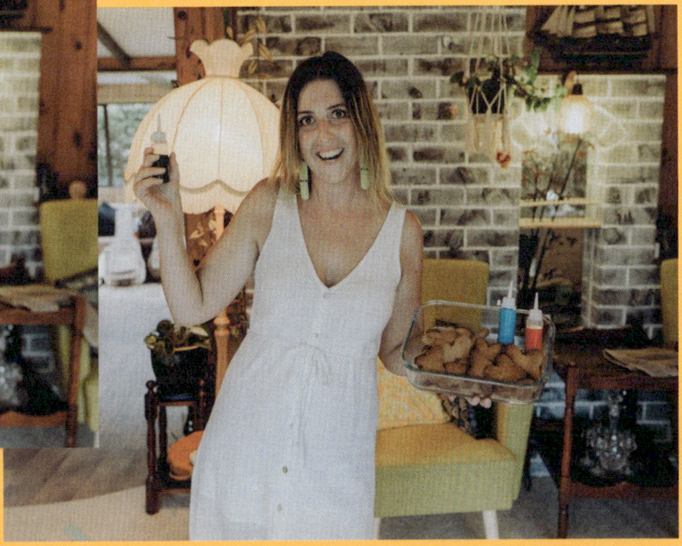
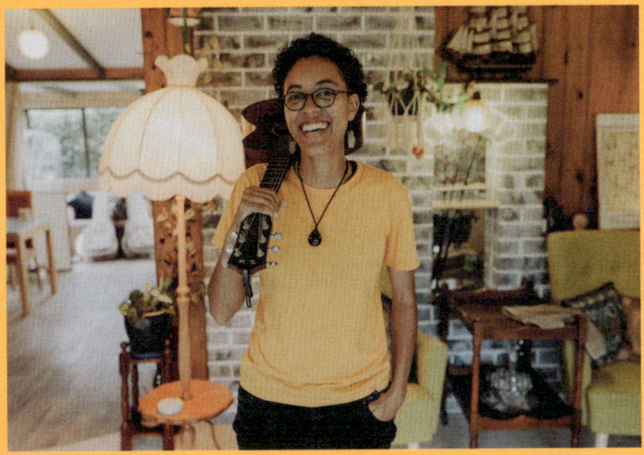
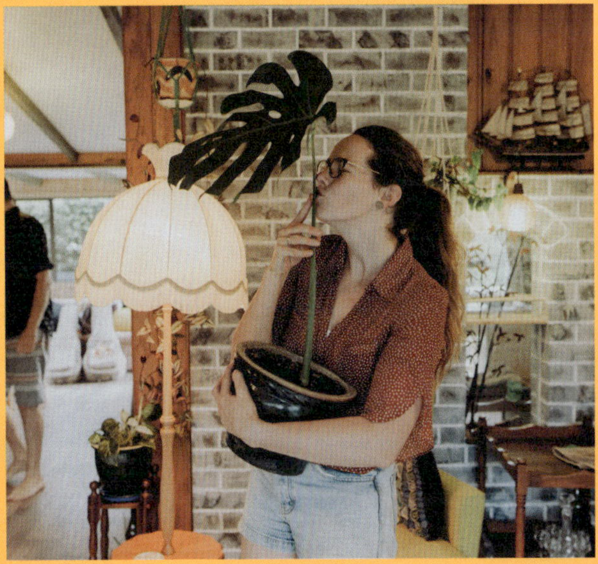

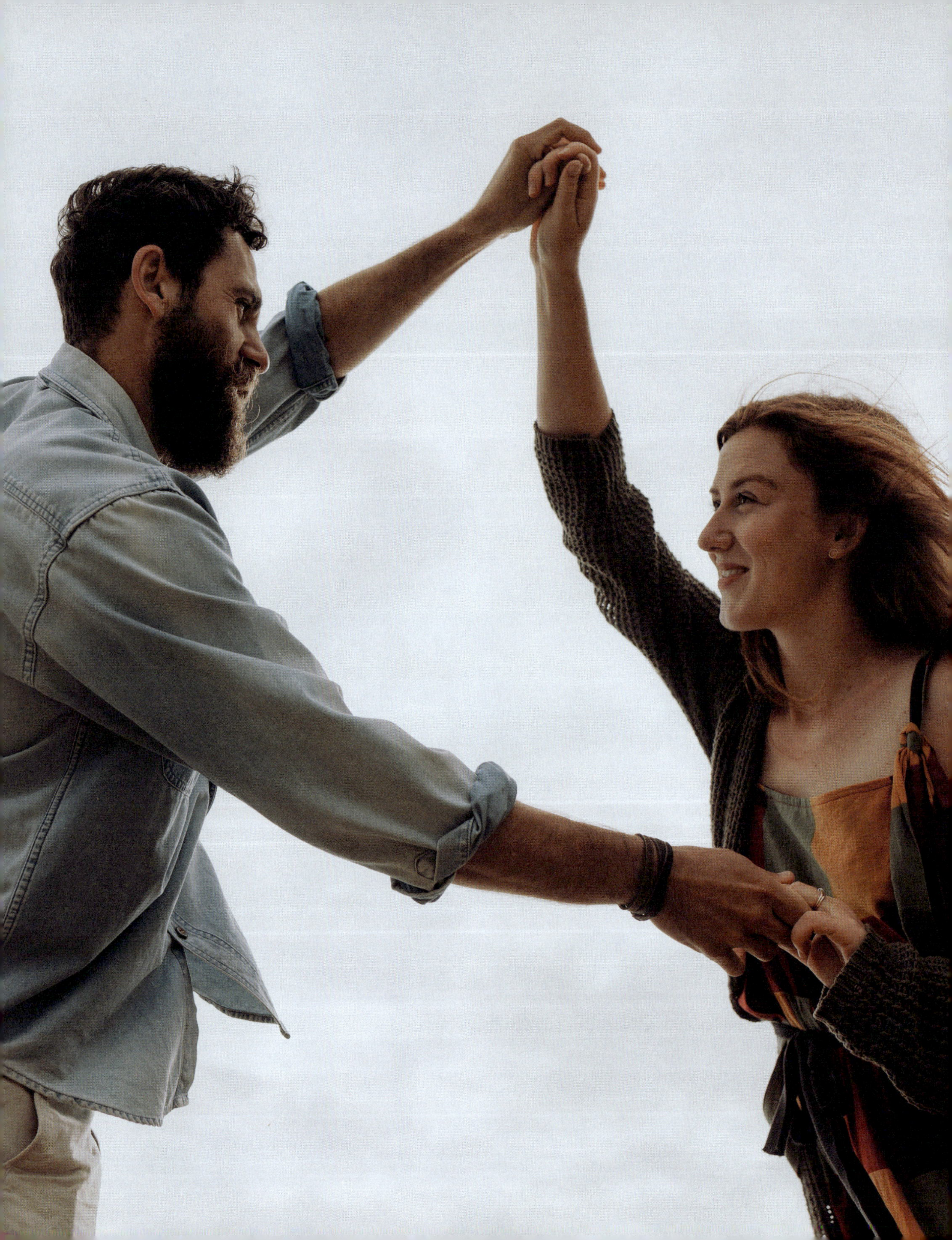

Romantic relationships

Aside from a couple of relationships when I was 14 that involved holding sweaty hands in the most awkward way possible at lunchtime, Tim was my first love. Although I am a little sad I didn't get to experience dating, because I know I would have loved it, being married to Tim is the best part of my life. He's not my soulmate (I don't believe in those) and I could live without him. But we choose to be together because life is best as a duo. We work hard to make our partnership an epic one!

How we came to be 'Tim & Kate'

Tim and I knew each other for quite a long time before we acknowledged each other as a potential couple. It's hard to identify the moment we started dating, but a Coldplay concert in 2012 was the catalyst. A group of us carpooled together in a van. It was the first time we connected outside of the church community we knew each other from. We sat beside each other at the concert and connected over music. We talked all night and arranged to start casually recording music together. Tim offered me his vest when I appeared cold, but I remember stubbornly refusing it because I knew that's what men did when they liked a girl in the movies.

I also made a list on our way home from the concert when sitting in the van. A list of all the reasons why I didn't like Tim and why a relationship wouldn't work. The list included things like *He's too outgoing and I want someone who's introverted and balances my wildness.* The age thing was on the list too; he was seven years older than me and I was aware a woman's life expectancy is higher than a male's, so I convinced myself it would be tragic to have such a lonely elderly life.

After frequently playing music together, we were asked to play our mutual friends down the aisle. Turns out you can only sing so many love songs before falling in love. Four years later, we got married ourselves. I metaphorically threw that list out the window.

Together, we've crafted a set of rituals and habits:

- Always touch when having a big conversation.

- Celebrate on the first night of my period.
- Say thank you.
- Never say the word 'interesting'.
- Sleep upside down on Thursday nights.
- Thoughtfully bring up important conversations (not always on the spot).
- First mouthful of food thankfulness.

Touching while talking

When big topics are broached, we make sure we're touching. If a conversation we're having starts to get heated, we move closer to each other and ensure at least one part of our body meets the other's. It's one of the hardest things to do, but it's even harder to come back from a conversation without it.

Touching while arguing or talking about something serious demonstrates that no matter what we are talking about, we still love each other. Regardless of the conversation, we still trust and respect each other and are in life together. Touching often diffuses the situation too. Occasionally we'll be in the heat of a conversation, about to erupt further, and one of us remembers we're not touching. When we reach out to each other at that moment, usually we start to laugh. Touching brings us back down to earth. Physical distance makes things worse; our body language pulls us apart. So when we touch, perspective is gained.

It also stops us from walking away. Tim and I are both conflict-avoiders and would love life to be happy and easy 24/7. In moments of combat, we'd prefer to walk away and sidestep the situation, but the touching rule means we have to continue and sort it out. More often than not, this is great — the issue is sorted far more quickly than if we both huffed and puffed and tiptoed around.

Period celebrations

On the first night of my period, you'll find Tim and I throwing a party for two. We celebrate life as a duo with no kids, we celebrate my body and what it's going through, and celebrate *living* in general. Drinking wine and eating chocolate are often the only things I want to do on the first day of my period too, so it's a lovely ritual.

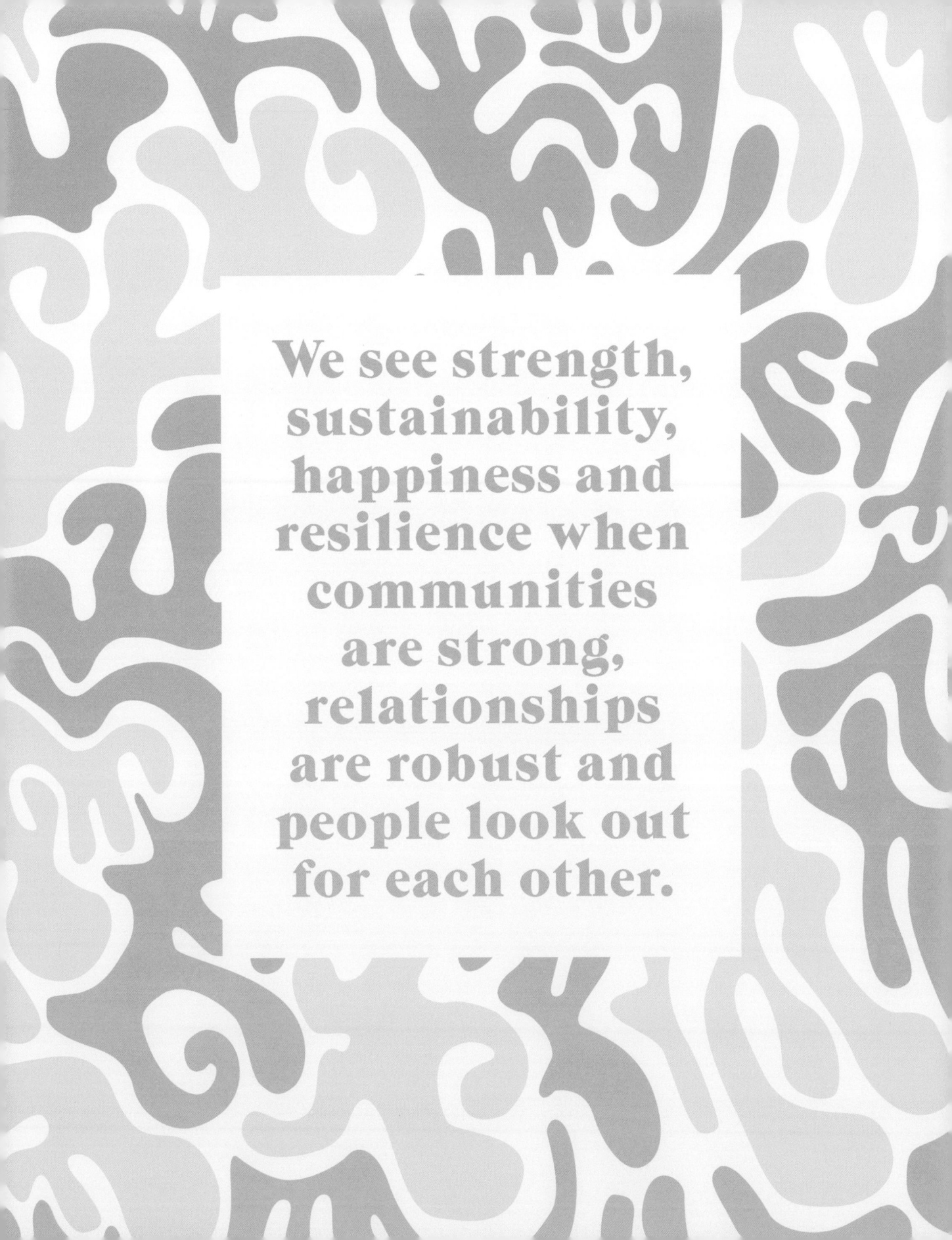

We see strength, sustainability, happiness and resilience when communities are strong, relationships are robust and people look out for each other.

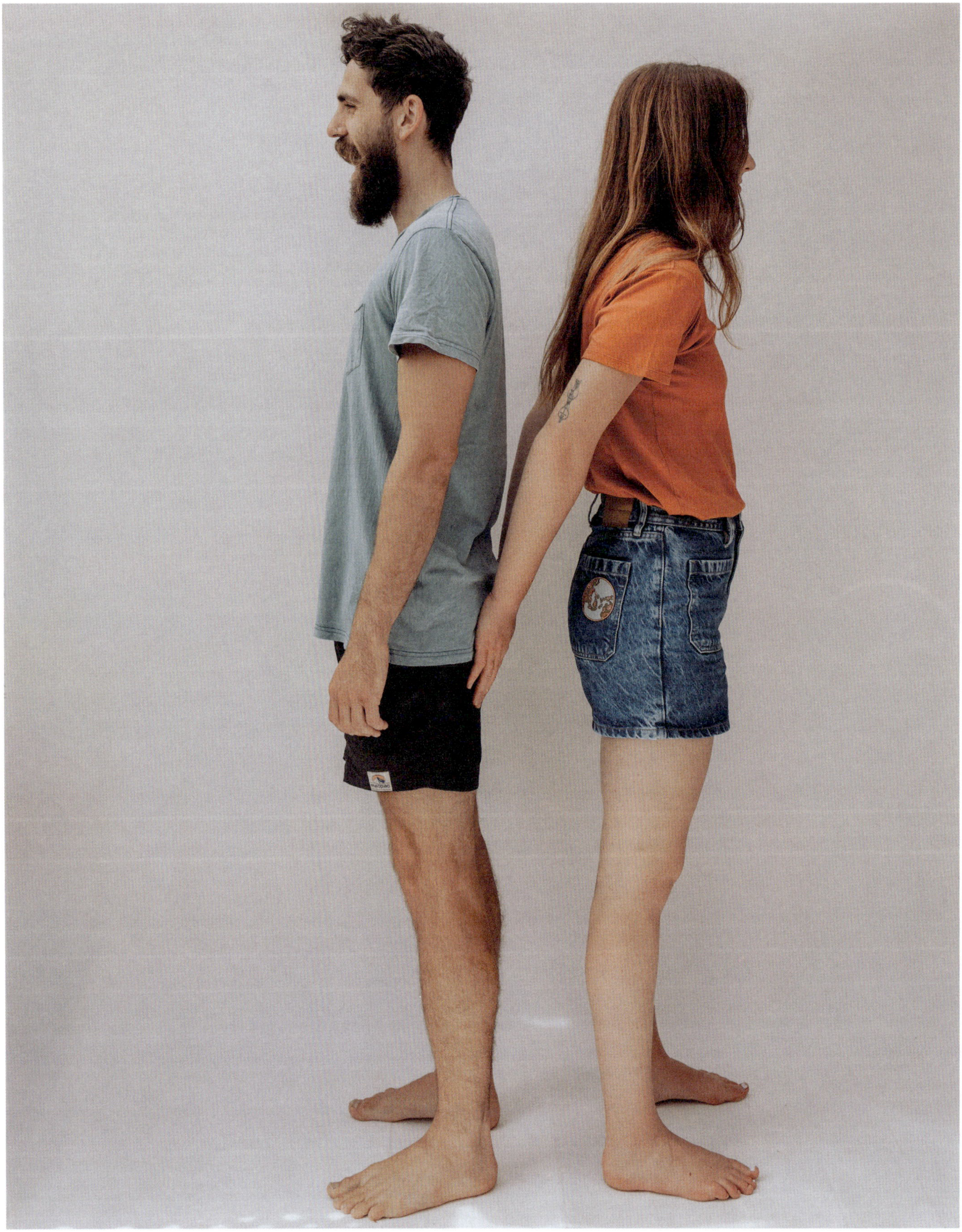

When I get my period, I let Tim know immediately so we can make plans and buy the snacks! If one of us has other plans on the first night of my period, we'll try our best to cancel it.

Be thankful, and say it

The power of words is underrated. We don't realise how powerful simple words can be until they're regularly missed out and cause problems far bigger than themselves. That's why Tim and I make an effort to thank each other for what we do.

'Thanks for doing the dishes last night.' Even though I made dinner and we take turns, I'm still grateful. So I say it.

'Thanks for fixing my earrings.'

'Thanks for baking those cookies.'

'Thanks for trimming the hedges.'

'Thanks for walking the dog.'

'Thanks for making me a cup of tea.'

'Thanks for sending me that funny llama video.'

Showing we're constantly grateful — because we are — is super small and hardly takes any time or energy, but I believe it's paramount to all relationships and one of the reasons why we work so well together. Sure, co-living means you both chip in and do things, but even if tasks are expected to be done, a thank you will go a long way to fostering harmony.

Never say 'interesting'

I bet you're interested in why we don't say interesting. This trick was borrowed from the superb movie *Captain Fantastic*. In the movie, the father banned the word 'interesting' from his children's vocabulary as it's a 'non-word'. When his children use it, their siblings shout 'illegal word!' Tim and I do the same. 'Interesting' doesn't add any extra explanation to what you think of something. 'Interesting' is often used as a filler word when you're too lazy to properly reply to someone. For example, Tim asks me 'How was the event you attended this evening?' If I were to reply 'Interesting', he would know nothing more about the event. Instead I could elaborate on what happened, what I felt, who was there, etc., which would properly answer his question. Removing the word 'interesting' helps us engage in conversation rather than avoid it.

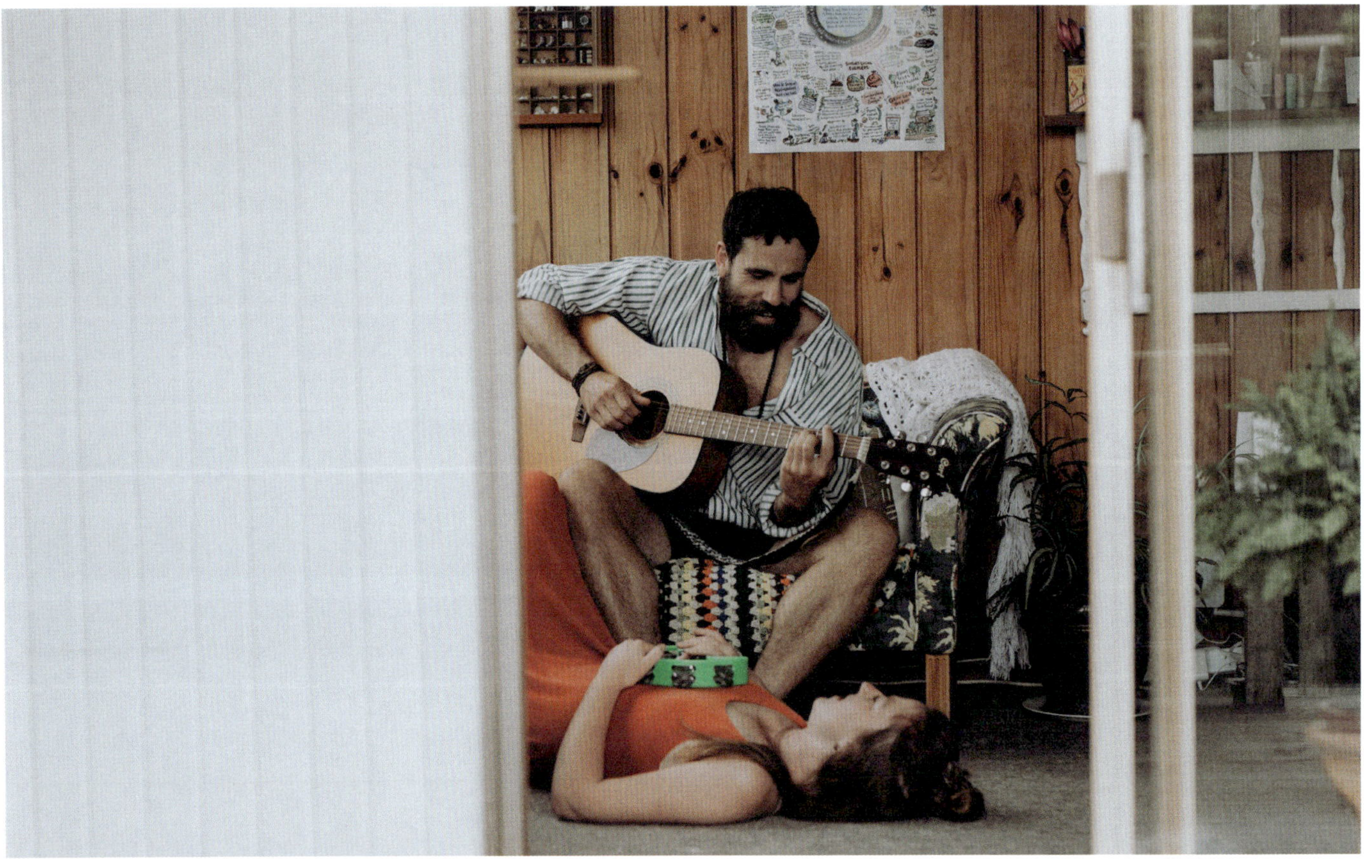

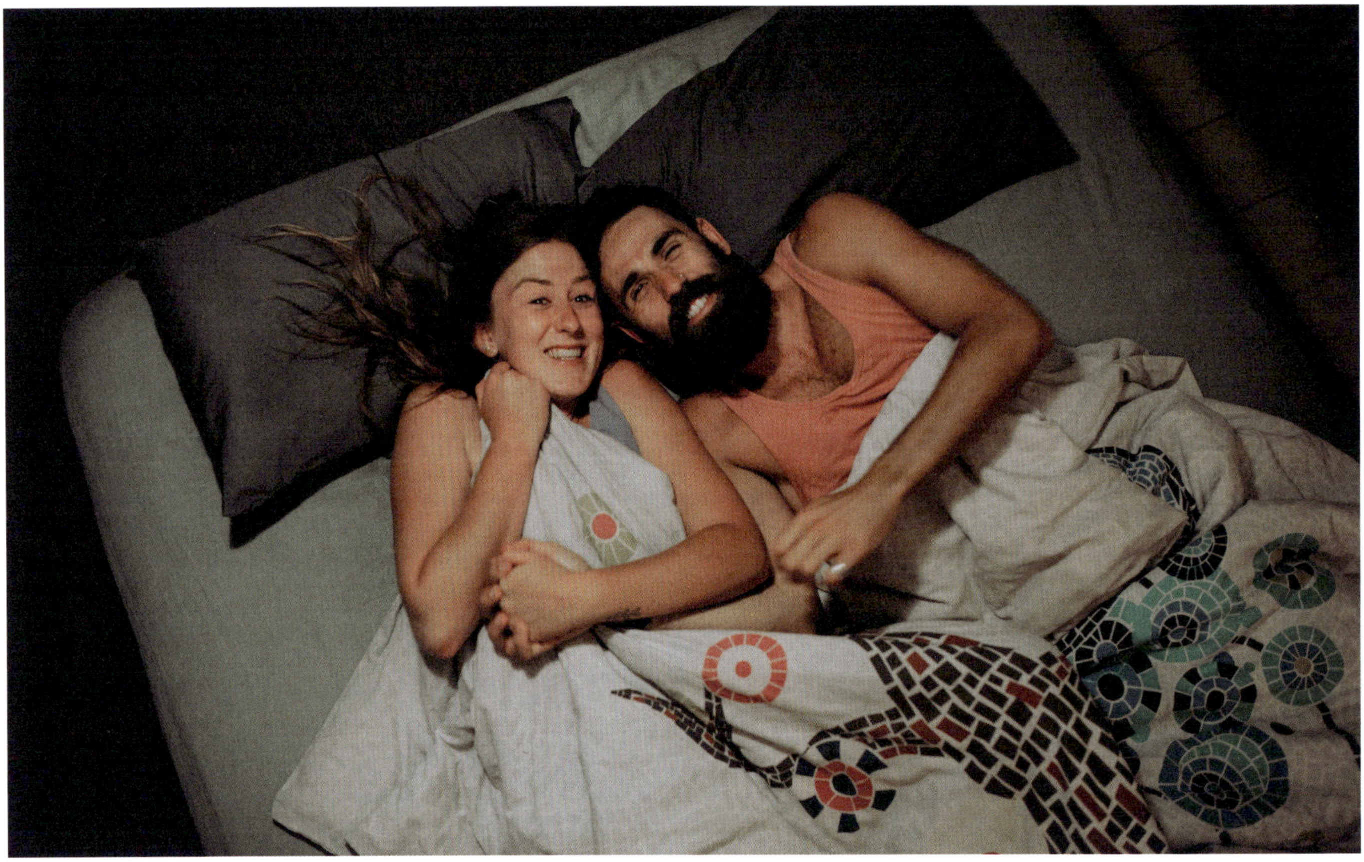

Sleep upside down on Thursday nights

Tim and I sleep upside down on Thursday nights and have done so since 2018. It was Tim's idea. Throughout our dating life, we talked about not having sides of the bed. But after getting married and moving in together, we quickly realised this was impractical. So one night, Tim suggested we sleep upside down. If you're imagining us sleeping like bats hanging from the ceiling, or top and tail, you've got the wrong idea. We sleep with our heads on the place where our feet usually are. After trying this once on a Thursday night, we made a pact to do it every Thursday night for the rest of our lives, and so far we've stuck to this 99 per cent of the time.

We take this ritual very seriously. One Thursday night, I came home super late from an event. Tim was already asleep but hadn't remembered to sleep upside down. I (rudely) turned the light on, startled him out of a deep sleep, and demanded he change the direction of the bedding! Even when we're away from each other on a Thursday evening, we sleep upside down in our tent or hotel room, and send each other an upside-down selfie.

Why?

Different perspective

Seeing our room differently changes things. My brain is so used to doing and seeing the same thing every single night. Getting into bed with a different leg, viewing our bedroom from an alternative angle, and noticing things I've never observed before in a space I frequent is great for the mind. This practice started out as a fun couple routine, but it genuinely strengthens my ability to gain a new perspective when it comes to problem-solving.

New ideas

On Thursday nights, Tim and I also try to hop into bed an hour earlier because we always end up talking a lot when we're upside down. The different outlook on life unconsciously provokes us to talk about topics we haven't broached before, and chat in a way that can only be described as a classic teenage sleepover. Thursday nights are our time to brainstorm what our new gate should look like, what we might get up to on the weekend, and generally think unconventionally because our minds are open and ready for it!

Strategic conversations

I'm often asked how to manage low-waste living with a partner who doesn't have the same sustainable-living values. It's a common challenge for many, and this tip is my main answer to that question, plus it applies to all conversations that are bigger than 'Pass me the tea, please'.

The trick is to not have the difficult conversation when you're in the moment with the difficult thing. Bring it up later — but make sure you bring it up.

For example, when we were making dinner the other night, I realised we had eaten meat a few days in a row. This isn't my preference and not something we had agreed to do. Although Tim shares similar values to my own, he prefers to have more meat in his diet than I do. Instead of storming into the kitchen and exclaiming 'We had meat last night! Why the heck did you get this out of the freezer!' I waited for a relaxed moment on the weekend. We had time to talk, and our emotions weren't heightened. Tim and I were able to have a constructive conversation about our individual meat-eating ethics and the conversation ended positively. If I had started this conversation in the process of making dinner, tied up with all my heightened emotions, the conversation would have ended in tears (for me) and zero positive outcomes.

Don't use this tip as an excuse to bottle up your emotions, but think more strategically about big topics you care about and want to discuss with your partner.

Meal thankfulness

I grew up saying grace before dinner and usually still say grace when eating with Tim. It just looks a little different. Before fully digging into a meal, Tim and I craft the best mouthful of food. We pick up all the different elements from our meal on our fork, eat it and send internal thanks to the people, plants or animals that made our meal happen. We don't remember to do this every single mealtime, but Tim suggested it one day and it has turned into a grounding practice that reminds us not to take our meals for granted.

Feel free to steal these ideas and make them your own, or take time to think about what rituals you could start with your partner.

Our wedding

Weddings can be massively wasteful events. I shudder to think of the mountains of waste they create. Although our sustainable values weren't as solid back in 2017, we still managed a low-waste wedding. We used our purchasing power to support local vendors and ensured the day was about the people in it, rather than matching napkins or Pinterest-perfect table settings.

Tim proposed in the middle of my favourite regional park, on a human treasure-hunt that involved an hour-hike before finding him in a glade singing 'I want to grow old with you' supported by our families playing instruments. Straight after our engagement, we sat down at a café to start talking about wedding arrangements. Immediately, we felt cornered by the constructs of weddings that have evolved out of trends and traditions that we didn't click with. We felt frustrated, it didn't flow, our decisions were confined and it wasn't fun. This was obvious when we started talking about who our bridesmaids and groomsmen would be. Some of our greatest friends were close with us both. I wanted both my siblings to be with me, but traditionally it's a few guys on one side, and a few girls on the other. The cost that comes with each person can be phenomenal too, so just a few is best — says the handbook.

Feeling this frustration, we threw the 'wedding handbook' out the window. We had a bridal team, made up of eighteen people who were important to us. One of them was the celebrant. They wore what they wanted, guided roughly by the colour blue, and helped along by a group second-hand shopping adventure. Our bridal team did their own hair and make-up because we think they look pretty beautiful without the help of professionals, and they arrived at the wedding with Tim in a bus!

A talented twelve-year-old friend braided my hair and another friend did my make-up. My dress was sustainably made by a company in India, my 'shoes' consisted of crocheted string that went over the tops of my feet and around my ankles, and I wore my grandmother's necklace. Dad grew sunflowers for our bouquets and a little caterpillar sat on my bunch as I walked down the grassy aisle. Tim wore second-hand shorts and shoes and an ethically made hemp shirt. We paid $243

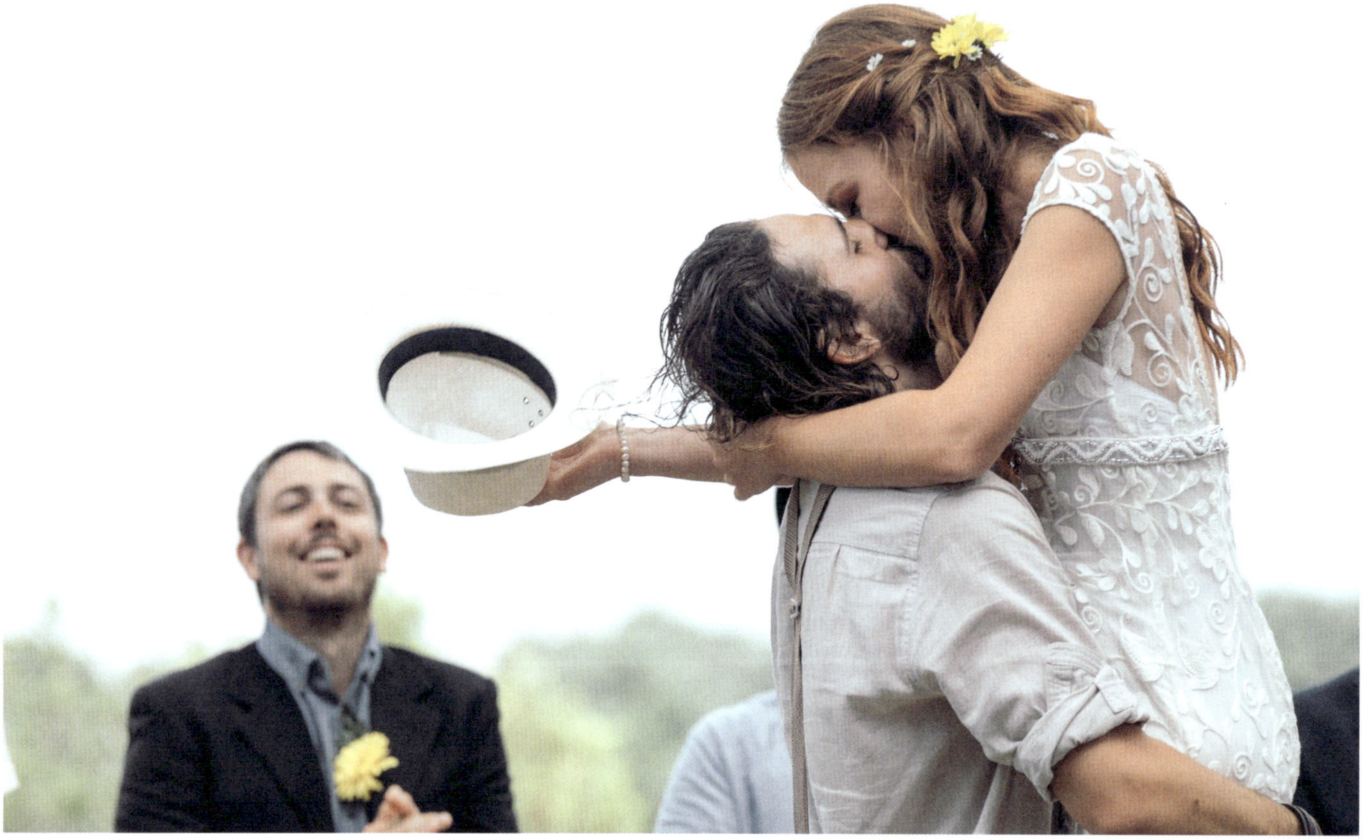

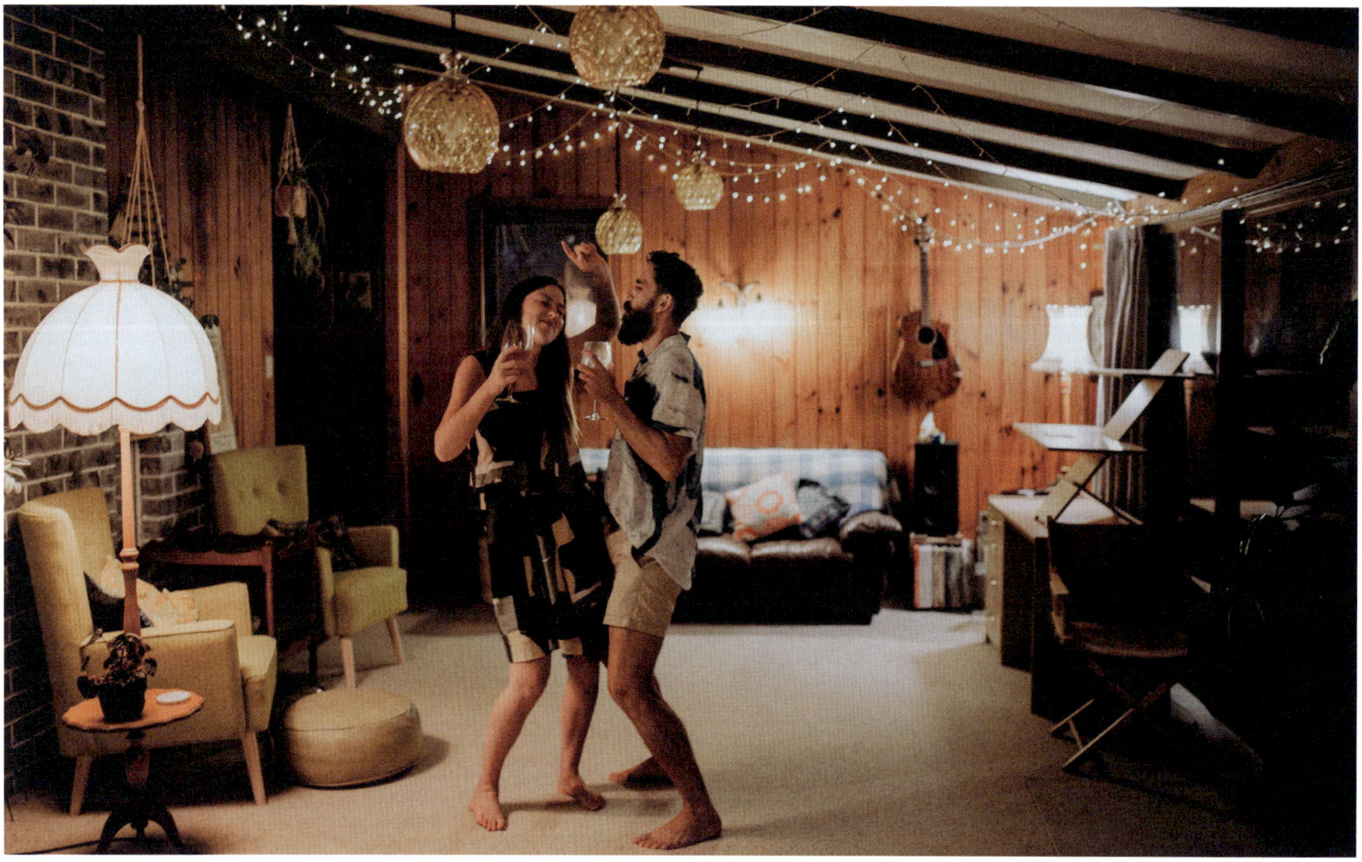

to have our ceremony at the same regional park where we got engaged, and our reception was at a house where the bridal team stayed for a few nights. Many guests brought afternoon tea instead of a gift and were all instructed to wear something they already owned and loved. Because the bride had none, shoes were optional for everyone.

The reception was called the 'FestivHall'. An old wooden boat looked after BYO drinks and ice, a borrowed teepee provided a quiet hangout space and vintage couches made up our dress-up photo booth. Picnic rugs were dotted across the lawn, with casual tables and chairs for those who needed more support. Cricket was played, a funky jazz band set off the vibe on the dance floor (field), and beer in kegs continued it. Our lovely guests lined up at three food trucks with lots of vegetarian options and were encouraged to write a few words to us on my typewriter. I contacted a local market to borrow all their fabric bunting and we hired festoon lights to top off the festival look.

Our wedding came in just under $10,000. With the average Aotearoa New Zealand wedding costing $30–35,000,[2] we were super proud of ourselves. We still had some of the best food trucks in Auckland, fed 80 guests, and didn't feel like we missed out on a single thing! Many weddings I've attended feel like a cookie-cutter, rinse and repeat kinda deal. Same structure, same event, different people. Consciously thinking about what you want your wedding to look like makes for a more sustainable wedding economically and environmentally. I may be biased, but I think it's 100 times more memorable too.

Family and gift ideas

I come from a unique family, so I'm told. At birthdays the birthday person has a special, exciting, coloured plate, and we go around the table and say what we like most about them. During Covid-related lockdowns, we each hosted a 'TEDg' talk (my maiden name is Gumbrell) on a topic of our choosing. Hypnobirthing, the five miracles of life, free will and where vegans get their protein from were just a few of the topics discussed. In Mongolia we travelled for a few weeks in a bus and Dad stopped to treat reindeer — I call it our 'Wild Thornberrys phase'. I think our time travelling overseas together, paired with the smaller home we grew up in, made us all strangely close. When my family and our partners are together, the vibe is electric. It's my happiest place.

For gifts, we've done a few things:

- Donate to particular charities that are related to the gift receiver's interests and hobbies.
- Gift vouchers of time and skills (e.g. my sister gifted us a voucher for her to come to our house and make dinner, set up a romantic date night and leave. We gave my parents a voucher for a bathroom clean and vacuum of their house.)
- Give second-hand things from thrift stores or our own homes.
- Spend time together instead, or spend money on a family holiday.
- Bring an activity to Christmas Day and skip the gifts (e.g. Tim and I bought lots of zero-waste, hand-made snacks. My brother and his partner led an acro-yoga class on the lawn.)

It's only been recently that I've realised how epic my family are. I composted since day one because my parents did, wore reusable nappies (because they were the only affordable option!), and was taught hand-me-downs are better than shopping malls. But no matter what kind of family you have, suggesting things like alternative gift ideas is a brilliant way to grow closer while reducing waste and bettering your impact.

Community action

Most of us are passive citizens. We have all sorts of strong opinions, but we don't take action because we don't believe our voices have an impact. Wrong! There are so many ways you can connect with your community to influence how it works. It may be difficult and tiring sometimes, but like everything in this book I encourage you to do what you can.

Talk to your local council

I walk a lot. Mainly because I have a dog, but it's also a meditative form of exercise for me. When I walk, I play a game with myself. I notice all the little spaces of lawn around the community that are redundant and I plan a community garden on them. I'm not talking about taking over parks that people sit in or dogs enjoy; those spaces are important! I'm thinking of the ones alongside public walkways and wedged on weird corners between houses. There are so many. It pains me to see so much unused land that could easily provide a haven for people to tend to plants or trees, and grow food for themselves and their community!

I have a plan to one day choose a plot of land and pitch this to my local council. This may sound like a pipe dream, but did you know that if you're in Aotearoa New Zealand, your local council has to take your call and arrange a meeting if requested? We have open access to engaging with our local councils, though most of us don't use it. Talk to your mayors! Go to the council meetings, and learn about your community so you can be a key part of it.

Give feedback on government proposals

If you're in places like Aotearoa New Zealand or Australia, the government is always proposing new legislation and ideas. Many of these go through a public submission process which involves hearing from everyday people, like you and me. Seek. Them. Out.

There's no point in constantly complaining about our terrible public transport systems if you're going to miss out on an opportunity (that takes three minutes) to make them better! Sign up to your local and national government email newsletters so you know when these submissions are open. The great thing about these submissions is that they can take you a minute or 60 minutes, depending on how much time you have and how much feedback you'd like to provide. Following along with groups, like 350.org and Greenpeace, is beneficial too. These groups frequently remind the public when submissions are open and provide templates that help you write your feedback in a quick but impacting way.

Learn from those less heard

When sustainable living is discussed, it often sounds like a new thing. It's not. Indigenous peoples have been living this way for many years; well before package free pantries began trending on Pinterest. Society wasn't always 'busy' and the individualistic mentality I have mentioned is not held in all parts of the world. I'd argue that for everyone to live better, bolder, and differently, we must learn from the voices that are often ignored or talked over. After all, sustainable living is not sustainable if it does not include everyone.

For me, learning from others has involved:

- Talking to my grandparents about how they used to live
- Learning Te Reo Māori (the indigenous language of Aotearoa New Zealand) and incorporating it as much as possible into my everyday life
- Actively reading books by authors who don't look like me
- Consciously noticing who is not in the room (literally and metaphorically) and questioning why
- Having conversations about privilege even when they feel awkward

'Now is the time to listen to the people and communities most impacted by the climate crisis, support their initiatives, and take action internally and externally to voice your solidarity.'

Eric Johnson, editor, Intersectional Environmentalist

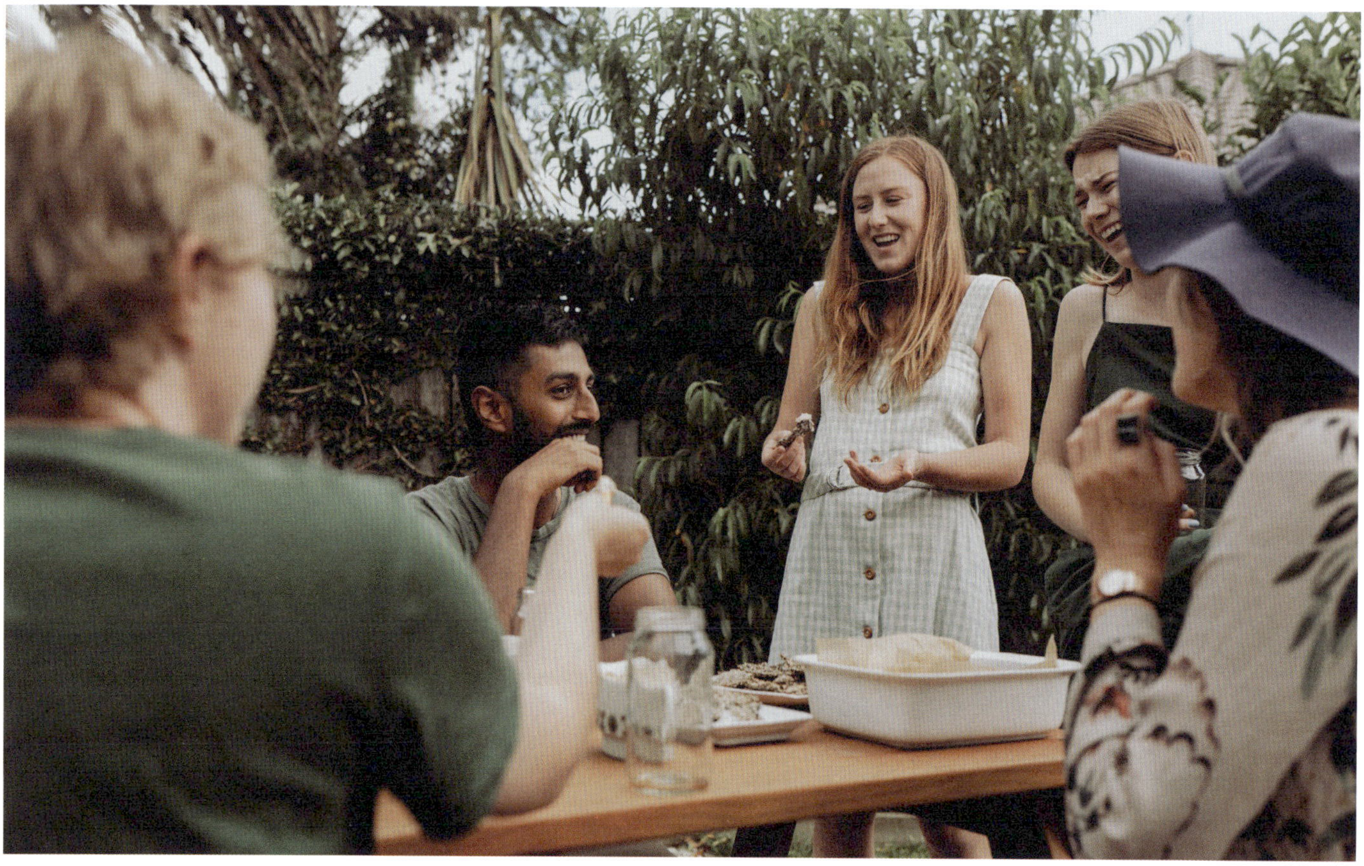

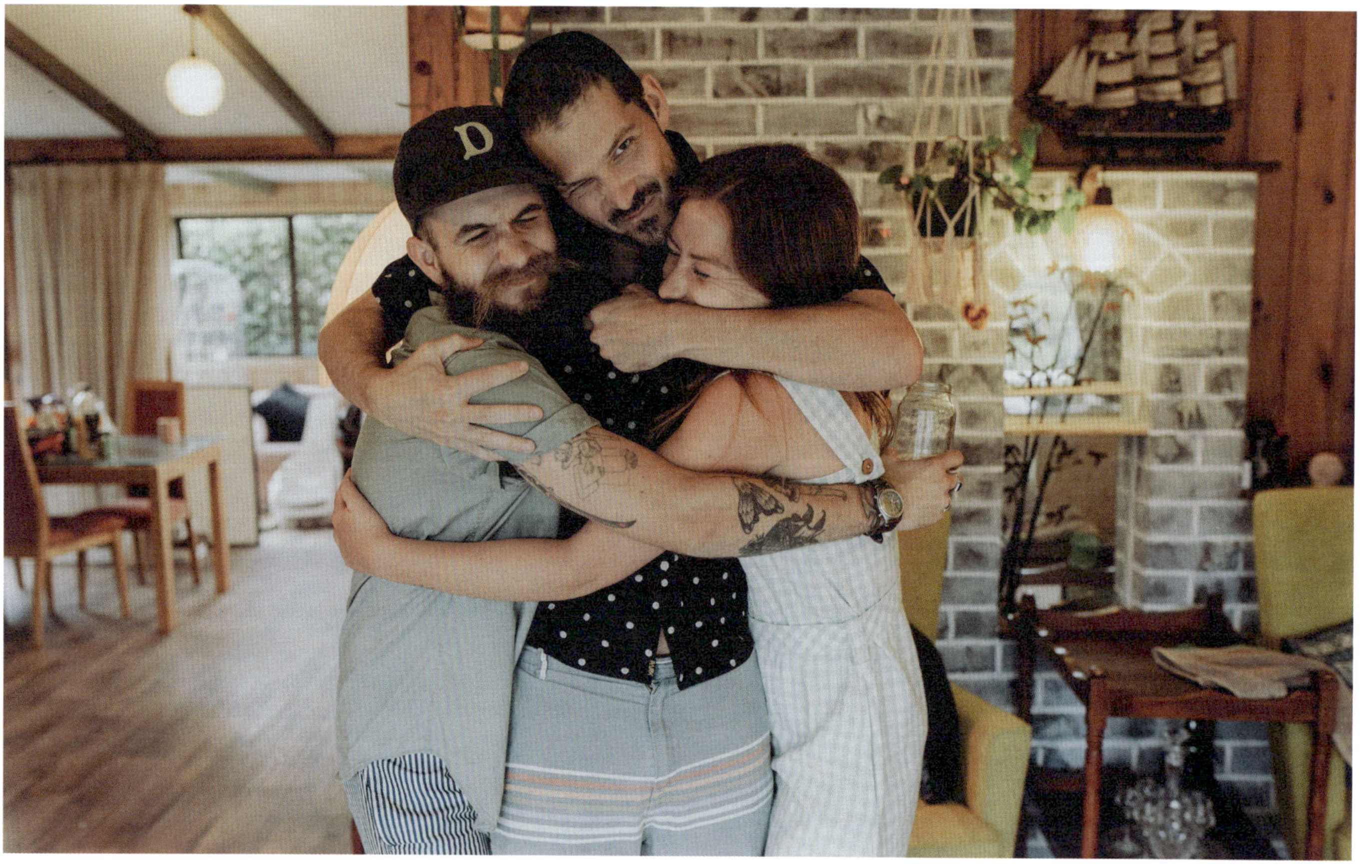

Join a community group

I belong to a few local community groups. Although I'm not consistently active in them, it's rewarding to be part of groups with a shared interest. I meet people I wouldn't have met anywhere else, and feel inspired knowing others in the community care. If you don't know of any community groups in your local area, start one! Your purpose and shared interest could be low-waste living, exercise, beach clean-ups or gardening — whatever you're passionate about. Joining community groups and thinking local is common advice I give to people when they suffer from eco-anxiety. Focusing on what you CAN do within your immediate surroundings is a constructive way to get out of an overwhelming funk.

Sign or make petitions

A petition is essentially a request or call for change that is signed by lots of people who agree with it. A group of us launched a petition in early 2020 to demand that the government bans single-use plastic disposable serviceware (things like plastic plates, cups and cutlery) and implement accessible reusable systems instead.[3] It was mentioned throughout national media, shared all over social media, and gained over 5000 signatures. Other petitions I've signed in the past few months are concerned with making it easier for people to repair items in our country, protecting precious marine resources, and stopping pesticides from being used in parks.

Petitions are frequently used as evidence to support cases presented in government. Signing a petition can take literally one minute, but when thousands of people sacrifice one minute, a lot of positive change can be made.

Connection is a critical part of sustainable living. Sustainable values are not (yet . . . I'm working on it) normal in society, so working together, sharing resources, focusing on sustaining your relationships and thinking of yourself in a group, not as an individual, are key actions to doing things differently. Need an encouraging push? Knock on your neighbour's door, search online for 'local community group near me', and always sleep upside down on Thursday nights.

In a nutshell:

- Share things!
- Spend time and energy on making your romantic relationships brilliant.
- Touch your partner while talking about big things.
- Have strategic conversations.
- If you're having a wedding or other major event, think of all the good you can do by planning it sustainably.
- Think differently when it comes to gifts.
- Talk to your local council.
- Give feedback on government proposals.
- Learn from those less heard.
- Join or start community groups.
- Sign lots of petitions or create your own.

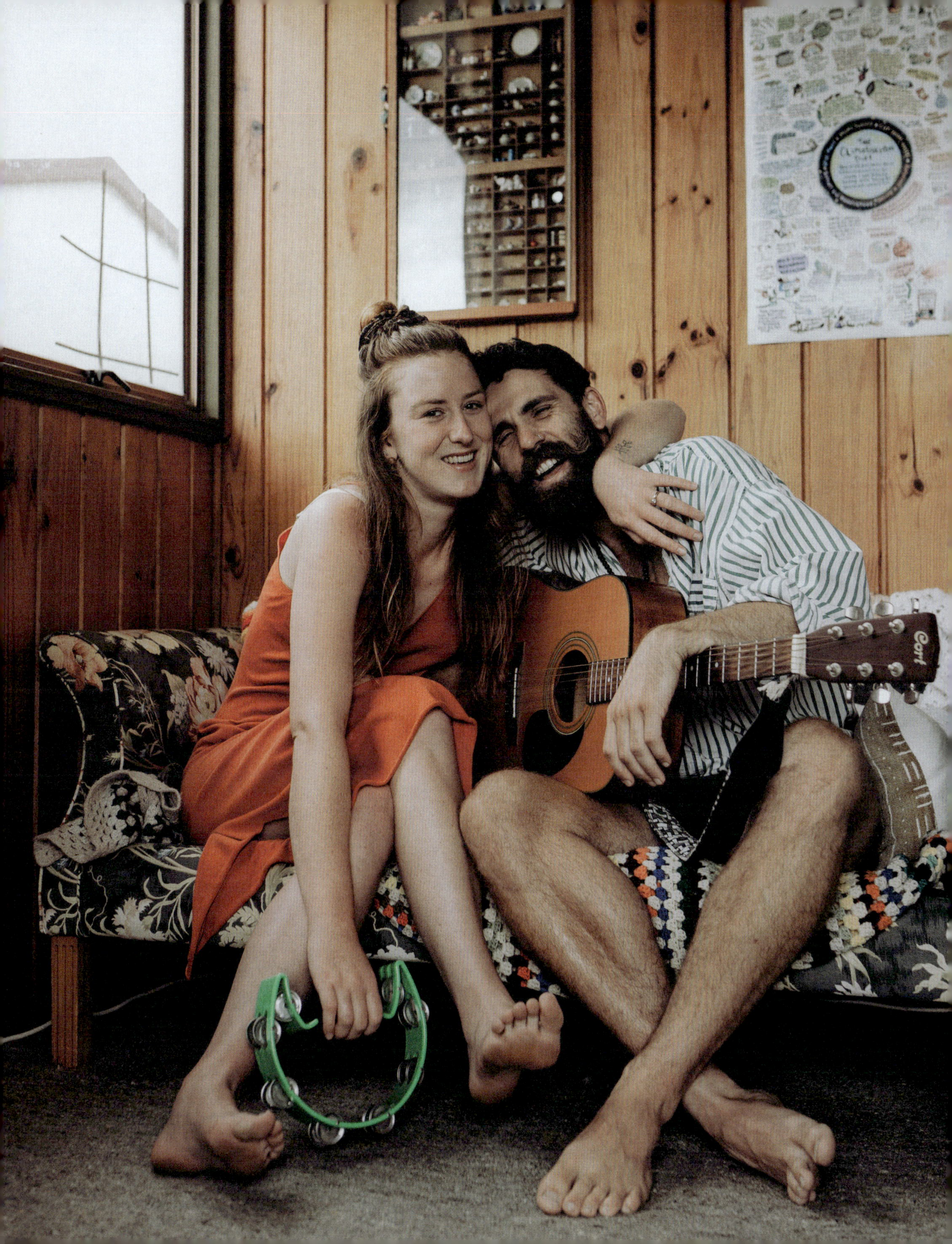
Cort

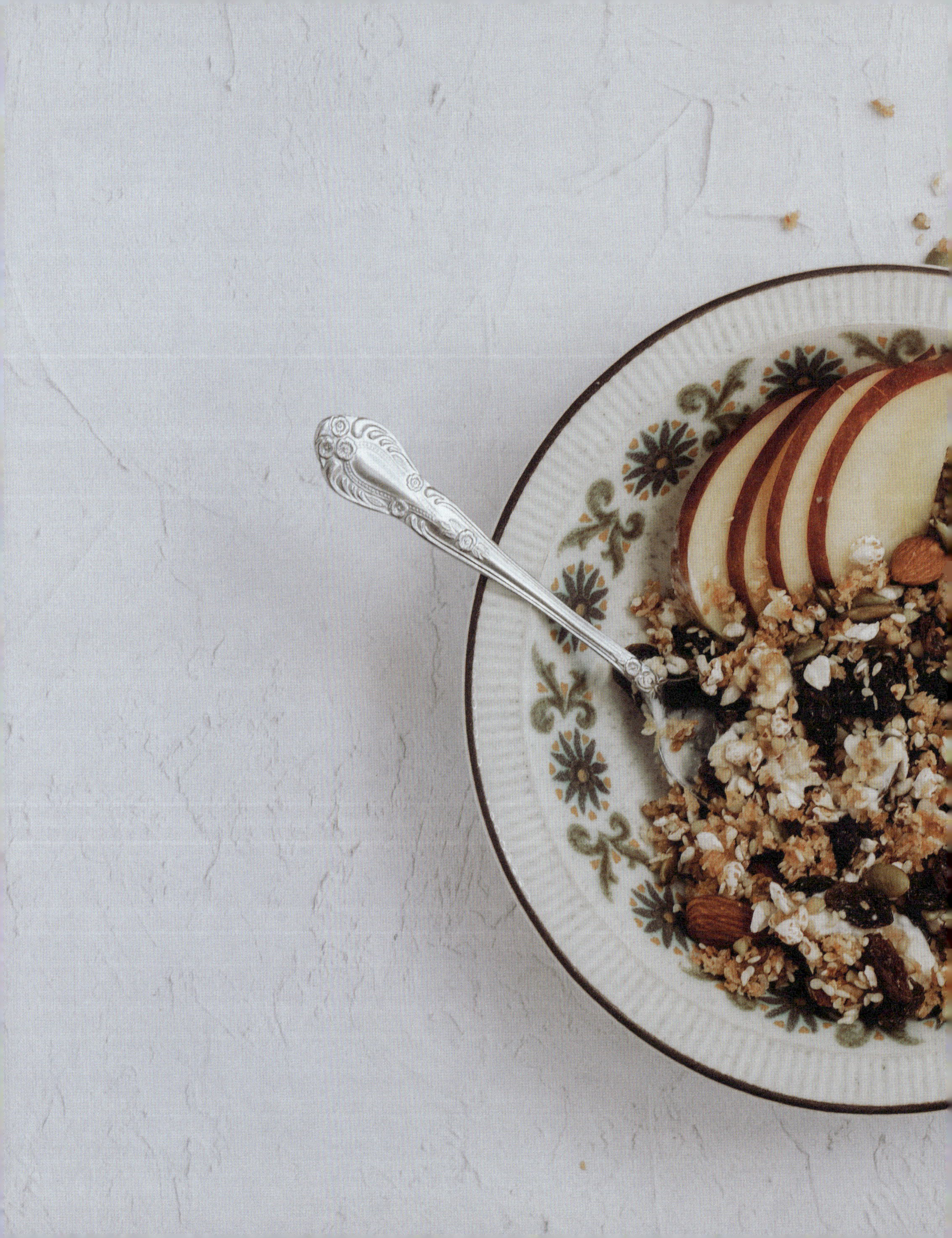

Food

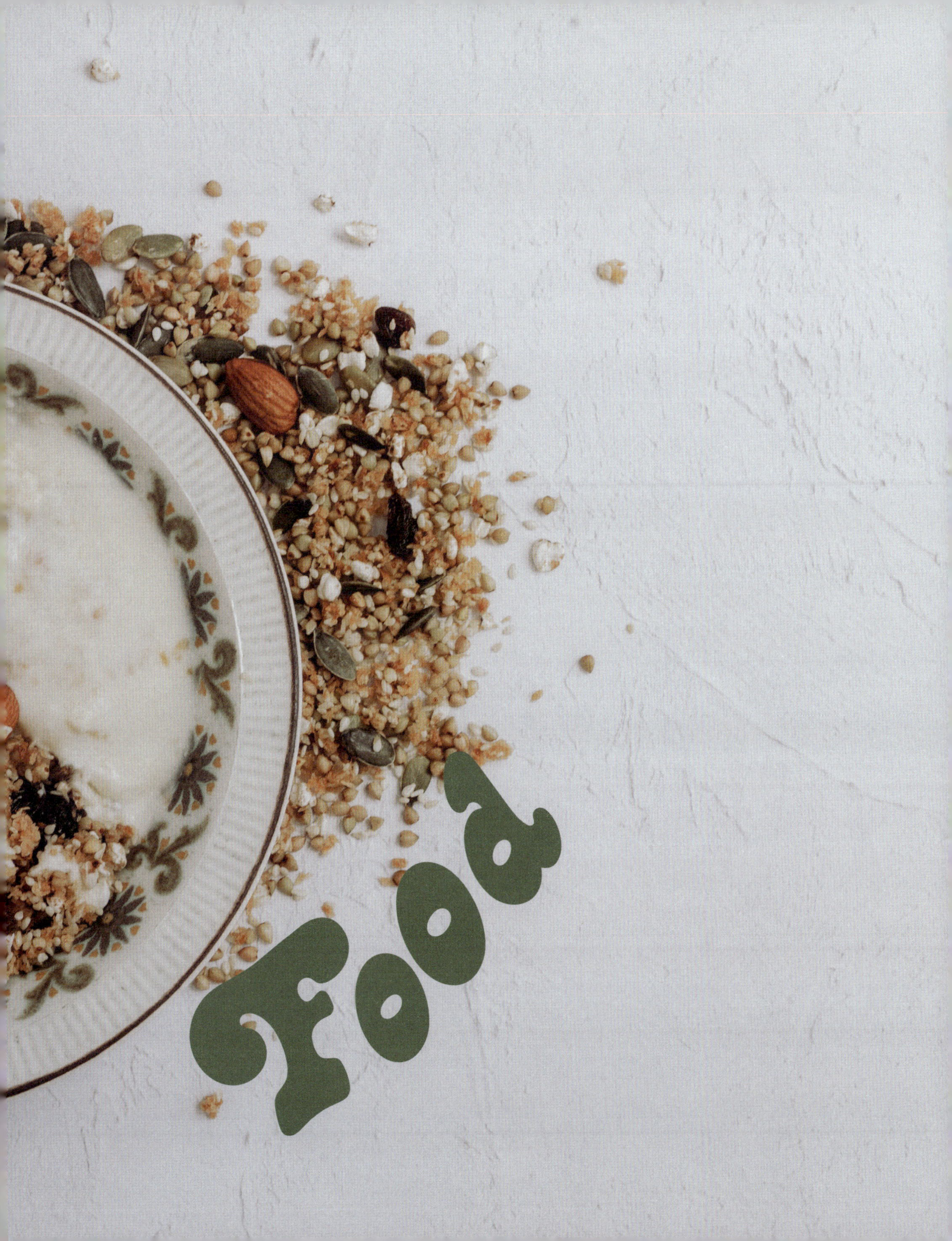

During winter, I have a jar of freshly squeezed grapefruit juice in my fridge that I refill regularly and take swigs from throughout the day. The grapefruit are from Tim's grandmother's tree. My pantry houses constantly brewing kombucha, beans in soaking phase and apple cider vinegar concoctions. I can count the recipe books I own on one hand; they're used sparingly for general inspiration. I gave up trying to follow recipes when I realised they are not helpful for eating in a way that utilises locally available low-waste ingredients.

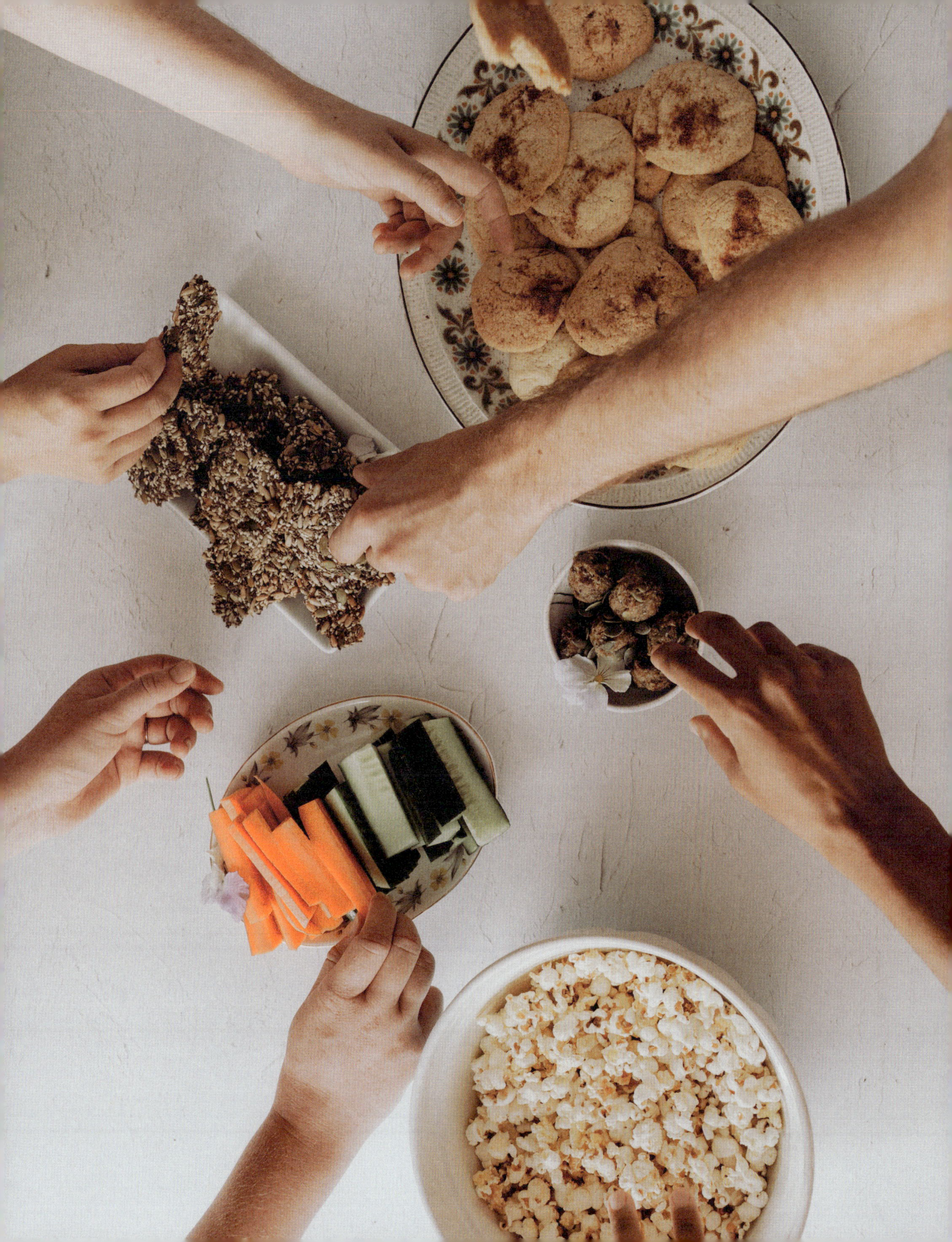

I grew up with a dad who ate carrots for dessert and a mum who passed on her love of chocolate.

I have cupboards full of jars, drawers full of beeswax wraps and, for me, a day spent creating a storm in the kitchen is a cup-filling day.

But I also buy plastic-wrapped papadums and corn chips, and don't always make it to the shop that stocks the refillable glass-bottle milk. Not all food items that fill my belly are made fair trade, and some foods travel thousands of kilometres to get to me.

Essentially, what I'm trying to paint for you, before I launch into my passion for good food and sustainable grocery shopping, is a picture of my imperfect sustainable pantry. A pantry based on the values of zero waste, fair trade and locally sourced, paired with consideration for the foods available to me, my limited self-control and love of socialising.

I've tried the 'no rubbish bin' thing, and it hurts. The first few months of my attempt to live with absolutely no waste in my pantry were tasteless. There's only so much dressing-free lettuce, boiled potatoes, plain rice and polenta a person can eat before they go slightly bonkers. So holding the philosophy of zero waste tightly, while letting go of perfection and shrugging off the 'all or nothing' mantra, was liberating. It has allowed me to eat well, focus on the waste I can reduce, and inspire others to do the same without being 'hangry' because all I've eaten is fried chickpeas.

Food is an intimate and personal thing. You cannot 'do' food right or wrong, but you can acknowledge that it's powerful. What we choose to fuel ourselves with has a big impact on, well, everything. When it comes to living life differently, living with less waste, considering ethical supply chains, optimising your health and thinking more sustainably, food is the most important category there is.

Grab an organic, fair-trade carrot to nibble on, and buckle in. To begin with, here are a few things I know about food:

- Food creates the most amount of waste in my rubbish bin.
- The power of good food is overwhelming. I only need to compare my wellbeing after eating a whole bag of potato chips to the feeling of eating a wholesome stir fry to understand the impact of food on my mental, emotional and physical health.
- Food is imported from all over the world.
- Needing to eat is one thing we all have in common.

- Food is a personal decision.
- Deciding what you eat and having an abundance of food is a privilege.
- There are many allergies and diagnoses that mean a person cannot eat in alignment with their environmental values (and that's okay!).

One of the most common assumptions I come across is that being vegan is the best diet for those who want to live a sustainable lifestyle. So let's get this out of the way first: I am not vegan.

Exclaiming that everyone should be vegan disregards cultures who rely on consuming meat to exist, and always have (like nomads in Mongolia who travel frequently and have no, or little, opportunity to grow food), ignores individuals whose good health is supported by consuming animal products, and assumes that everyone is not okay with taking an animal's life for their own sustenance. Like all values, it shouldn't be expected that we have identical opinions on life and death, and one diet for all human beings in all parts of the world simply does not make sense.

I am also a coeliac. This means I have to eat a strictly gluten-free diet otherwise I become violently ill. But most importantly, I'm a self-proclaimed climatarian.

What you choose to nourish your body with has a big impact on your own health, the health of those in places where your food was made, the earth where your food packaging and waste will go, and everyone who transported your food from farm to table.

Grow what you can. Share. Shop at farmers' markets. Avoid food waste. Eat more plants. Support regenerative agriculture. Sidestep food packaging. Consider who made your food.

What is a climatarian?

This term was introduced to me by fellow eco activist, author and friend, Em Ehlers.[1] Having constantly struggled to explain to people how I eat without writing them a ten-page essay or saying I'm a vegetarian just to get them off my back, the term climatarian is so important to me that I have a poster explaining it (illustrated and created by Em) on my wall.

I've never been one for labels, but climatarian is a label I proudly wear. It encompasses all elements of a diet that makes people, the planet and yourself happy and healthy. Less waste, more plants. Less food miles, more fair wages. Less fast food, more slowing down. Less exploitation, more respect.

A climatarian has a few key values, but above all, a climatarian is less worried about exactly what food groups they're eating — they're focused on stopping global warming, reducing their carbon footprint and addressing our climate crisis, and they make food choices according to these values. Because nature wants these things too, being a climatarian ultimately leads to a balanced and healthy diet that respects people and the planet in the process. The 'rules' that are followed by a climatarian aren't rocket science and can hardly be argued over; they make a lot of logical sense.

Grow what you can

There's a certain feeling that comes from growing your own food that I can only describe as euphoric. So many parts of our lives are disconnected from the natural world; we usually grab food from a supermarket without thinking about how it was made, drive cars, walk on concrete and live on our phones. Growing your own food stirs something inside that reminds us how and why we are alive. Put simply, without the gushing philosophical stuff: growing your own food is rewarding and nourishing for all aspects of your health.

Growing your own food requires being out in the sunshine, getting your hands dirty in soil and inhaling fresh air — all great things for anyone's wellbeing! Consuming vegetables and fruit you've grown yourself also means you're more likely to be eating a seasonal diet. Nature works in wonderful ways; generally, the plants that grow during certain seasons contain the particular nutrients your mind and body need more of in those seasons too.[2] Put that together with the added control of knowing what chemicals your food was grown with (or without!) and the feeling of accomplishment from eating what you've lovingly tended to, and you have a recipe for a healthy human.

Developing green fingers also reduces 'food miles'. On average, our food travels 1640 kilometres (1020 miles) to get to our plates.[3] That's a lot of petrol used and carbon released into the atmosphere. With multiple meals a day and billions of people, the carbon footprint of food is exponentially increasing and playing a big role in furthering our climate crisis.

The truth is, 56 per cent of humans now live in cities,[4] and this percentage is predicted to keep on rising. Unfortunately, we cannot all have gardens at our doorsteps, but that's where we regroup and go back to the words 'grow what you can'. If you're in an apartment building, grow herbs in little pots on your kitchen counter. Care for a tomato plant in a small planter box on your balcony, or try your hand at a hydroponic system that can come in the shape of a tower and take up little space. If you're a serial plant-killer, again, regroup and go back to the words 'grow what you can'. Can't grow anything? Seek help, learn tips from your community, trade for garden goodies, or play to your strengths and buy local instead.

On our property, you'll find three big planter boxes, a herb garden, plus lemon, peach and plum trees, with a beautiful passion fruit vine covering our fence.

I currently fertilise my plants with:

- compost that we make with our food waste
- seaweed
- worm wee from our worm farm.

One of the planter boxes also has an in-ground worm farm.[5] It's essentially a bucket with holes (around 2cm diameter) in the sides. The bucket is dug into the garden bed with 10cm popping out the top. Some

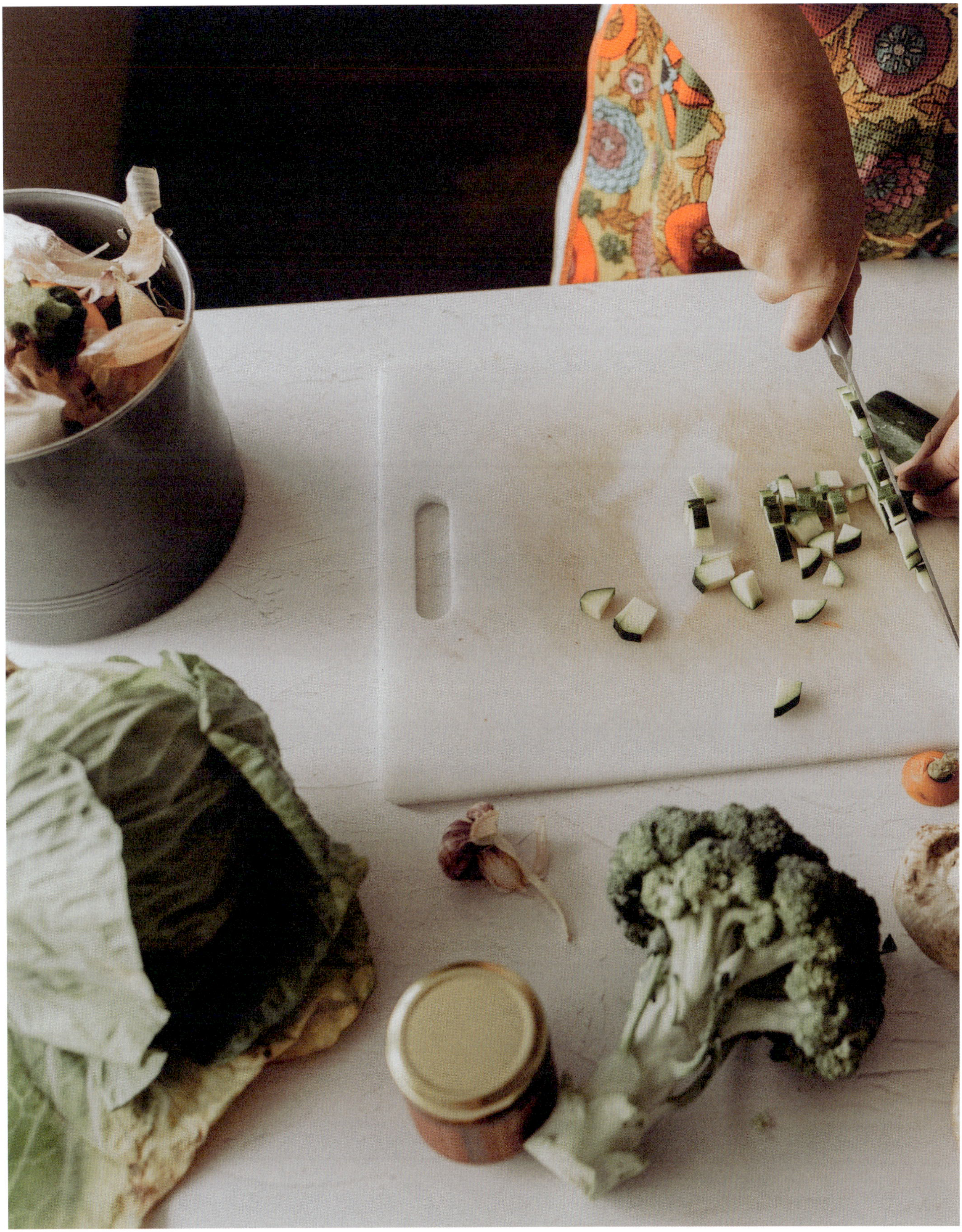

established worm-farm soil and worms need to be added to kick it off, and then food scraps are put in the bucket to keep on feeding the worms and nourishing the garden. An in-ground worm farm adds nutrients to the plants around it. The worms can wiggle around the garden as they please, and then come back to the worm farm for more kai.

My plants come from:

- seedlings from a local nursery (200 metres from my house)
- seeds from an organic-certified grower
- seedlings and seeds from friends and family
- seeds that I collect when my plants go to seed.

I remember when I used to be terrified when a plant would 'go to seed'. I believed it signified the end of the plant's life, and the end of it producing food. However, I've learnt how to collect seeds and use them for next time! My seed saving will always be a work in progress, but saving the seeds from my plants helps keep costs low and is a therapeutic activity.

Seed-saving basics:

- Save seeds from the best plants, not sick ones.
- Research how to save seeds for particular plants — every plant is different.
- Dry the seeds really well before storing them.
- Experiment! Don't be afraid to get it wrong.

Share

Remember that you don't have to exchange money for every commodity. Through sharing, resilience is built and communities are strengthened.

Considering the supermarket as our only option for food is an outdated ideology but an easy trap to fall into. The sharing economy works beautifully in the world of food, and I am privileged to have so many talented food-makers around me. A climatarian sees resources as

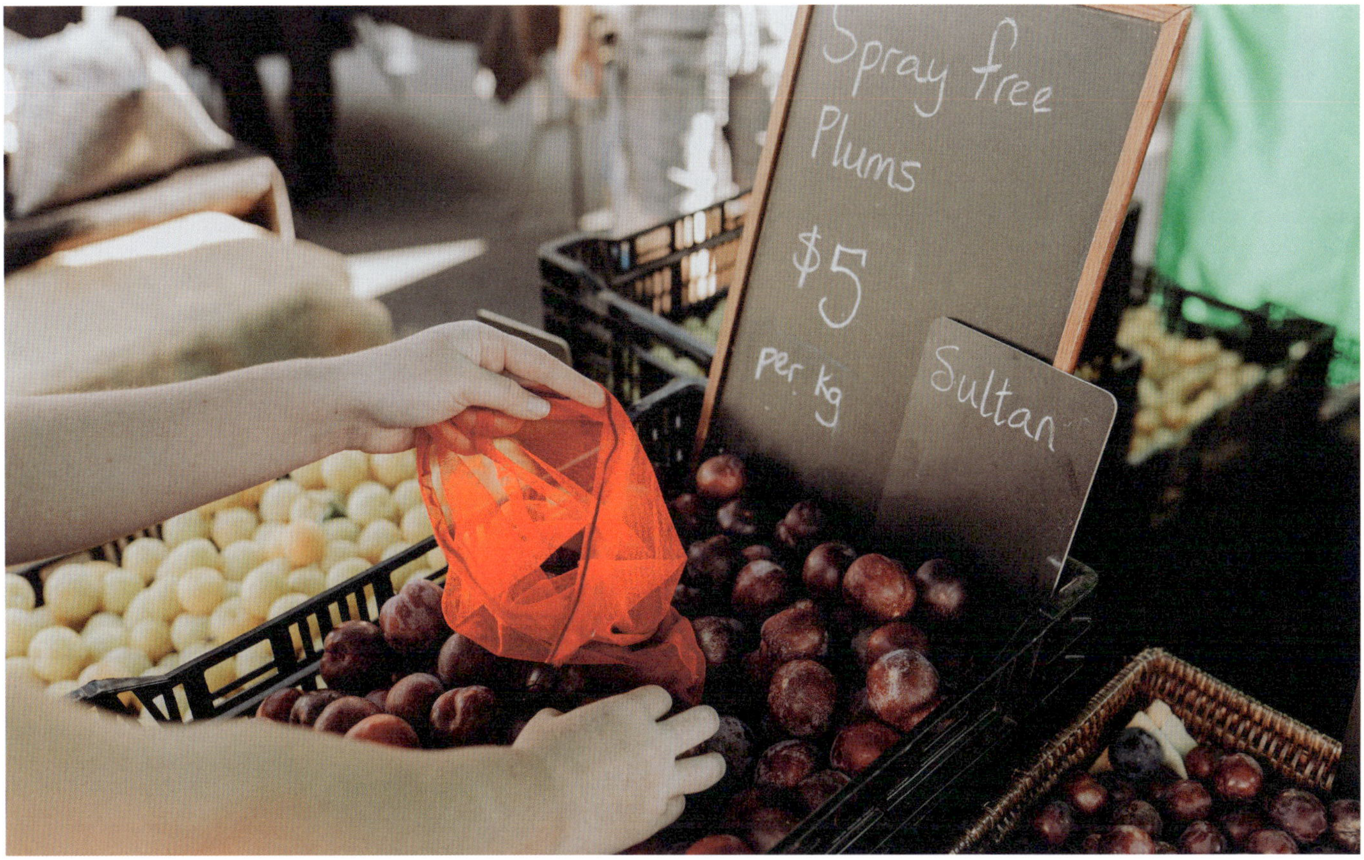
Spray free
Plums
$5
per kg
Sultan

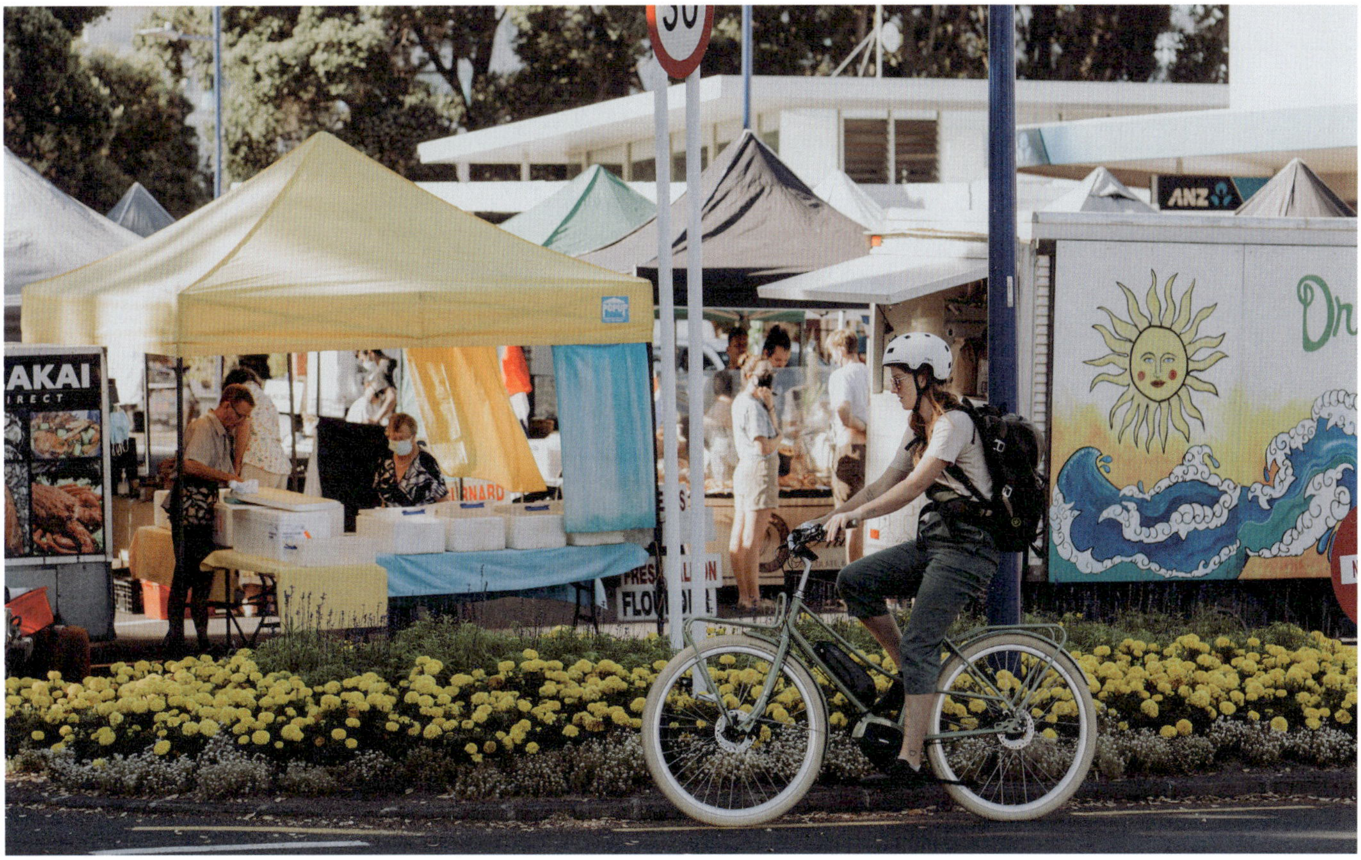
AKAI
ANZ

collectively owned, and thinks uniquely to make sure their community has what they need and little is wasted.

When you embrace the sharing economy, play to your strengths. Most weeks, I leave a bundle of green things from my garden on my neighbour's doorstep and borrow her electric vehicle when I need to. My dad grows the best kale, I grow the best carrots (and make sure Dad knows my carrots are better than his), and I swap seedlings with friends when I have too many. A friend, Tanya in Katikati, has delicious honey and avocados. I have a knack for kombucha making.

Shop at farmers' markets

Farmers' markets are a big part of a climatarian's routine, including my own! First, they provide smaller farmers with an entry point for selling their goods, without having to start with a big, booming business or even have the need to grow into one. Second, on average, farmers' markets provide cheaper organic produce to the community than supermarkets and can educate their customers on the foods they're buying and how to eat and cook them.

Locally grown food is generally more flavourful, contains more nutrients because there's a shorter time between harvest and table, and benefits the local economy by keeping money in the community. Local foods also decrease the chances of a contaminated food supply; the fewer steps there are to getting your food to your plate, the less likely there are to be food-safety issues.[6]

The vast difference between farmers' markets and supermarkets is incredibly obvious to me every Sunday morning. My weekly ritual involves biking to the farmers' market, gathering all the produce that I can, and then stopping by the supermarket afterwards to purchase anything I haven't been able to source from local growers and makers. At the farmers' market, I am welcomed by smiling faces who know my name. I'm filled with a sense of belonging and connection. I look into the eyes of the person who grew my cucumber, make small talk with the woman who produced my honey, and check in on the family who tends to the chooks who plopped out my eggs. I'm outdoors, so I welcome the benefits of fresh air. I can bring my containers back to the person who grows strawberries in summer. I can provide feedback to the growers or request particular things. It just feels so right. So normal. So human.

I don't go to the farmers' market simply for food. I go for my mental health and my physical wellbeing. This experience, including lugging my food home on my bike, makes me more grateful when I eat meals, and acutely conscious of reducing my food waste so the work of the growers and makers wasn't for nothing.

Avoid food waste

I made soup for lunch today. The recipe involved a leek. I cut off the bottom of the leek and placed it in a shallow bowl of water to regrow roots. In 2-4 days I will replant it in the garden and it will grow another leek! The other scraps of vegetables that cannot be used in the meal, e.g. potato peels and onion skins, can be cooked in salty water to make vegetable stock for my next meal, and then composted.

The average Aotearoa New Zealand household throws away 164kg of food per year, and over half of this amount could be easily avoided.[7] Meanwhile, there are so many wonderful ways we can rescue food!

I regularly buy our vegetables from an online store that sells only rescued food from supermarkets or growers who have older produce that is absolutely safe to eat but cannot be sold due to imperfections or strict selling guidelines. There are several apps popping up that connect people with places like cafés who have unsold, edible meals.

A climatarian has a healthy idea of what foods are safe to eat (newsflash, a bruised apple won't kill you!) and understands food isn't an infinite resource. I'm the weirdo who grabs the wonky carrot and buys the brown bananas. Over time I am witnessing this behaviour becoming less weird. I love it.

Eat more plants

We need to eat more plants. The rate that we currently produce and consume meat is unsustainable on many levels.[8] The amount of people who believe a meal is not complete without a meat product is concerning — this ideology has made the meat industry boom, but the industry cannot meet demand without pillaging more land and exploiting animals.

Eating more plants not only takes strain off the meat industry, it also helps our soils and reduces carbon emissions by creating a demand for more plants in the ground.[9] The more plants that are growing, the more oxygen is produced and the more carbon dioxide is taken out of the atmosphere.

A climatarian eats a large variety of vegetables, whatever is in season, and lots of them. I personally fluctuate in how much meat I eat. Sometimes my diet is vegan or vegetarian, other times I'll have a sustainably sourced steak. The majority of our meals at home do not include meat, and when they do, we try our best to eat meat that is sourced ethically (e.g. eating animals that have lived happy lives, free of confinement).

Support regenerative agriculture

The term 'regenerate' means to transform to a higher state. To be formed or created again. To change for the better. So when you add the derivative word 'regenerative' to 'agriculture', you get a term that describes farming that doesn't take from the land and environment, but adds to it.

Regenerative agriculture is a systems approach to farming.[10] It values soil health and biodiversity, both above and below ground. The goal of regenerative agriculture is to mitigate all negative impacts of farming, return carbon and nutrients to the soil, and ultimately combat our climate crisis. Before I start to get too detailed, to sum it up, when regenerative agriculture practices are applied, the natural habitat is rehabilitated and enhanced, not depleted. This way of farming works with natural systems, rather than against them.

You won't see fields being tilled or chemicals being used, or whole fields of one single plant or animal. You'll see compost fertilising a diverse array of plants, animals naturally nourishing the land with their droppings, strategic layers of shrubs, natural water-trapping systems and livestock grazing where you'd normally think they shouldn't be. The usual neat rows of one type of plant that we've become accustomed to seeing don't often exist in the world of regenerative agriculture, because one type of crop grown en masse in the same place can destroy biodiversity and make for a barren and unsafe place for insects and wildlife to dwell in. Many different plants growing together, with

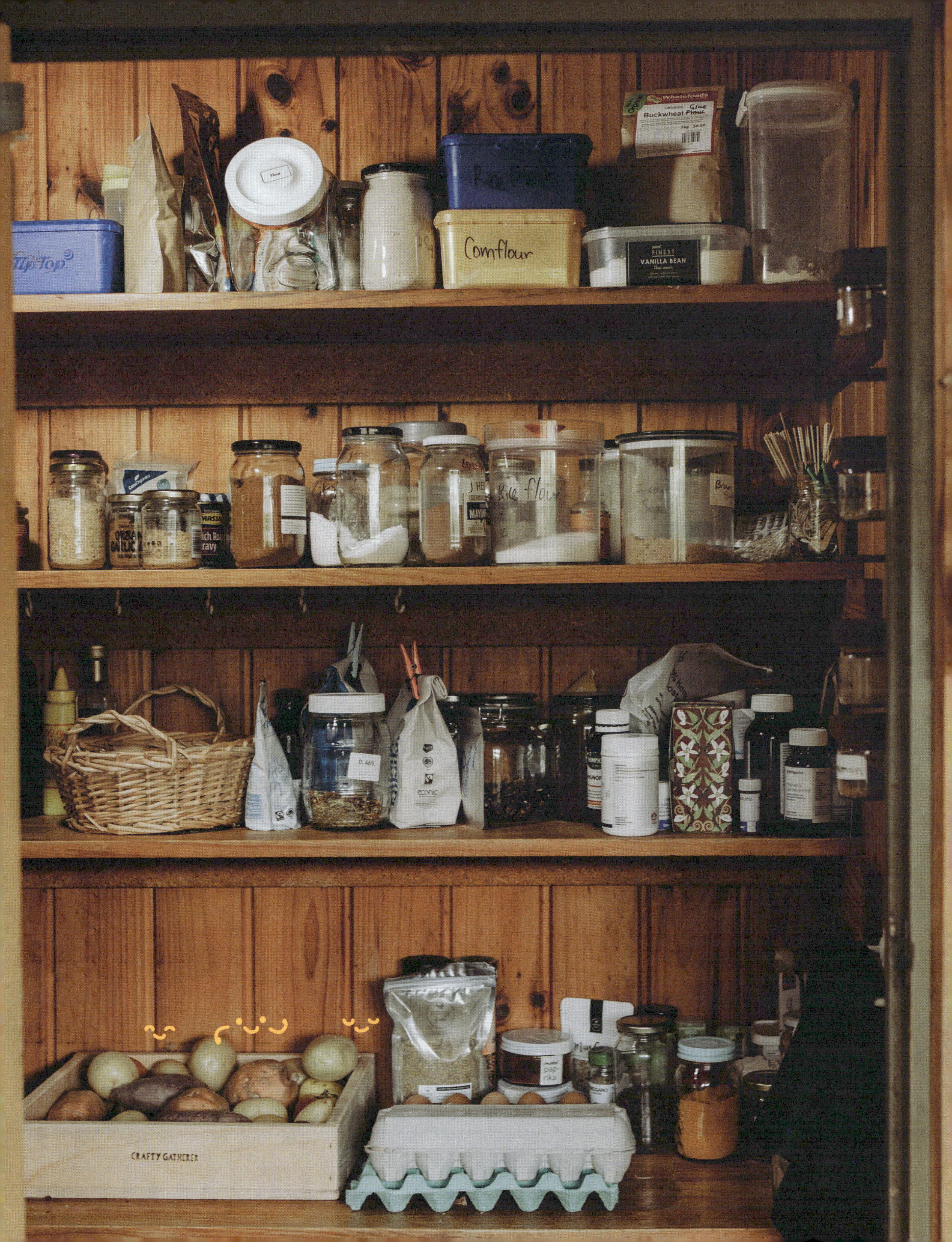
Tip Top
Wholefoods
ORGANIC
Buckwheat
Cornflour
FINEST
VANILLA BEAN
Rice flour
econic
CRAFTY GATHERER

varieties of animals in between, cultivates healthy terrain. Regenerative farms usually look a little wilder — the way nature was intended.

Climatarians support regenerative agriculture. They prefer to eat crops that are grown in this way, and consume meat from animals that are part of a regenerative system. For example, we eat meat from a New Zealand company which hunts wild animals. We don't buy fish and only eat what Tim catches himself. Sometimes we have the opportunity to have lamb from a friend's farm. In this case, we are able to trust the animal is cared for respectfully throughout its lifetime and killed humanely.

Terms to look out for that fall under regenerative agriculture:

- organic
- permaculture
- biodiversity
- agro forestry
- composting
- crop diversity

Sidestep food packaging

Climatarians aim to buy food that is unwrapped; free of plastic covers and polystyrene trays. They'll shop around the outside of the supermarket, where the unpackaged food usually sits, and buy more unprocessed foods because of this. It's difficult to find food products on their own. Most food requires you to also purchase the product around it: the glass bottle, the aluminium can, the plastic wrapper or the paper box. All waste, regardless of its recyclability, requires energy to create, strips the planet of resources (e.g. trees and oil) and can harm ecosystems when discarded.

Climatarians grab the tomatoes on the vine instead of in the boxes. They'll bring their own fabric bags to the bakery or supermarket to pop their bread in, and a reusable container to the butcher, and if there's no other option, they'll choose the glass jar of mayonnaise and reuse the jar for a hundred different things. Single-use plastic is a no-no and often climatarians are avid DIYers who buy naked food and use those ingredients to make things from scratch.

Less packaging is a great goal, but I say 'less' instead of 'no' for a reason. I am an able-bodied person who can cut my own vegetables. Some people who suffer from arthritis, for example, are unable to do that on their own. It's important throughout this entire chapter to constantly remind ourselves of the privilege that comes with eating in a way that aligns with our values and acknowledge there may be areas where we are able to eat in a way that respects our planet, and areas we cannot.

Consider who made your food

Unless you have a thriving food forest in your own backyard that feeds you sufficiently, your food was made by someone — usually, many people. Being a climatarian involves ensuring the people who made your food were treated with respect and paid fair wages. Fair treatment should extend to all makers in the supply chain of your food: the people who grew the ingredients and the people who loaded those ingredients into a truck to transport it to the factory; the people who used those ingredients to make a yummy product; and the people who maintain and fix the machines that stir, whip and cook it.

Climatarians acknowledge that the environment and people need to be respected in the production of food. Food is a social and environmental concern; you cannot focus on one without the other.

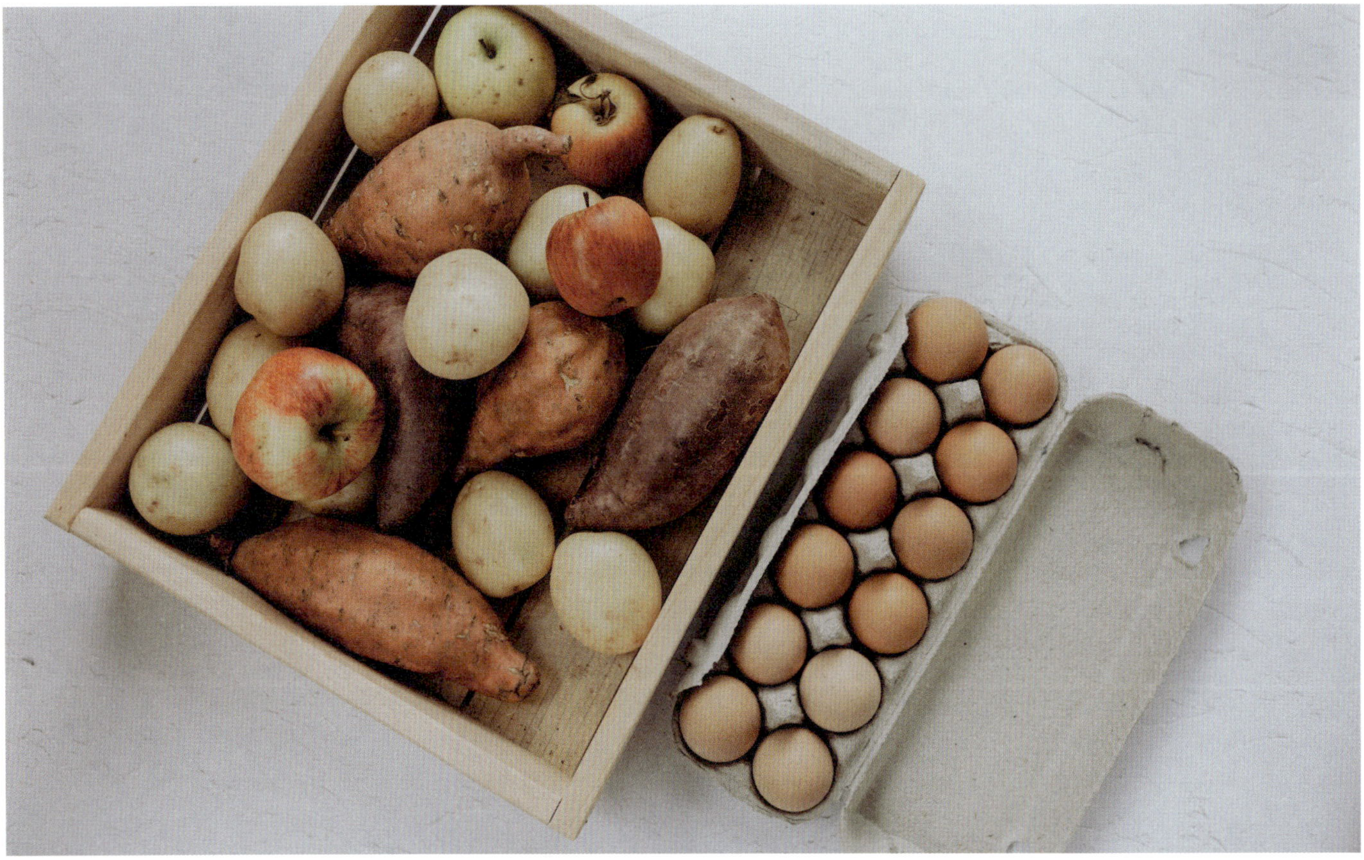

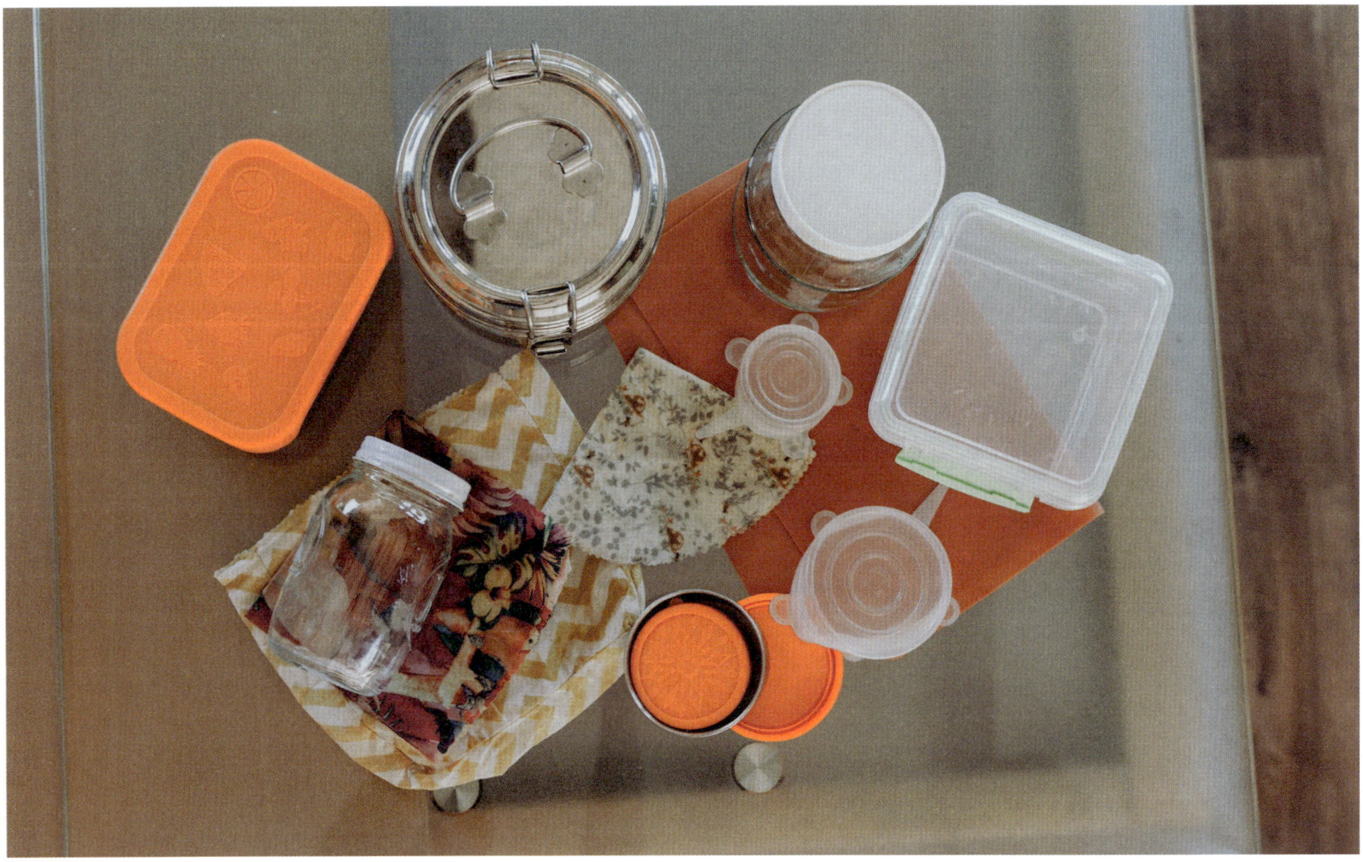

Storing food

When you pair food-waste avoidance with less packaging, you get a bunch of naked food and therefore the need for a strategy to save it all from spoiling. Storing your food properly is an important part of living more sustainably; it helps to preserve the food's nutrients and avoid food waste.

Beeswax wraps (cotton cloth set in beeswax)

These are excellent for wrapping around sandwiches, covering vegetables when you don't need the whole thing, sealing over the top of salad bowls (the heat from your hands melts the beeswax slightly as you push it around the bowl rim) and wrapping up on-the-go snacks.

Containers

You don't have to go out and buy fancy matching containers. Use what you have, take advantage of the containers that end up in your life when you buy the products inside of them, and scout second-hand shops for them too.

Jars

Jars are my best friend in the kitchen. I use them for rolling out pizza dough, making kombucha, storing leftovers and transporting food. I have multiple different sizes of jars in my 'jar cupboard' (yes, a cupboard specifically for jars) for all my different needs. I've never bought a new jar; they're all second-hand or have come holding some sort of food I've purchased or been given.

Freezer

The freezer is your best friend. I used to think freezers were only meant for bread and freezer meals, but I was so wrong. When fruit and vegetables are super close to rotting and I know I won't be able to eat them immediately or make a meal with them, I put them in the freezer. Lemons, avocados, bananas. I blanch spinach before putting it in containers (boil, then toss in ice-cold water), and peel bananas first so they're easier to use. I freeze cookies when I make too many and know I should slow down on my cookie consumption, and juice lemons in winter so I have the exact portions of lemon juice to make hummus with during summer. A freezer is the best food-waste avoider!

Fridge

Second best is a fridge. When I was a nanny, I cared for a family who put their packets of chips and crackers in the fridge. I thought they were bonkers, but it kept them crispy for so much longer! Temperature plays a big part in the longevity of food. Consider finding an extra second-hand fridge or freezer to increase your food-saving capacity.

Takeaways

I've proudly boycotted places like McDonalds for several years. But that doesn't mean I don't adore a Friday-night curry. Takeaways are something we eat sparingly, because we don't know exactly where the ingredients have come from or how much waste has been produced in the making of the meal. On a takeaway night, we'll grab our reusable containers and let the place know we are bringing them. We arrive slightly earlier, so they can take our containers out back to the kitchen, but it's never more than a few extra minutes' wait.

When I am out and about, I keep a little kit of reusables on me at all times. These items help me avoid food packaging and still eat when I need to! You don't have to buy anything new; take things from your kitchen, or find lightweight reusables in a second-hand shop.

Label key

1. Metal straw (even if I don't need a straw to drink my beverage I hand it to the server so they don't put a plastic straw in).
2. Wooden spork
3. Cloth napkin
4. Foldout carry bag
5. Collapsible silicon bowl
6. Handbag
7. Collapsible silicon cup
8. Stainless steel drink bottle

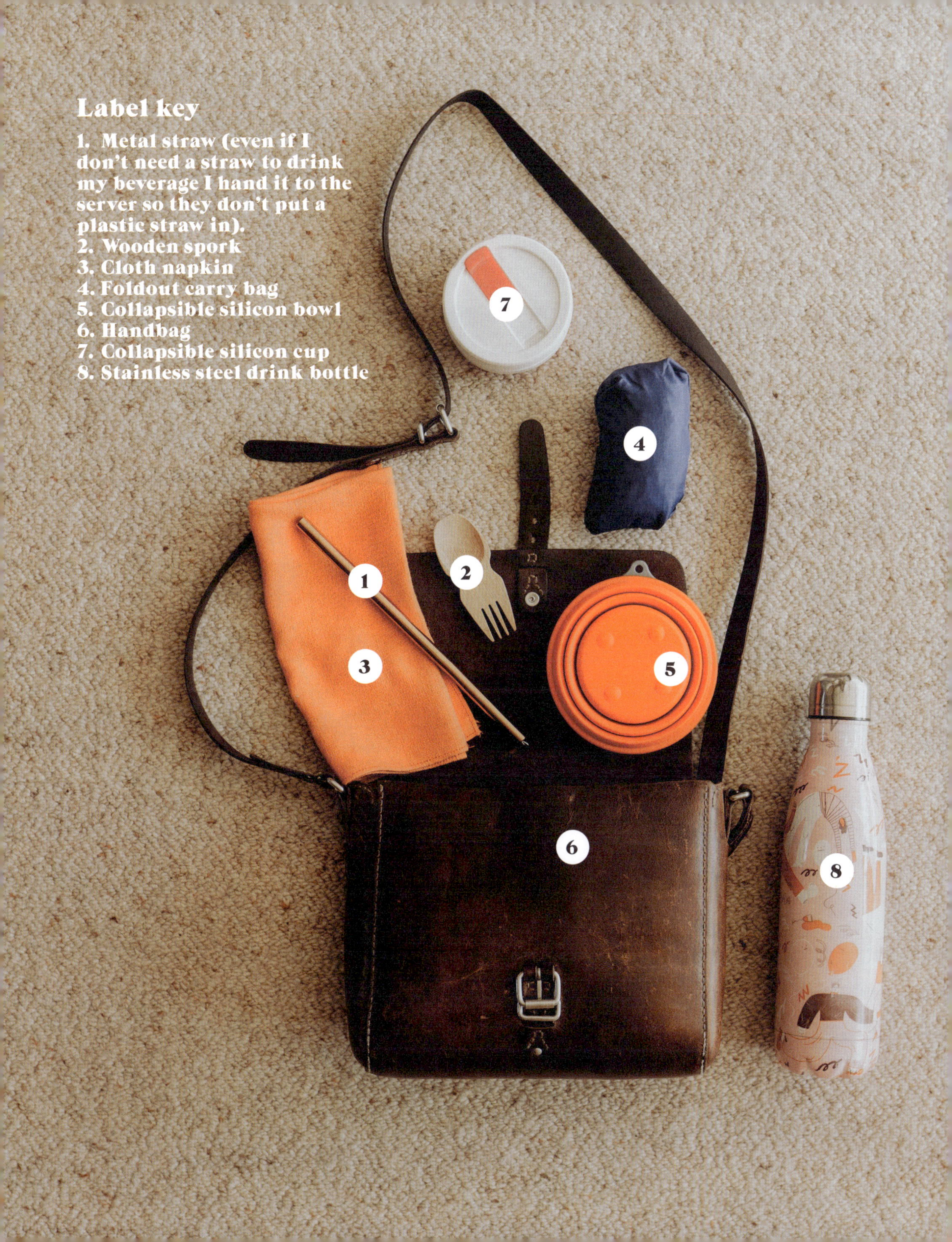
7
4
1
2
3
5
6
8

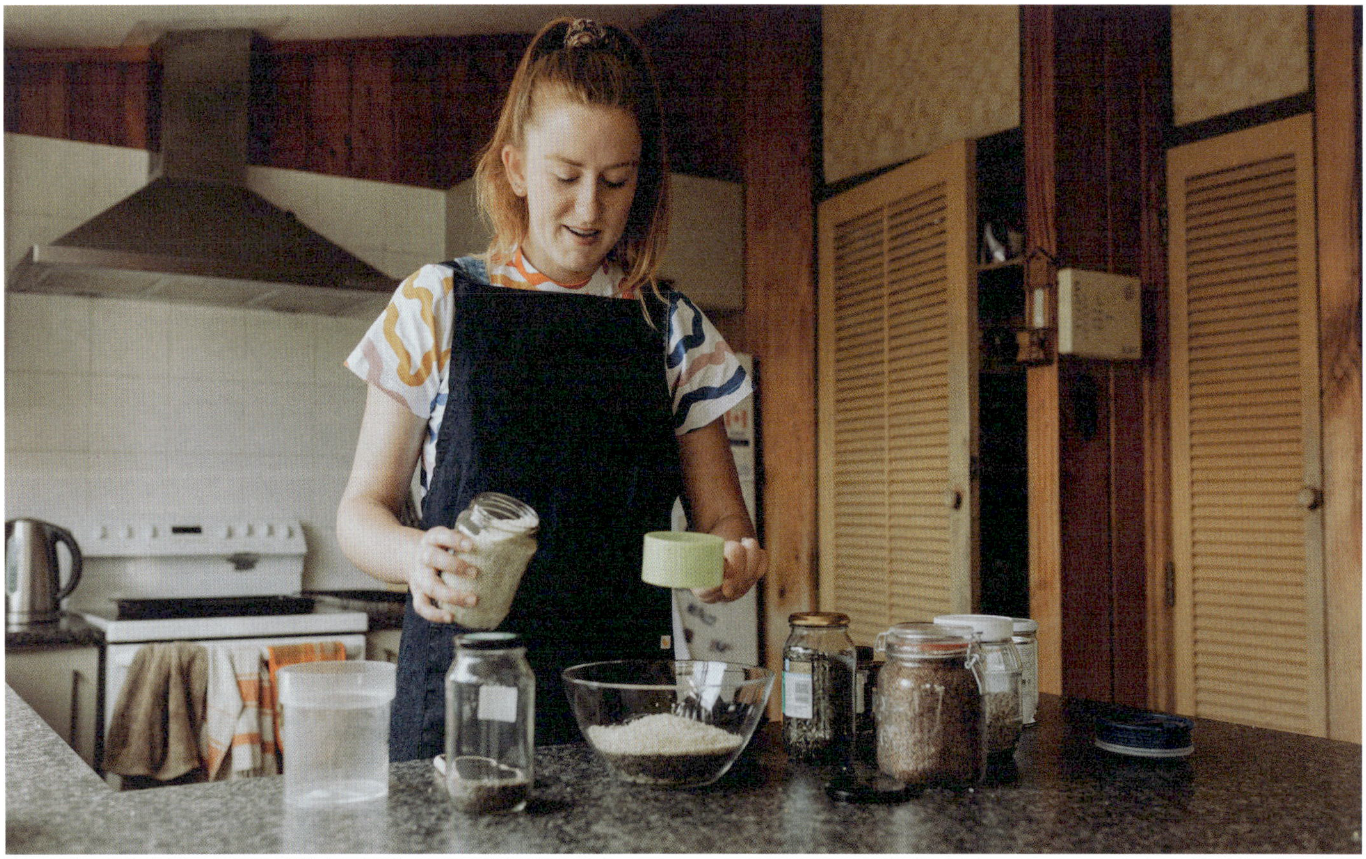

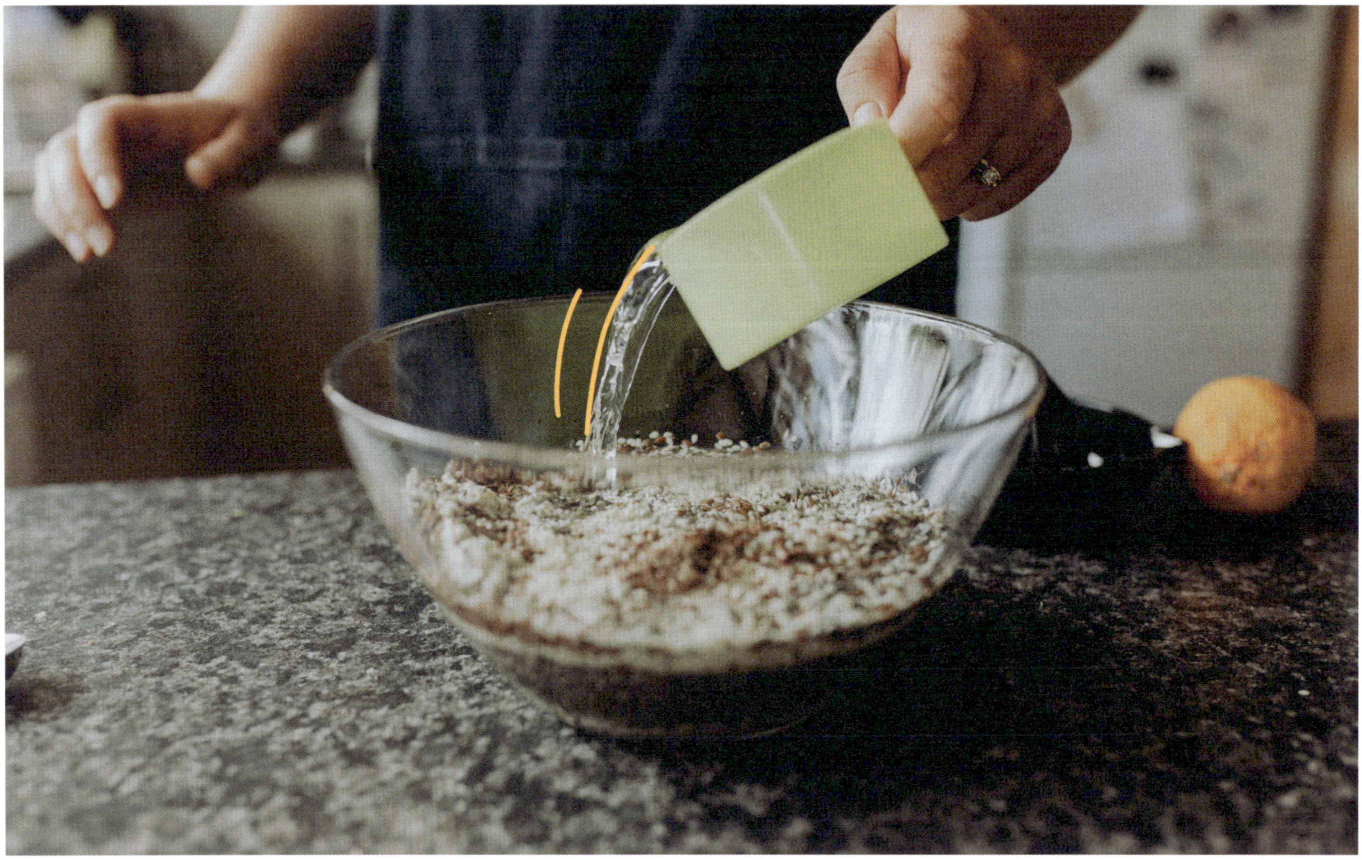

What I eat

As I've said, I'm not so into recipe books — so I won't turn this book into one. I get inspiration from having meals at other people's homes or by watching flatmates cooking to see how they use different ingredients.

Imagine you're in my house. You're propped up on a stool, staring intently from the other side of the kitchen bench as I walk you through a mini food-diary and throw splashes of food inspiration at you.

It's breakfast time!

I take some of my homemade bread from the freezer (it only takes me 6 minutes and 37 seconds to make it with 500g of a 10kg bag of gluten-free bread mix) and pop it in the toaster. I'll spread some jam from my local farmers' market on it or some peanut butter that's made locally too. Perhaps some avocado or tomato from a company who rescues vegetables from the bin, or an egg from Anni's beautiful farm. On another day, you might see me roast a mixture of honey and oil-drizzled seeds and nuts to make cereal. It's really that simple! Mix it, roast it.

No access to a farmers' market? Choose the jam in the glass jar instead of the plastic one.

Can't make your own bread or cereal? Find a local business who can or reuse your plastic bread or cereal bag to freeze things like fruit in.

The key ingredient to my breakfast routine is my cup of tea. Loose-leaf black tea from a bulk bin store paired with a drop of milk is my morning must. The milk I usually use is purchased from my local vegetable store, which has a reusable glass-bottle return scheme. I paid around $8 to purchase the milk and the bottle, and whenever I bring the bottle back and buy another, I pay $4. If that's not in the fridge, I make my own almond milk. I blend water and almonds and strain that mixture through a thin fabric bag. If I wasn't coeliac, I'd drink oat milk! One of the cheapest, most sustainable, and easiest milks to make.

Morning tea
It's 10:30am, so I'm getting a tad hungry. Back in the kitchen we go . . . I'll grab a piece of fruit, a cold boiled egg, or perhaps a bliss ball.

Bliss balls

½ cup dates, soaked in boiling water for 10-15 minutes
1 tbsp coconut oil (softened, but not runny)
¼ cup sunflower seeds
½ cup chia seeds
desiccated coconut, 1 tsp cocoa powder, chopped apricots or walnuts (optional)

Simply blend these together. Add more dry or wet ingredients as needed, until it's the right consistency to form into balls in your hands. Place in the fridge to set.

You don't have to use these exact ingredients. Dates and coconut oil are key, but apart from that you can use whatever you have in your pantry. If not bliss balls, dried fruit, nuts and seeds await me in their glass jars — also purchased from a package-free shop.

Lunchtime
If past Kate hasn't made enough dinner the night before for leftovers, I'll cook up my 'usual' (spaghetti or spiral pasta, any vegetables I have, cut up well, with soy sauce, sweet chilli sauce and lots of grated ginger) and wash it down with a glass of my homemade kombucha.

Afternoon tea
By the afternoon, I'm a little peckish and need to have energy for my evening exercise. I'll munch on an apple, make a smoothie (with frozen fruit that was about to go off), or if I'm lucky there will be a frozen fruit popsicle in my freezer! Investing in some cool stainless steel popsicle sticks or scoring some at a second-hand shop is a game changer. You can blend all your slightly old fruit and vegetables to make cheap iceblocks.

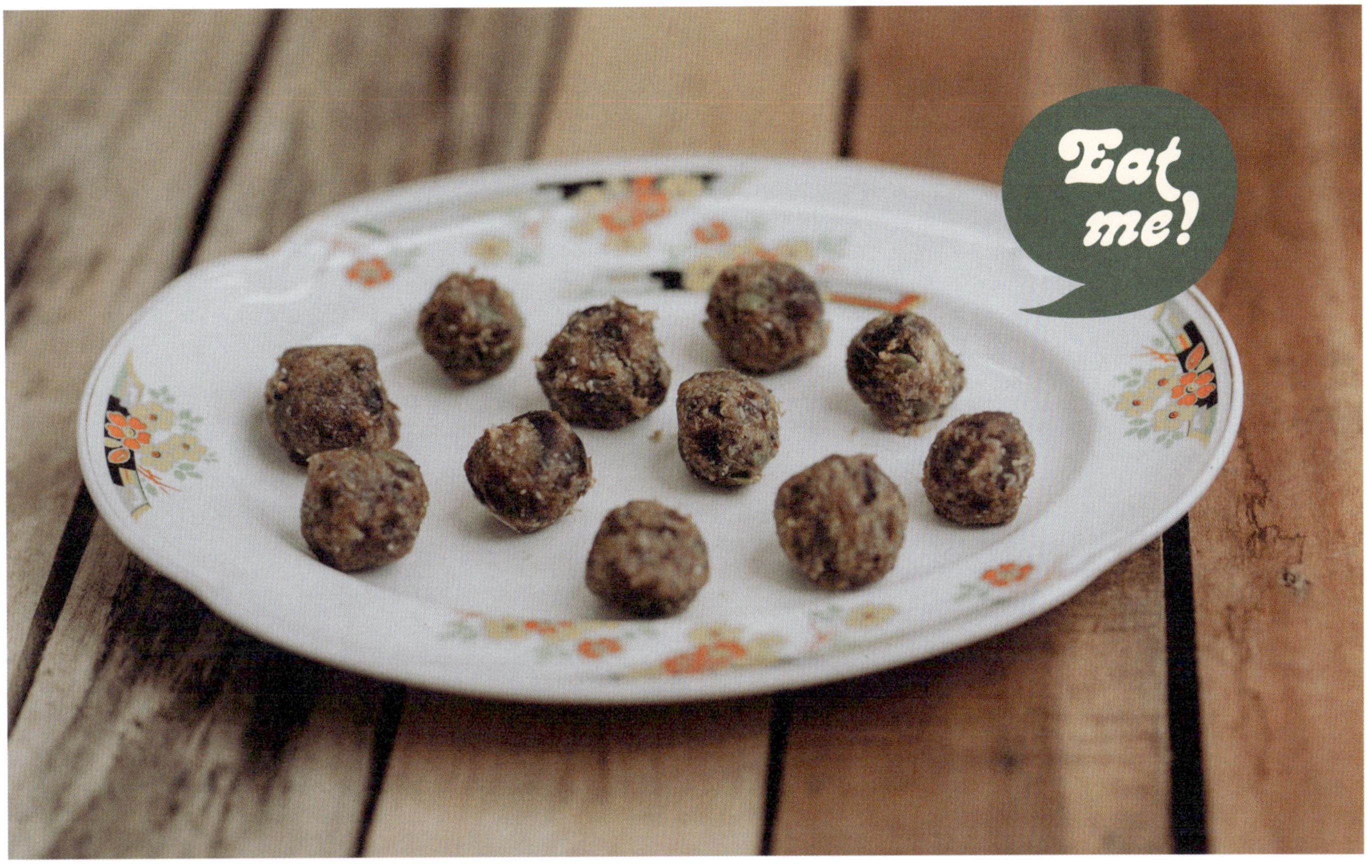
Eat
me!

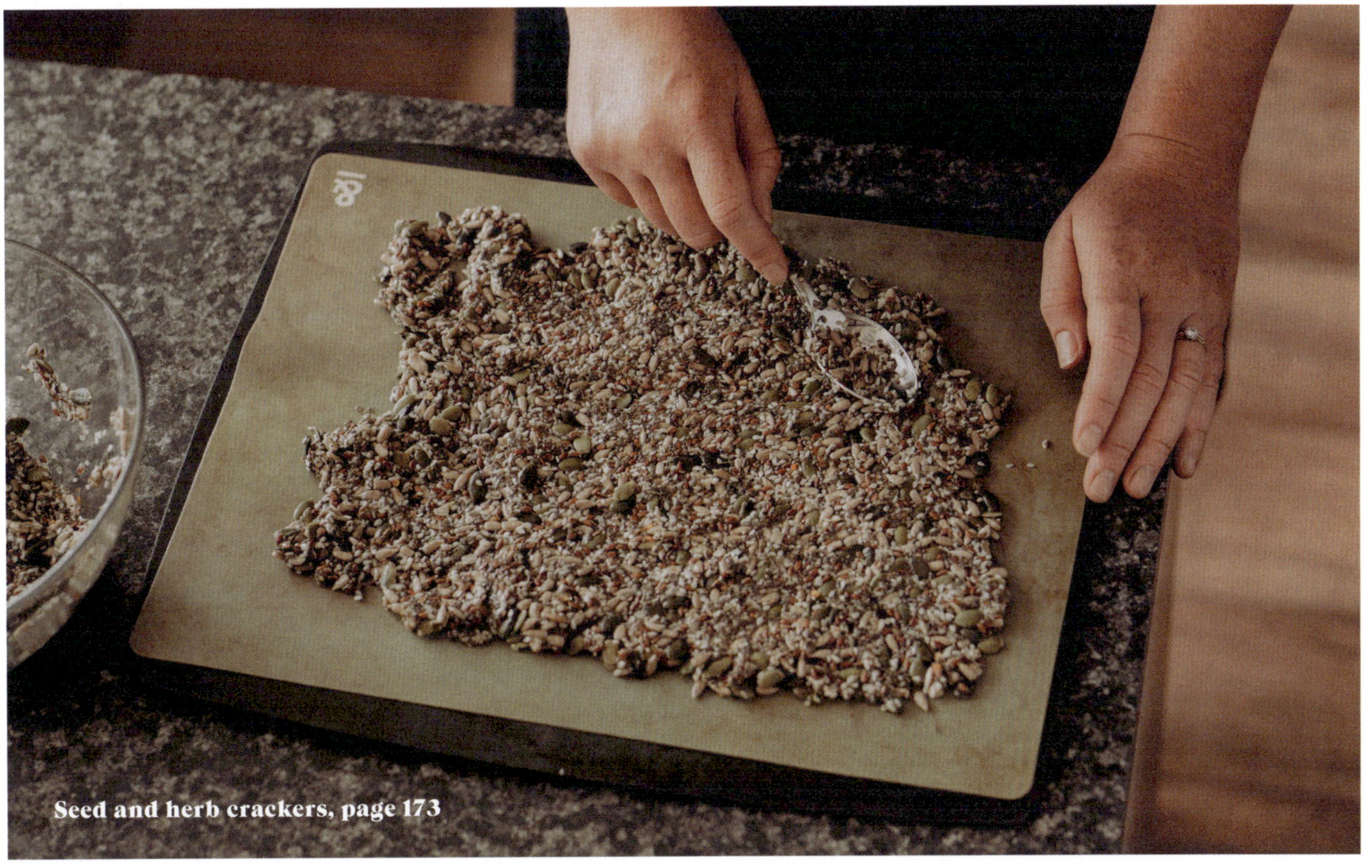

Seed and herb crackers, page 173

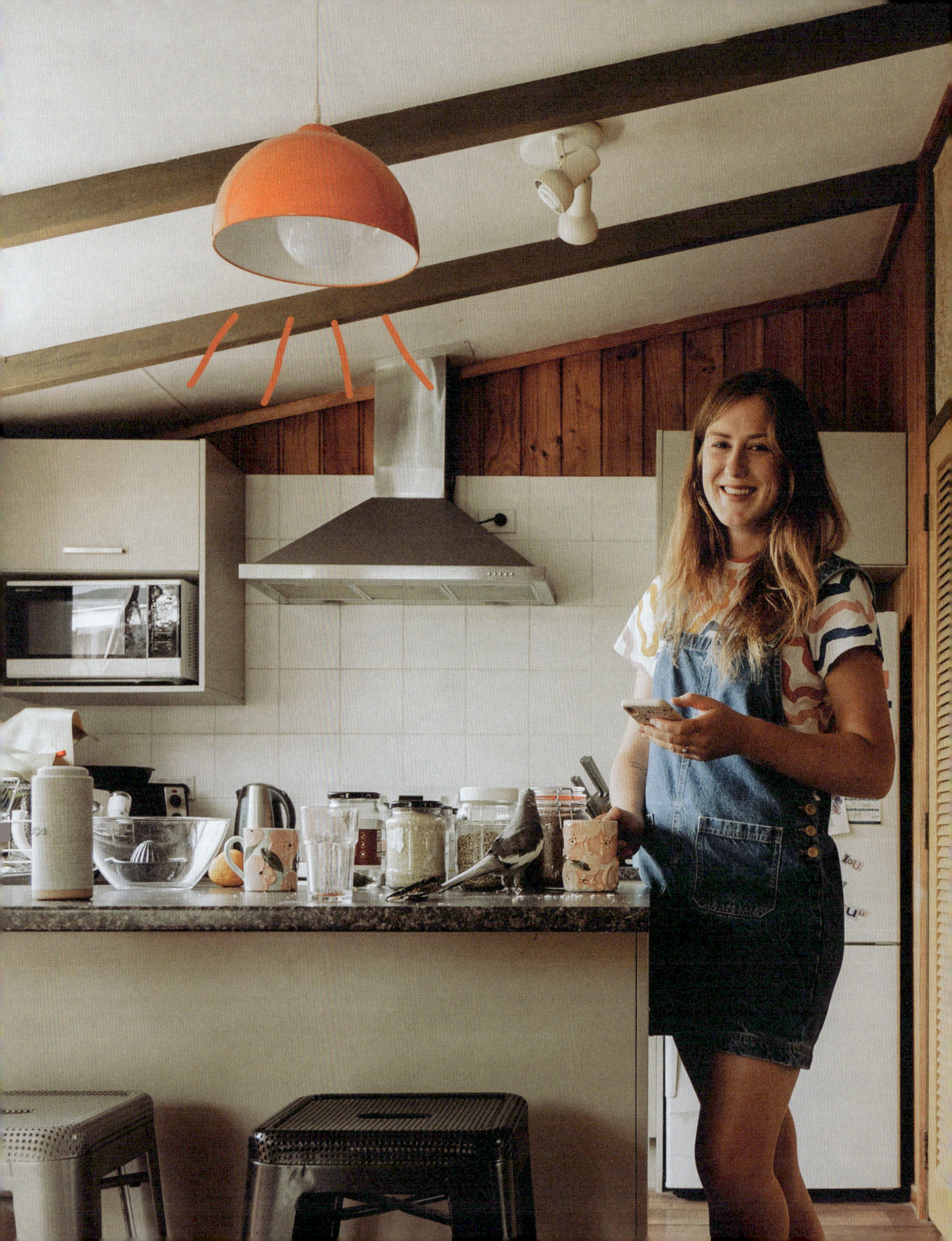

Snacks

My favourite snack, which I bring to most pot-luck meals, is low-waste hummus and crackers. The cracker recipe comes from the Quite Good Food website[11], and the hummus recipe overleaf comes from the Inspired Taste website.[12]

Seed and herb crackers

1 cup sunflower seeds
¾ cup pumpkin seeds
½ cup chia seeds
½ cup sesame seeds (I use a mix of black and white)
¼ cup flaxseed/linseed
1 tsp salt
1½ cups water
1 tbsp dried herbs of your choice
1 tsp chilli flakes (optional)

Heat oven to 150°C.

Mix all ingredients together and then leave for 10 minutes.

Spread mixture out on a baking tray and bake for 10 minutes (you may need to do more than one batch if there's too much mixture to fit on the tray). Keep a close eye on them.

Flip over (you can break it up into crackers at this stage, or flip the entire thing). Bake for a further 10 minutes.

Note: If you don't have these exact quantities of seeds, just swap them out for another seed listed.

Hummus

¼ cup (60ml) well-stirred tahini
¼ cup (60ml) fresh lemon juice
2 tbsp (30ml) extra virgin olive oil, plus more for serving
1 small garlic clove, minced (I often sneak in 2-4!)
½ tsp ground cumin
salt to taste
1 can chickpeas, rinsed, or 1½ cups (250g) cooked chickpeas
2-3 tbsp (30-45ml) water or aquafaba
dash ground paprika or sumac, for serving

Combine the tahini and lemon juice in the bowl of a food processer and process for 1 minute. Scrape the sides and bottom of the bowl then process for another 30 seconds. This extra time helps to 'whip' or 'cream' the tahini, making the hummus smooth and creamy.

Add the olive oil, minced garlic, cumin and half a teaspoon of salt to the whipped tahini and lemon juice. Process for 30 seconds, scrape the sides and bottom of the bowl then process for another 30 seconds or until well blended.

Add half of the chickpeas to the food processor and process for 1 minute. Scrape sides and bottom of the bowl, then add remaining chickpeas and process until thick and quite smooth, 1-2 minutes.

If the hummus is too thick or still has chunks of chickpea in it, with the food processor turned on, slowly add 2-3 tablespoons of water or aquafaba until you reach your desired consistency.

Taste for salt and adjust as needed. Serve hummus with a drizzle of olive oil and dash of paprika or sumac. It will keep for up to a week stored in an airtight container in the fridge.

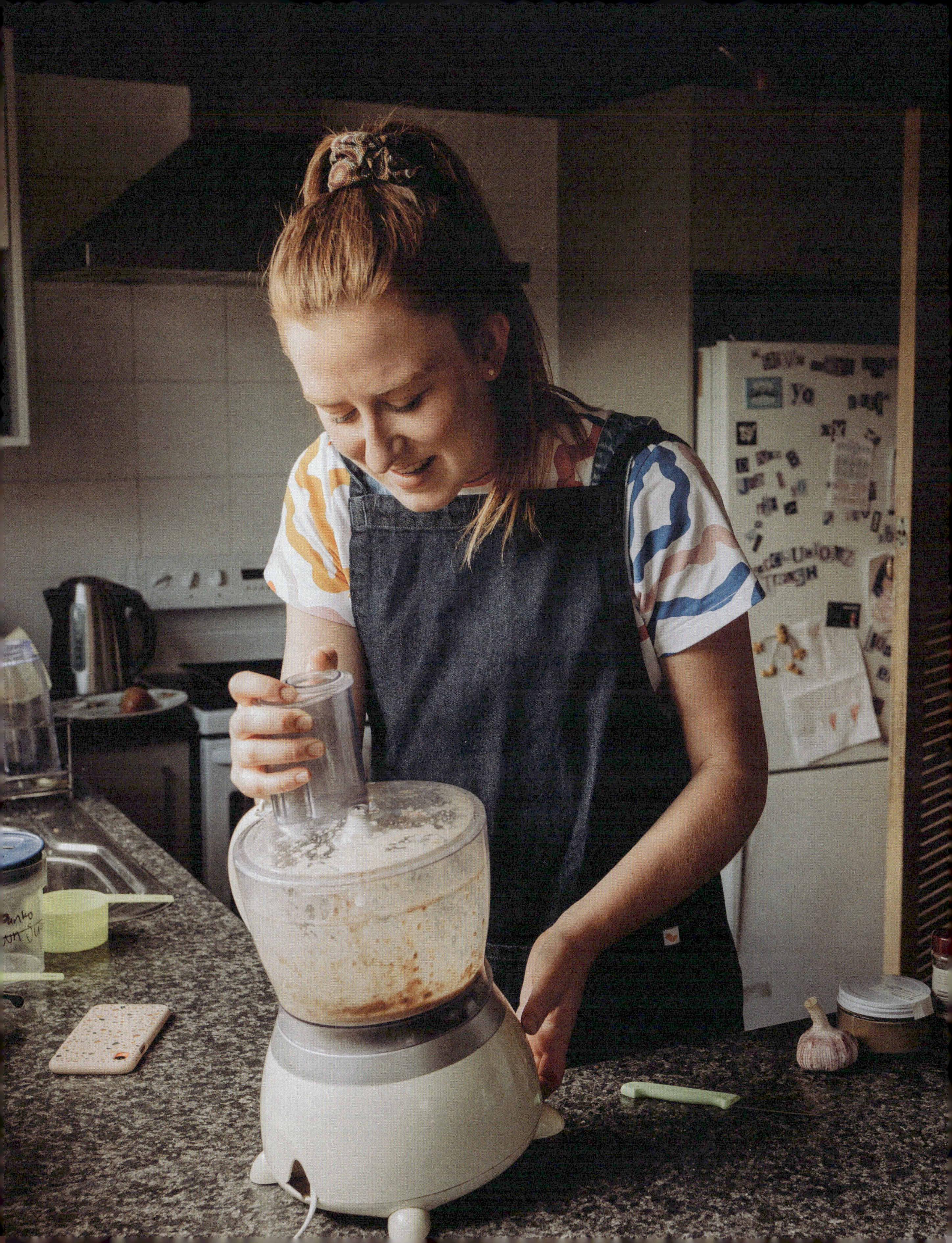

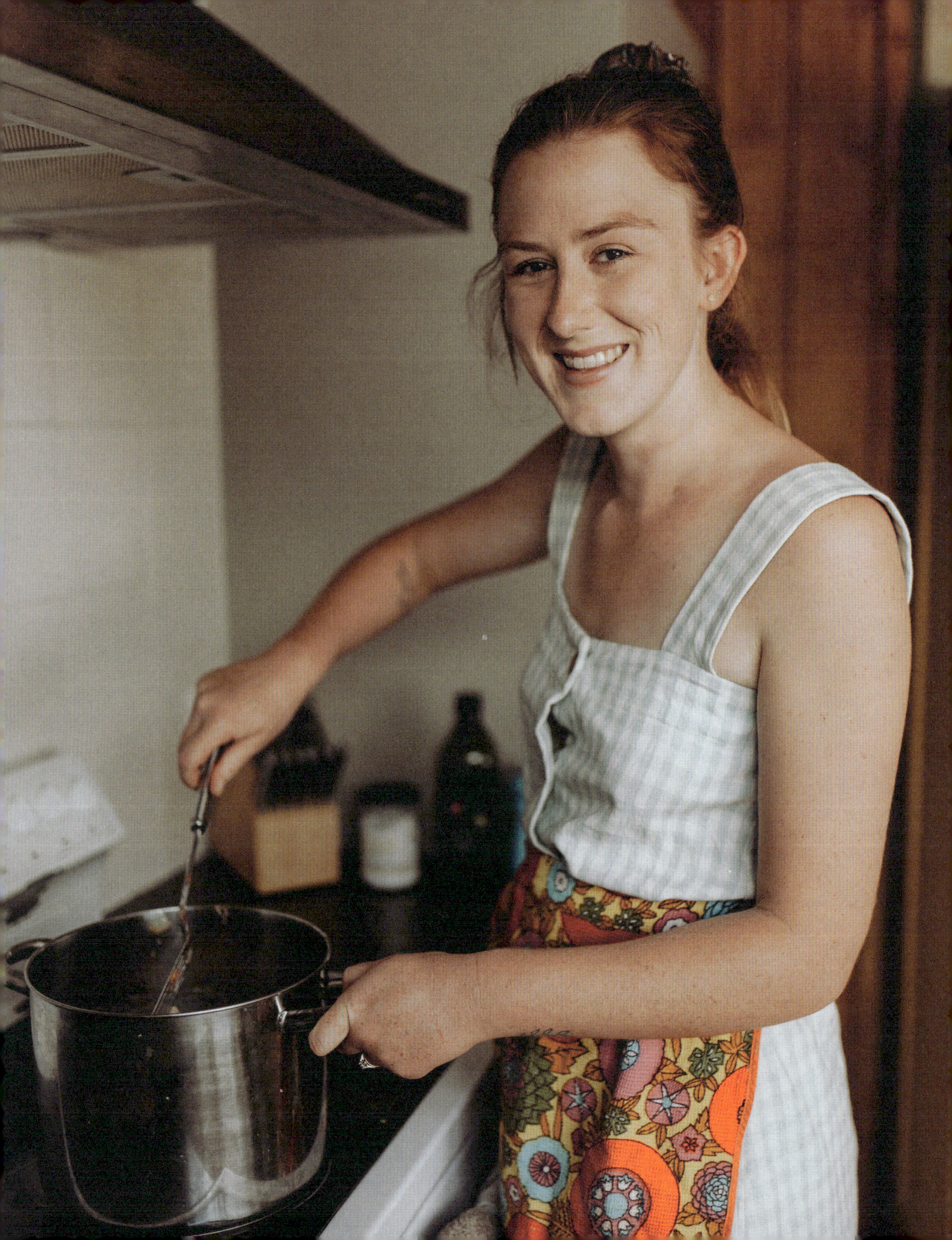

Dinner

At dinnertime, you'll often find Tim and me in the kitchen cooking together. Our go-to is vegetable curry. Sometimes we'll add fish that Tim has caught; meat purchased in our own containers from our local butcher or from a company which only kills wild beasts; or free-range, organic chicken that comes in a home-compostable bag.

Curry

1 kūmara, diced
1 potato, diced
1 tbsp oil
2 large cloves of garlic
1 onion
mixed herbs of your choice (optional)
curry paste of your choice
½ head of cauliflower, roughly chopped
1 big handful of mushrooms, sliced
1 large carrot, diced
salt and pepper
1 can coconut milk (or fresh coconut milk)
1 can chopped tomatoes (or fresh tomatoes, blended)
rice or quinoa, to serve

Boil the kūmara and potato in a large pot of salted water until soft, about 10 minutes.

Heat the oil in a frying pan or wok, and add the garlic, onion and herbs (if using). Sauté for 3-5 minutes. Add the curry paste, kūmara and potato. Cook for 5 minutes.

Add the cauliflower, mushrooms, carrot and any other vegetables you want to use up! Stir and cook for 5 minutes. Season with salt and pepper. Add the coconut milk and chopped tomatoes. Stir and let bubble for 5-10 minutes. Serve on rice or quinoa.

Popcorn

Potentially the easiest and best snack of them all. It only takes a few minutes more to make popcorn waste-free and more nutritious, too. Ditching those two-minute popcorn bags that are wrapped in plastic is a quick and easy sustainable snack win! Use a saucepan with a glass lid if possible, so you can check on the popcorn.

> ½–1 cup popcorn kernels
> 1 tbsp oil (any vegetable oil will do)
> 50g butter (you can use less or more, depending on how buttery you like your popcorn)
> 1 tsp salt

Okay, you're sitting in my kitchen, watching me make popcorn. This is what you'll see . . .

I set one stove element to 'high' and put the saucepan on it. Inside the saucepan is one popcorn kernel plus the tablespoon of oil. I wait for a second, probably doing a little stretch or boogie, until the kernel pops. When it has popped I pour in the rest of my popcorn kernels and put the lid on.

Every 10 seconds, I toss the popcorn by holding the handle of the saucepan and shaking it. Once the popping slows down, I turn the element off, give you a wink, and tip the popcorn into a bowl.

I melt the butter in the saucepan or in the microwave, and drizzle it over the popcorn while I shake in the salt, too. A bit of a toss around, and I dance out of the kitchen and lead you into my TV room for a movie.

 Waste

Now I've talked about what we eat, what about the stuff that we don't eat? We don't eat cardboard or plastic wrap. So, where does that go?

The 'out of sight, out of mind' mentality doesn't work. Not if we want to continue thriving on planet Earth. When a rubbish truck takes away our rubbish, the rubbish does not disappear. I believe we all have a responsibility to make sure our rubbish bins are as empty as possible by treasuring the resources we create rather than making them, using them and throwing them into landfill.

One of the best ways to reduce your rubbish is to become aware of it.

How to complete a home-waste audit

1. Keep all of your waste for 3-7 days.
2. Lay a sheet on a flat surface outside, and grab a pair of reusable gloves (it's about to get messy!)
3. Separate your waste into piles: landfill, recyclable (check with your local council or recycling centre), glass, metal, paper, compostable/organic matter, reusable (the things you threw in the rubbish bin absentmindedly but now realise you could fix and repurpose).
4. Weigh those piles and make notes. Record common themes, the key items in your landfill pile, if you've had any big events or unusual activity during the time you collected your waste, and how much waste others (e.g. flatmates) may have contributed.
5. With this information, focus on the biggest waste stream first (e.g. wine bottles or bread packages). For example, if it is glass wine bottles, investigate local wineries who may have wine on tap. Perhaps you could bring your own bottles and refill them! If choosing the biggest waste stream is not within your current time/mental/emotional capacity, start with the easiest change first.
6. Complete a home-waste audit every six months to see where you're at and celebrate your progress.

Recycling

Often people tell me 'I'm living sustainably, my recycling bin is so full!' Yes, recycling is an important part of taking responsibility for your waste, but if you're truly living with sustainable values in your home and pantry, you'll start to recycle less.

Just like all rubbish, it's best to avoid an item you need to recycle. For example, think of a cardboard box containing cherry tomatoes. After you place the box in your recycling bin, it is transported by a fuel-powered truck to a plant to be recycled. More fossil fuels are burnt for the recycling plant to turn that cardboard into pulp and then into a new material. To add to the complexity, this whole recycling process only happens if there is no human error or interference along the way. The cardboard could get blown out of the recycling truck. The recycling plant may have not accepted any more materials that day so the whole load was dumped into landfill. Plus, many materials can only be recycled a few times. They'll be downgraded and turned into something less valuable than what they were before, and ultimately end up in landfill some time soon. Recycling is great in some instances, but it often only keeps the item out of landfill for slightly longer.

Avoiding recyclable materials as much as you do waste is vital to living more sustainably.

When it comes to *how* to recycle, the answer is not simple. It also varies depending on where you live. Here are some simple recycling rules that are generally the same worldwide.

- **Clean and dry:** Every bottle needs to be rinsed out and dried, every piece of paper needs to be dry and free of contaminants. Your recycling should be so clean and dry that you would feel comfortable having it sit on your kitchen table or laying it across your lounge floor.
- **Separated materials:** Each item must contain one type of material. For example, a piece of paper covered with glitter either needs to be put in the waste bin, or the glitter needs to be completely removed. A pack of batteries has a plastic cover and paper backing; the two

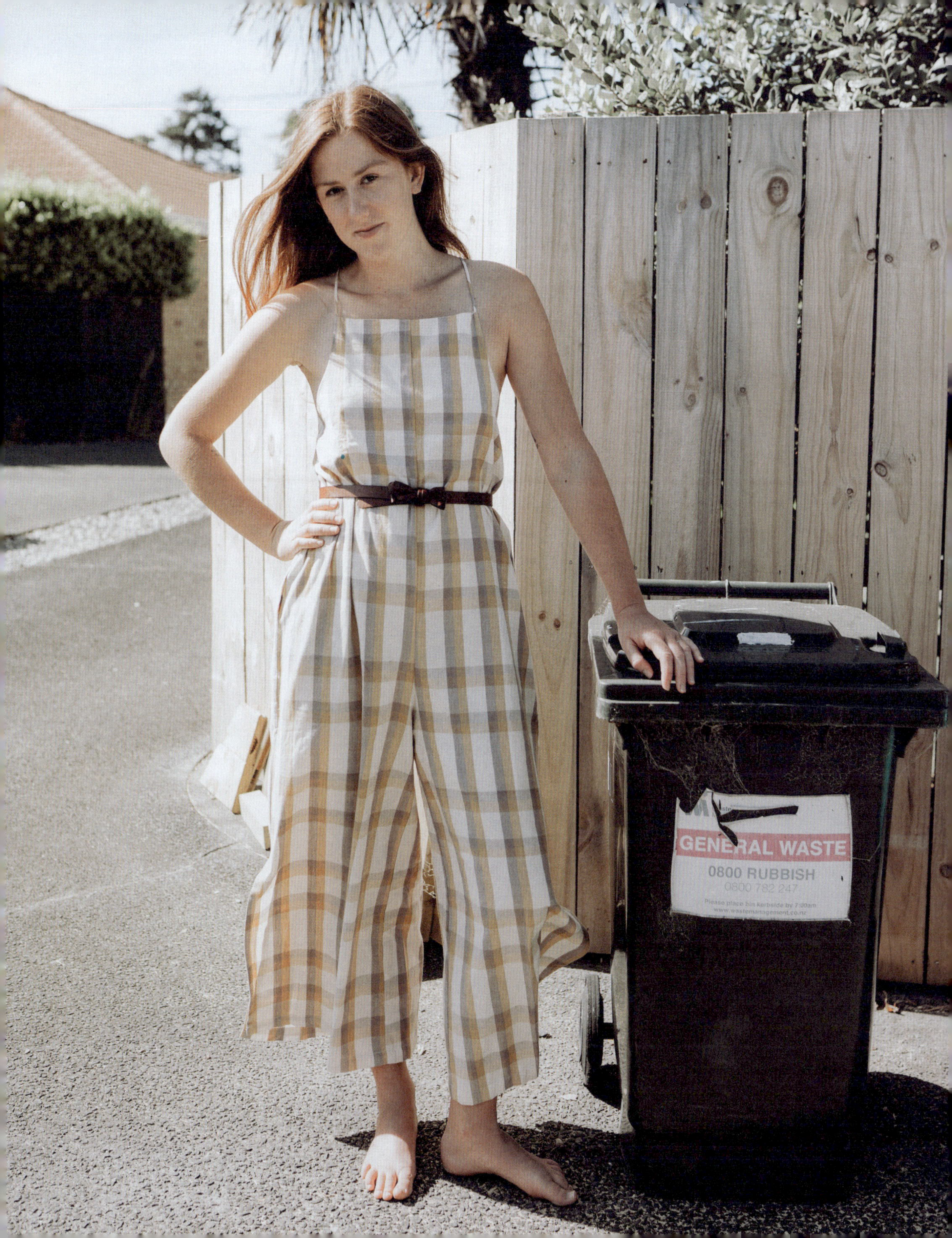
GENERAL WASTE
0800 RUBBISH
0800 782 247
Please place bin kerbside by 7:00am
www.wastemanagement.co.nz

need to be separated because a recycling plant generally cannot separate materials (although there is room for a small percentage of contaminants that the industry calls 'outthrow').
- **Repurposing:** Can you repurpose the item? Often recyclable materials can serve a purpose. A glass bottle can become a vase or a pencil holder. Cardboard boxes could be used to store things. Think before you chuck it in!
- **Consult your local council:** Check what type of materials can be recycled in your area. For example, there are many types of plastics and not all of them can be recycled in all places. The type of plastic is identified by the number on the item. Plastics number 1 and 2 are recycled often. Plastic number 5 is recycled sometimes. Plastics number 3, 4 and 6 are rarely able to be recycled, and plastic number 7 is almost never able to be recycled.

Understanding recycling can seem overwhelming, but following these basic guidelines and listening to your local council is the best way to feel confident when recycling your waste. Understanding what you can recycle is also a brilliant way to cut down your rubbish. If, like me, your local council recycles numbers 1, 2 and 5 plastics, you can check the plastic container during your supermarket shop to make sure it's recyclable.

Move beyond the idea that composting is just a way to dispose of your waste. Choose to see it as a way to have fun and create a valuable product.

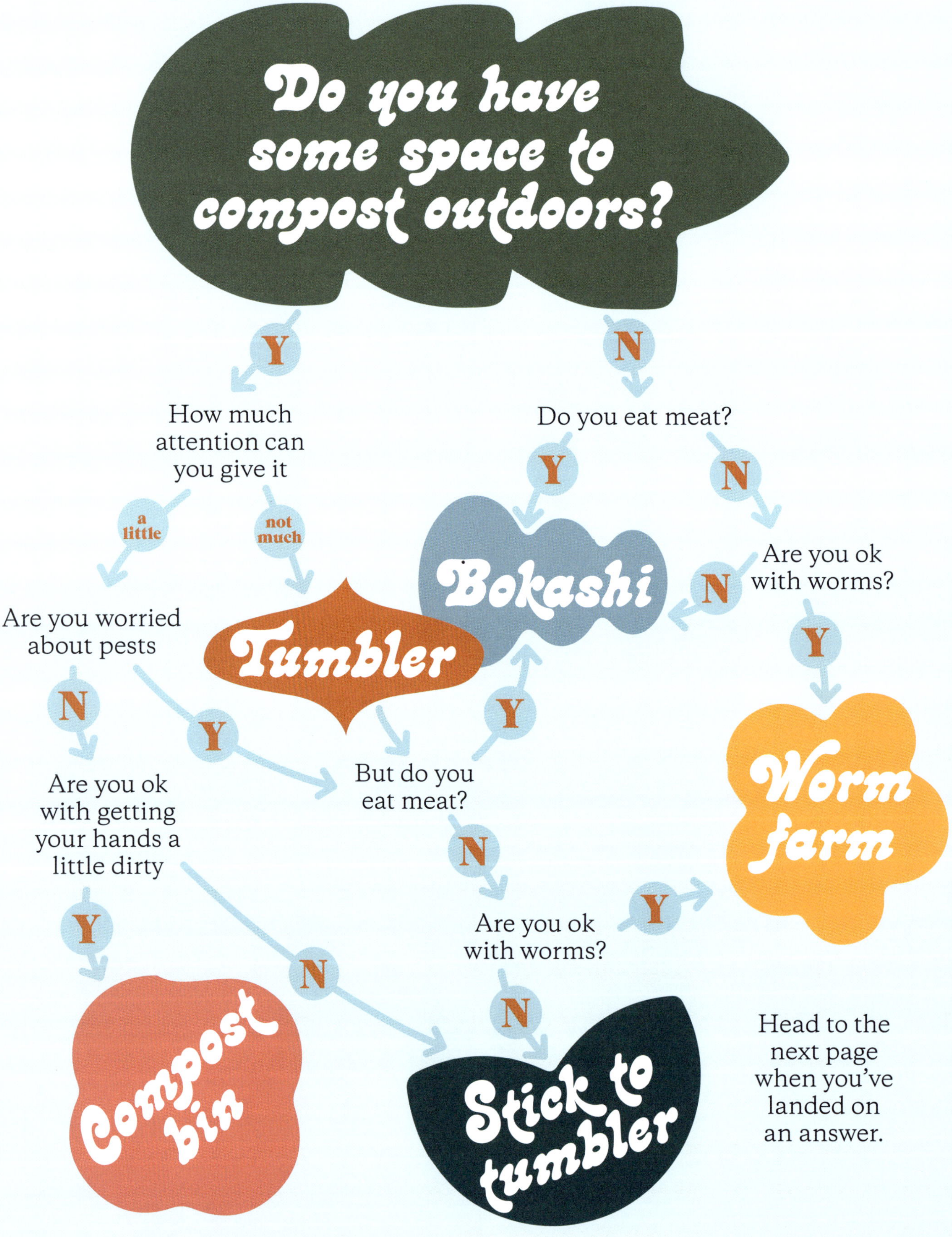

Do you have some space to compost outdoors?
Y
N
How much attention can you give it
Do you eat meat?
Y
N
a little
not much
Bokashi
Are you ok with worms?
N
Are you worried about pests
Tumbler
Y
N
Y
Y
But do you eat meat?
Worm farm
Are you ok with getting your hands a little dirty
N
Are you ok with worms?
Y
Y
N
N
Compost bin
Stick to tumbler

Head to the next page when you've landed on an answer.

Organic waste and composting

If you only do one thing that I suggest in this entire book, I hope it's composting. Technically, this section could be in the 'wellness' or 'self' part of the book because it's a hobby and a wellness-inducing pastime. Composting shouldn't be treated like a waste stream, though it's okay if your situation means you need to treat it like that in the short term. Composting is the process of turning organic matter, like the food you don't want to eat or clippings from plants, into rich, delicious soil that grows more food and harbours all sorts of thrilling nutrients.

I realise it's hard to hear 'you should compost!' if you're reading this in a tiny apartment in the middle of a city. But stay with me, because composting is possible for most people, no matter where they live.

On average, a person's household waste is around 50 per cent organic matter[13] that can be composted. Composting can cut your waste in half, save you money (the finished product is valuable soil), and is an ideal way to understand and fall in love with circular, sustainable systems. Turning unwanted organic matter into soil is also incredibly rewarding. I have a compost, bokashi, hot compost and a worm farm. It's safe to say I am obsessed. I've experimented with all types of organic food-waste systems in my own home and set them up for kindergartens and homes, and guided apartment dwellers, too. Although there are always hurdles to leap over and problems to solve, everyone can do it!

In an attempt not to overwhelm composting beginners or to make you think I'm utterly bonkers with the amount I love compost (I am), I'll keep things practical and simple.

Types of organic waste solutions

Type of organic waste solution	What is it	What I put in	What I don't put in	Picture
Compost (cold compost)	My favourite type of organic food waste disposal, composting involves the food matter decomposing with the help of microorganisms. Although micro-organisms do most of the work in a compost, it's also a home for worms and insects of many kinds. Composts look like the common black square bins, tumblers that stand on a metal frame, simple heaps on the ground, mounds in repurposed bathtubs, or piles with wire netting bundling things together	Fruit and vegetable scraps, fresh lawn clippings, paper, egg shells, newspapers, dried leaves, vacuum dust (if your carpet is wool, not synthetic). I/ also put our fully fermented bokashi matter in our cold compost.	Meat, dairy, commercially compostable packaging, faeces, invasive weeds, processed foods	
Worm farms	In a worm farm, worms consume organic matter, eating up to 50 per cent of their body weight in food each day! Worm farms are popular because they are ideal for people who don't have much space, and they can be stored indoors	Fruit and vegetable scraps, fresh lawn clippings, paper, egg shells, newspapers, dried leaves	Strongly acidic foods like onions or chilli, spicy food, meat, dairy, commercially compostable packaging, faeces, invasive weeds, processed foods, oil	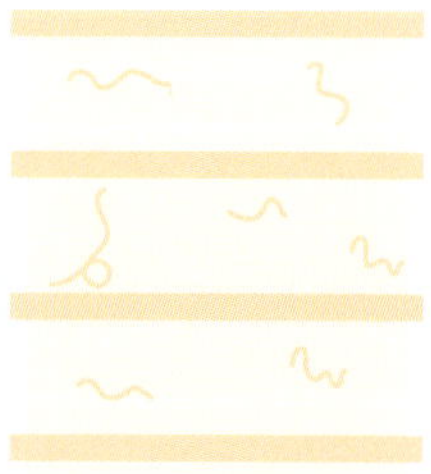

Type of organic waste solution	What is it	What I put in	What I don't put in	Picture
Bokashi	Bokashi is an anaerobic system that ferments food waste. You put your food scraps in, push them down to remove as much air as possible, add bokashi sprinkle (resembles sawdust and is full of microbes that help with the fermenting process) and repeat. The liquid that builds in the bottom needs to be released every few days (it's great for cleaning out your drains!). Small bokashi systems can sit on kitchen benches or under the sink	Meat, dairy products, citrus fruits, onions, vegetables, green lawn clippings, bones, shells, coffee grinds, cooked and processed food	Lots of liquids (like milk), paper, dried leaves	
Hot composting	You'll be absolutely surprised to know that a hot compost is just like a compost bin, but hotter. A hot compost is created more strategically so it reaches higher temperatures and breaks matter down faster	A hot compost is often used to break down things like thick branches and garden clippings. It's generally created and then left for several months to years to get really hot, rather than aerated and added to frequently like a cold (standard) compost	There's hardly anything a hot compost won't break down!	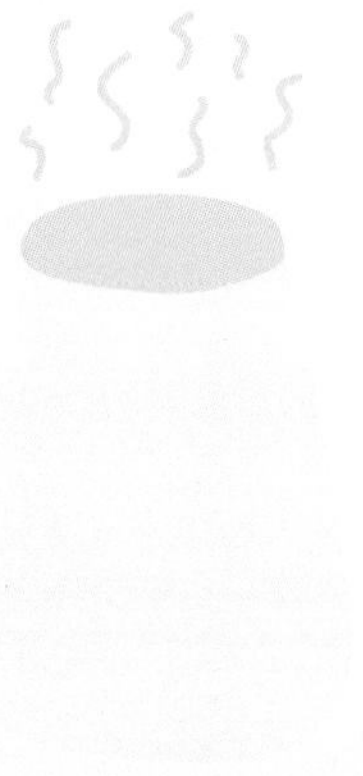

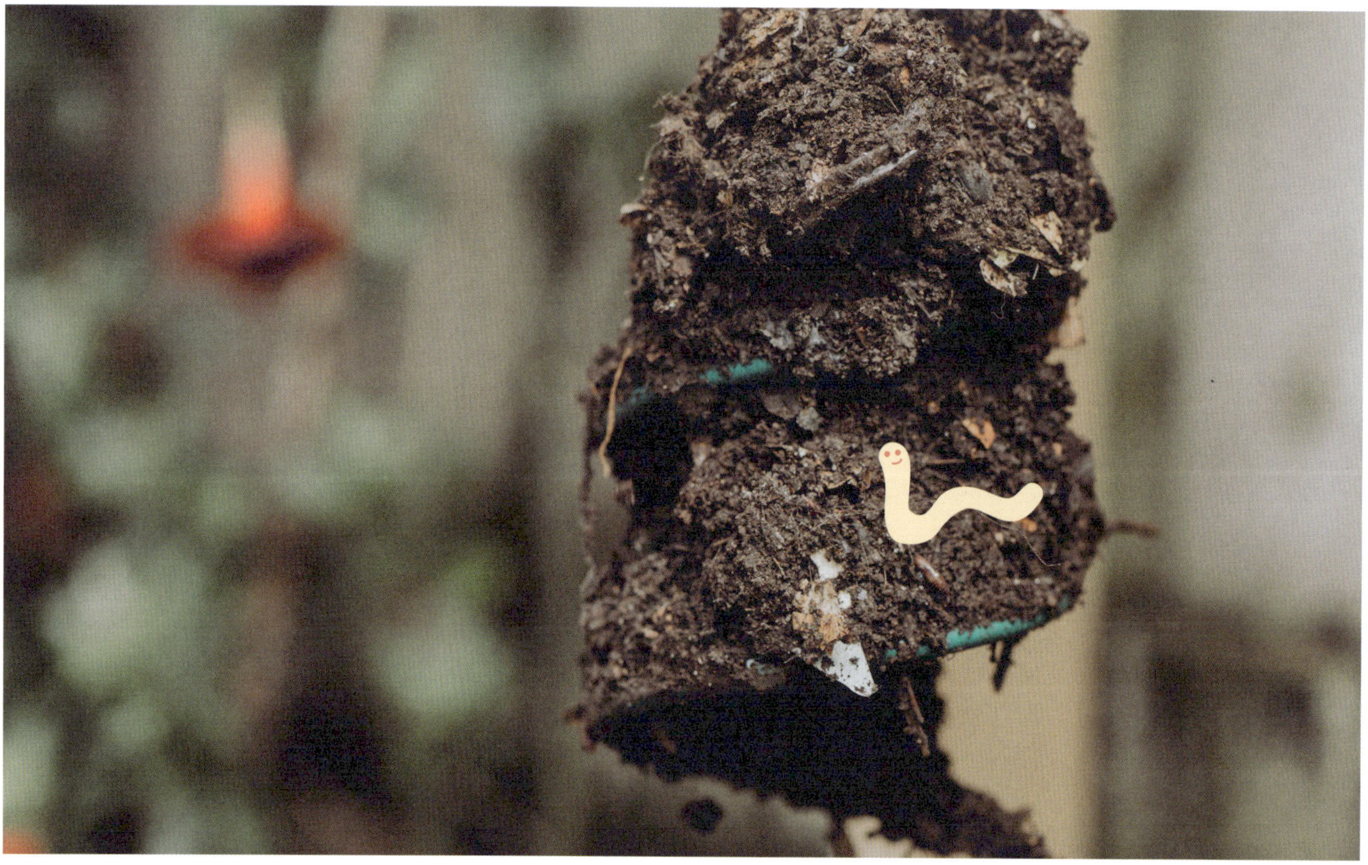

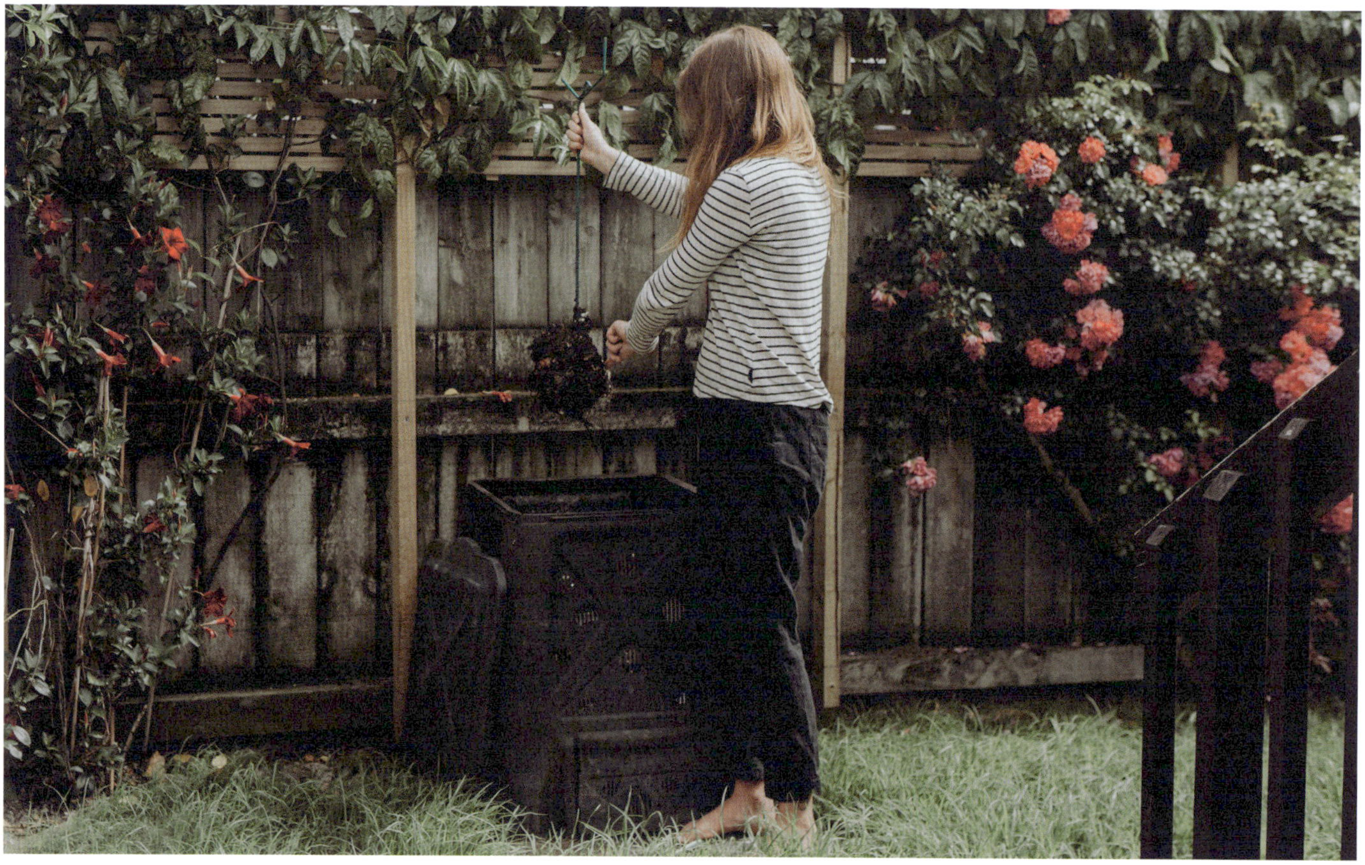

Commercial compost

You know those coffee cups that say 'compostable' and those sneaky trays of food that say 'plant-based'? Most of the time, these items are only commercially compostable. No matter how great you are at home composting, those items will not break down in your home compost. A commercial compost is like your compost at home, but done in a far more strategic way and on a larger scale. A commercial compost has the right levels of elements, like nitrogen and carbon, at all times, and gets far hotter than your compost at home.

Sharewaste

Sharewaste is a global system that connects composters with people close by who have organic food waste.[14] It may sound strange, but if you cannot compost in your own home, someone else will definitely want your scraps! Food waste is valuable, especially for people with large gardens who need compost for nourishing their plants. Most people who give their food scraps to someone else to compost will freeze them until they can drop them off. Some even receive a gift in return for their waste.

Your wilted lettuce leaf will not break down in landfill. Your compostable coffee cup won't either. Even if you close your eyes and wish really hard as you throw them into your rubbish bin, they're still going to sit in landfill for hundreds of years very slowly *breaking up*. This may surprise you, but because landfills don't have oxygen flowing through them or any other lovely elements that allow organic matter to break down into soil, your wilted lettuce and compostable coffee cup will create methane, which is a more powerful greenhouse gas than carbon dioxide. So, when you next have capacity for change in your life, start a compost, consider a bokashi or sign up to Sharewaste — and avoid any single use coffee cup, no matter what it's made from.

What you eat is a deeply personal matter, and no one should control that for you. Food is nourishing, connecting and obviously an essential part of life. How you choose to eat isn't my concern, but I'd wiggle my hips in a celebratory dance if you chose to eat with the planet and people in mind. Taking these values I've outlined and some of the recipes you've 'watched' me make in my kitchen, feel equipped to eat how you want to while remembering it's not all or nothing. You could reduce your meat intake while still consuming plastic. You could shop solely fair trade and continue to learn more about what organic means.

In a nutshell:

- Try your best to grow as much food as you can.
- Consider sharing the food you grow and make.
- Shop at farmers' markets if they're accessible to you.
- Reduce your food waste.
- Eat plants.
- Support regenerative agriculture.
- Lower your food-packaging consumption.
- Think about the wellbeing of the people who made your food
- Store food strategically.
- Use reusables.
- Do an audit of your rubbish bin.
- Make compost.

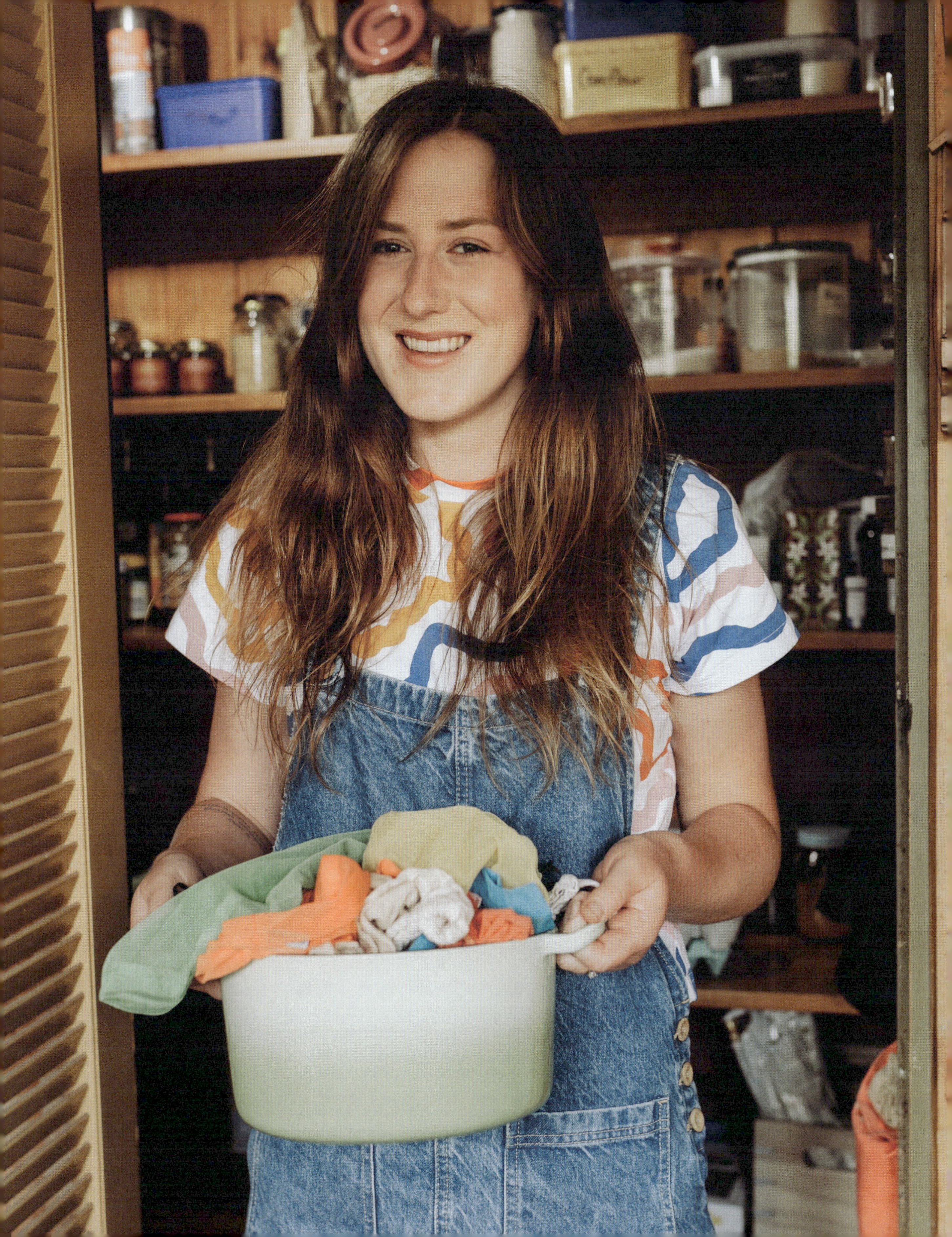

Clothes

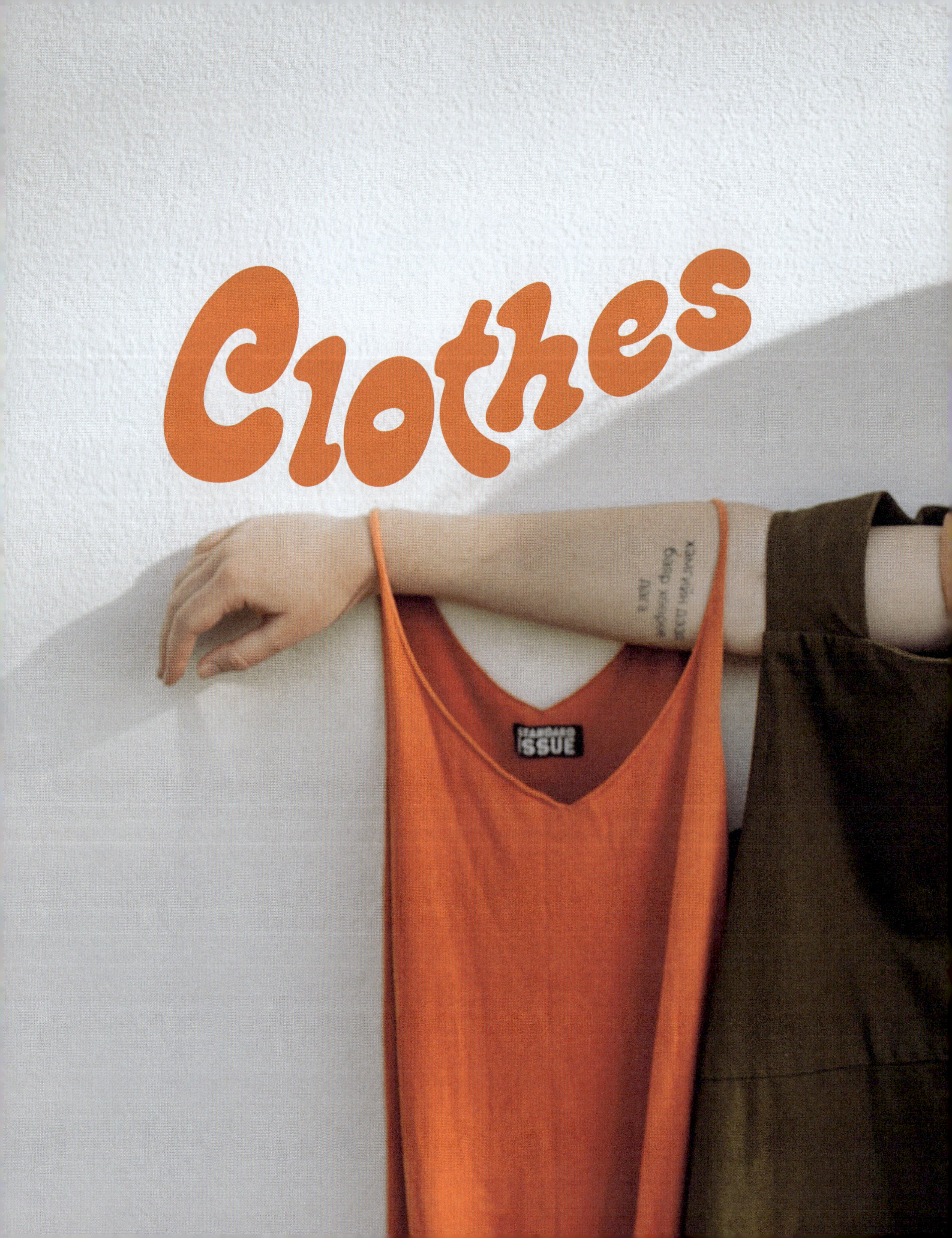
STANDARD
ISSUE

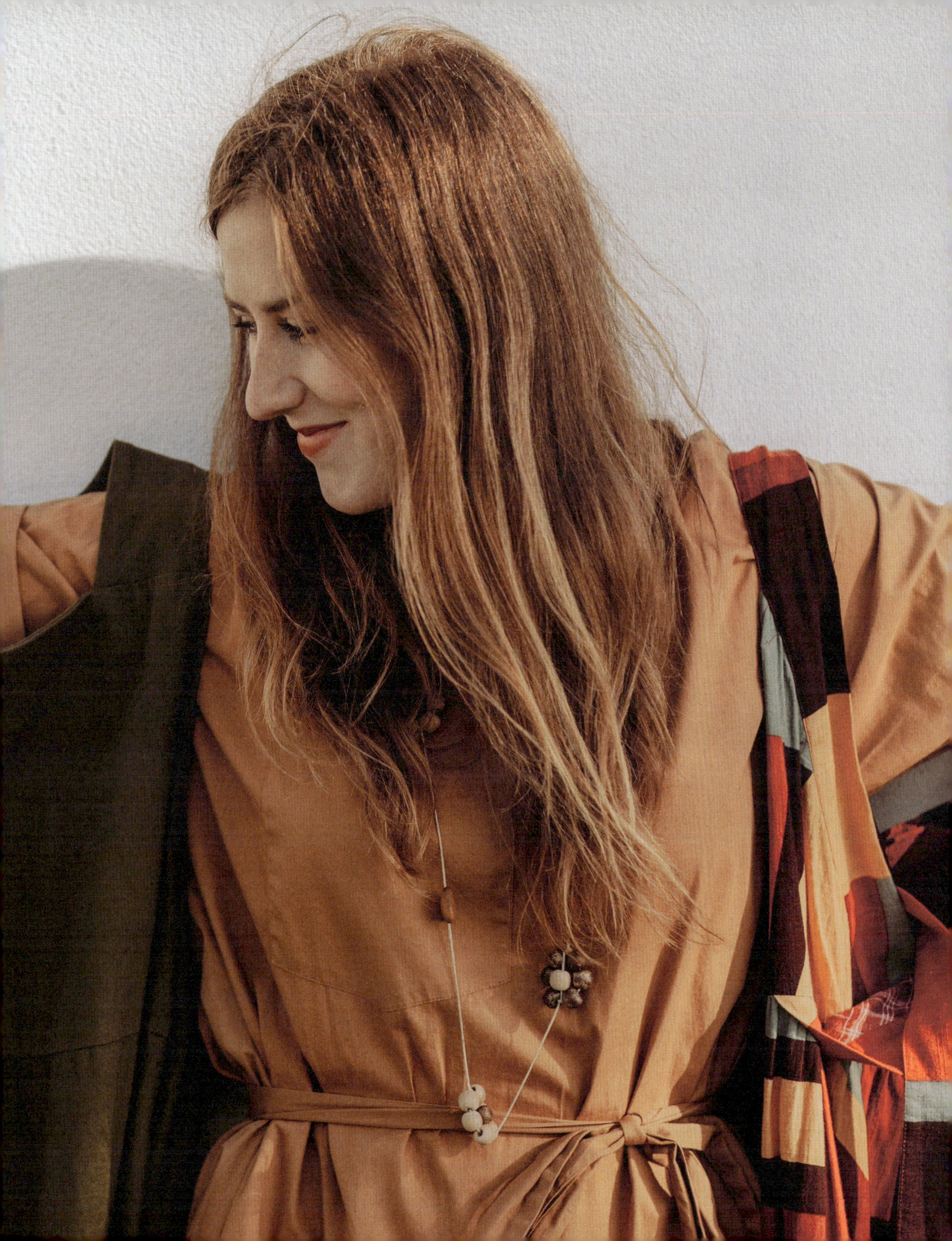

I was that kid who stripped off their clothes every five minutes and changed into something else. I loved the way clothes made me feel (oh, and I loved being naked) and the variety of personalities they could reflect with just one change. No matter what you feel about fashion, if you're someone who takes pride in their wardrobe or buys clothes because the alternative option is illegal... if you wear clothes, this section is for you.

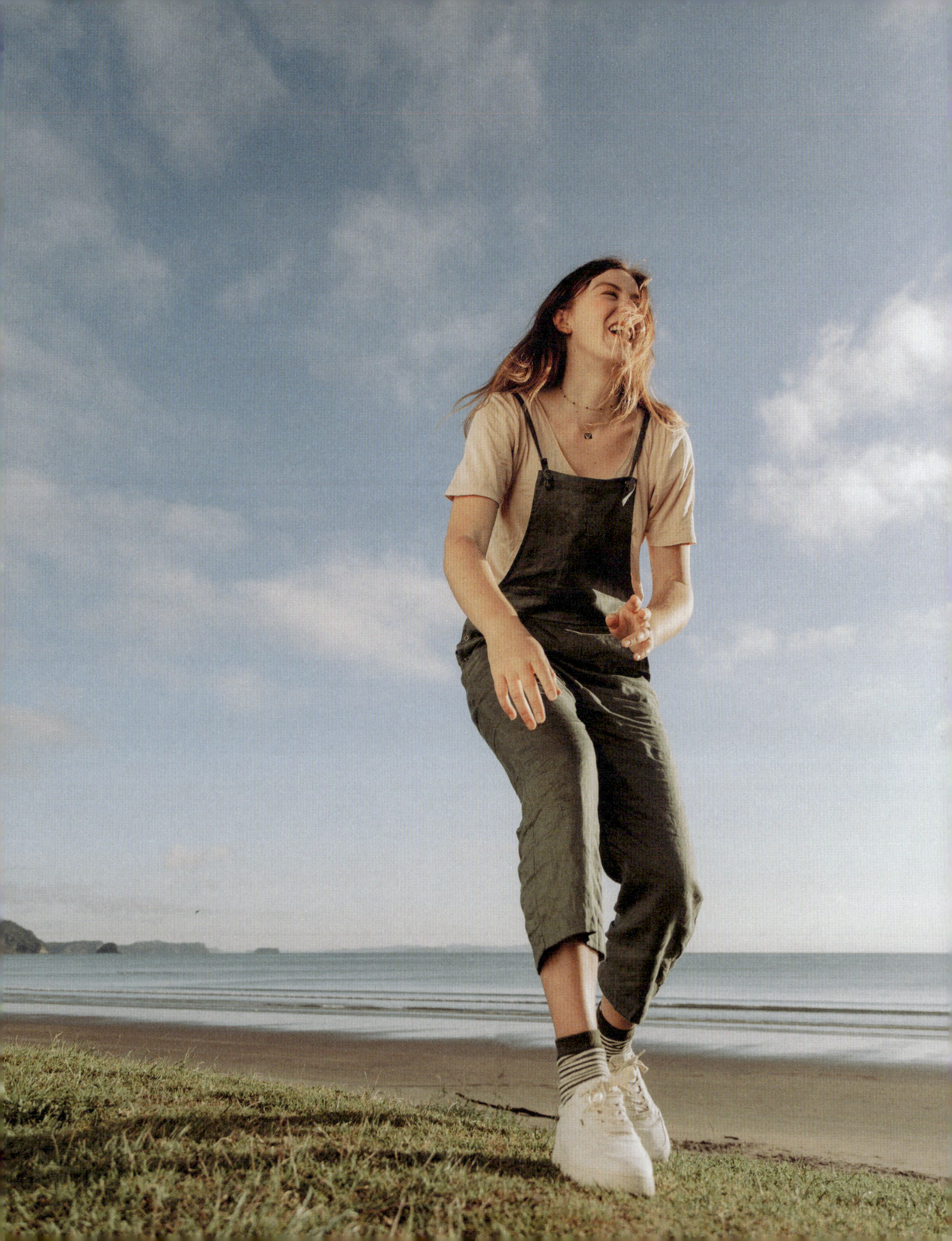

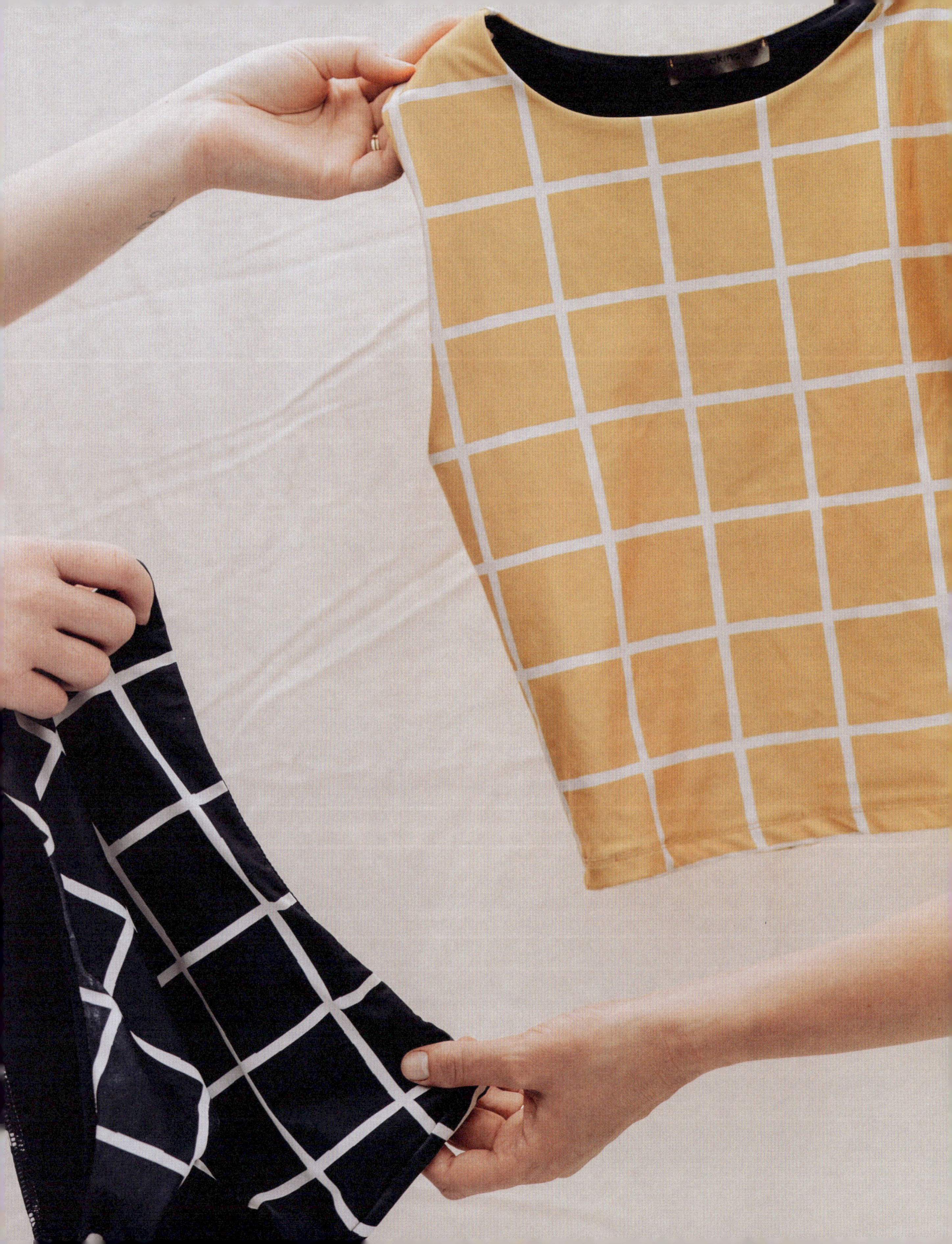

We demand clothes at a rate that is unsustainable for us, the planet and the people who make them. We all have messy wardrobe situations. For some of us, figuratively *and* literally.

Since 2015 I have approached my wardrobe in a sustainable fashion. I've learnt how to avoid those pull-my-hair-out-what-do-I-wear moments, and I don't mean to brag about it, but I enjoy my wardrobe far more than most people I know. Getting dressed in the morning is fun, instead of stressful. I save money, I am happier, my wardrobe is tidy and I save time, too.

I've achieved this through three key principles (see overleaf) and a practical list of eight tools (see page 212).

Often when it comes to sustainable fashion and purchasing mindfully, we're told the classic messages 'stop buying', 'buy ethically made', or 'shop second-hand'. You probably expected me to stop here and elaborate on the famous three. Yes, these three things are brilliant and I partake in all three, but they are inaccessible for many people.

Why?

- Stopping *all* purchases is impractical. Everyone changes size, style and circumstance during their lifetime.
- Ethical fashion costs more upfront. It relies on the person to have disposable income and excludes people who live week to week.
- Second-hand shopping isn't for everyone. People living rurally, who require larger or smaller sizes and who have health issues or accessibility requirements cannot always shop second-hand.

Ultimately, one wardrobe does not fit all. We need to move past these three messages and think outside the box!

My sustainable wardrobe philosophy

My philosophy is led by three guiding principles:

- I know where my clothes come from.
- I look after my clothes.
- I don't give in to consumerism.

I know where my clothes come from

As I mentioned earlier, in August 2015, I watched a documentary called *The True Cost*.[1] Eight of us gathered in Tim's lounge, with tissues on hand and a desire to know more about the fashion industry and what it was doing to people and the planet. I wish I remembered the exact date we watched the documentary, because it was the first time in my life I have ever had an actual 'lightbulb' moment. It was as if I woke up the next day with a literal lightbulb above my head like a cartoon character, and a new perspective on my wardrobe and my relationship with clothes.

Since then, before buying any piece of clothing, I have tried my best to find out who made the item and what it is made from. I wholeheartedly agree with Mahatma Gandhi's famous quote 'There is no beauty in the finest cloth if it makes hunger and unhappiness.' *The True Cost* documentary, and other fashion-industry reports, showed me that the majority of clothes made today are only profitable for their manufacturers because they are made by people who are hungry and unhappy.

I believe every person, no matter where they are in the world, deserves to work in a job that brings them joy and makes them proud of their work. Most garment-factory workers are forced to make low-quality clothes at unattainable speeds, placed in workrooms without proper air conditioning or basic health and safety precautions, and paid minimum wage or below. Personally, I'm not okay with buying something that was made by someone who was exploited for their expertise. But knowing who made your clothes is really difficult.

Supply chains are complex; many hands touch a garment before

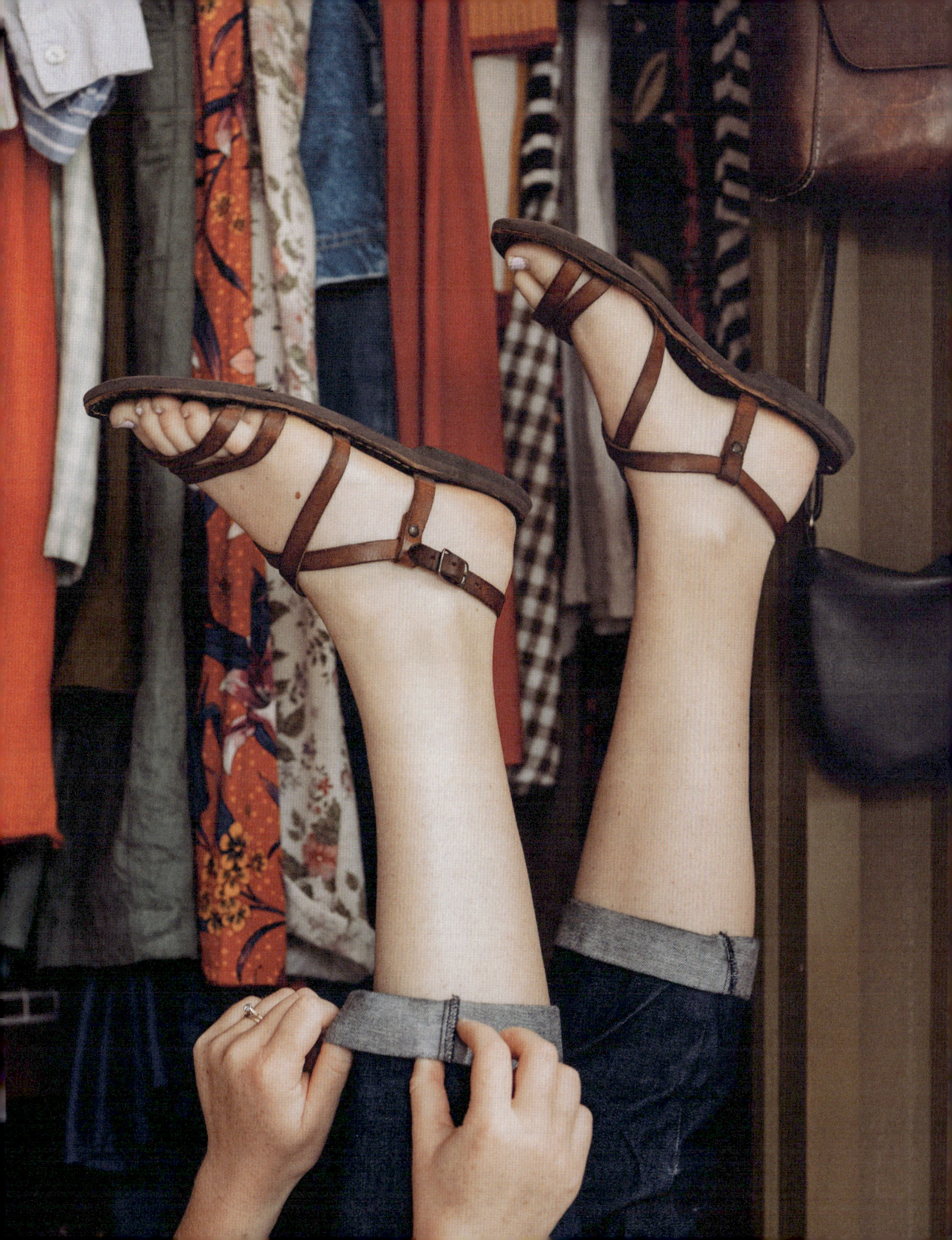

it arrives in the purchaser's possession. Even people who design and sell clothes generally don't know who made their garments, if they were paid fairly and how the person was treated. From a consumer perspective, it sounds like a simple question: Who made my clothes? But when you understand the complexity of supply chains and how murky the fashion industry is, you realise it's not that straightforward.

For example, last I checked no one in the world can track the complete supply chain of a zip. Therefore no one can deem any zip 'ethically made' (made by people paid fair wages and given basic human rights). No one. That's why ethical fashion brands often avoid using zips in their designs, or use 'deadstock' zips that were excess from a large company's orders and would have become rubbish if they weren't reused.

Although it's difficult, I always try my best to find out as much as I can about how the garment was produced, no matter what I am buying. From socks to frocks; I investigate before a purchase.

My first task in a quest to find out more about a garment involves hunting around the company's website for answers. If all details are not specified, I email them questions or message them directly on social media. I have my favourite ethical fashion companies that I follow closely and constantly go back to, and I'm always on the lookout for new sustainable fashion brands.

At first, I was skeptical and shy about being such a 'nosy' and curious consumer. But over time I realised the value for both myself and the brand in connecting and communicating.

Here are a few questions I ask a company before purchasing:

- Where are all your products/materials sourced (details of each material type)? e.g. countries, certifications, including swing tags, packaging, etc.
- Where do your products end up at the end of their life? How can they be kept in the resource loop?
- How are your products shipped to customers? e.g. what kind of packaging is used; is carbon-neutral shipping utilised?
- Who makes your products? (As specific as possible please.)
- How do you ensure the people who make your products are paid a fair wage?

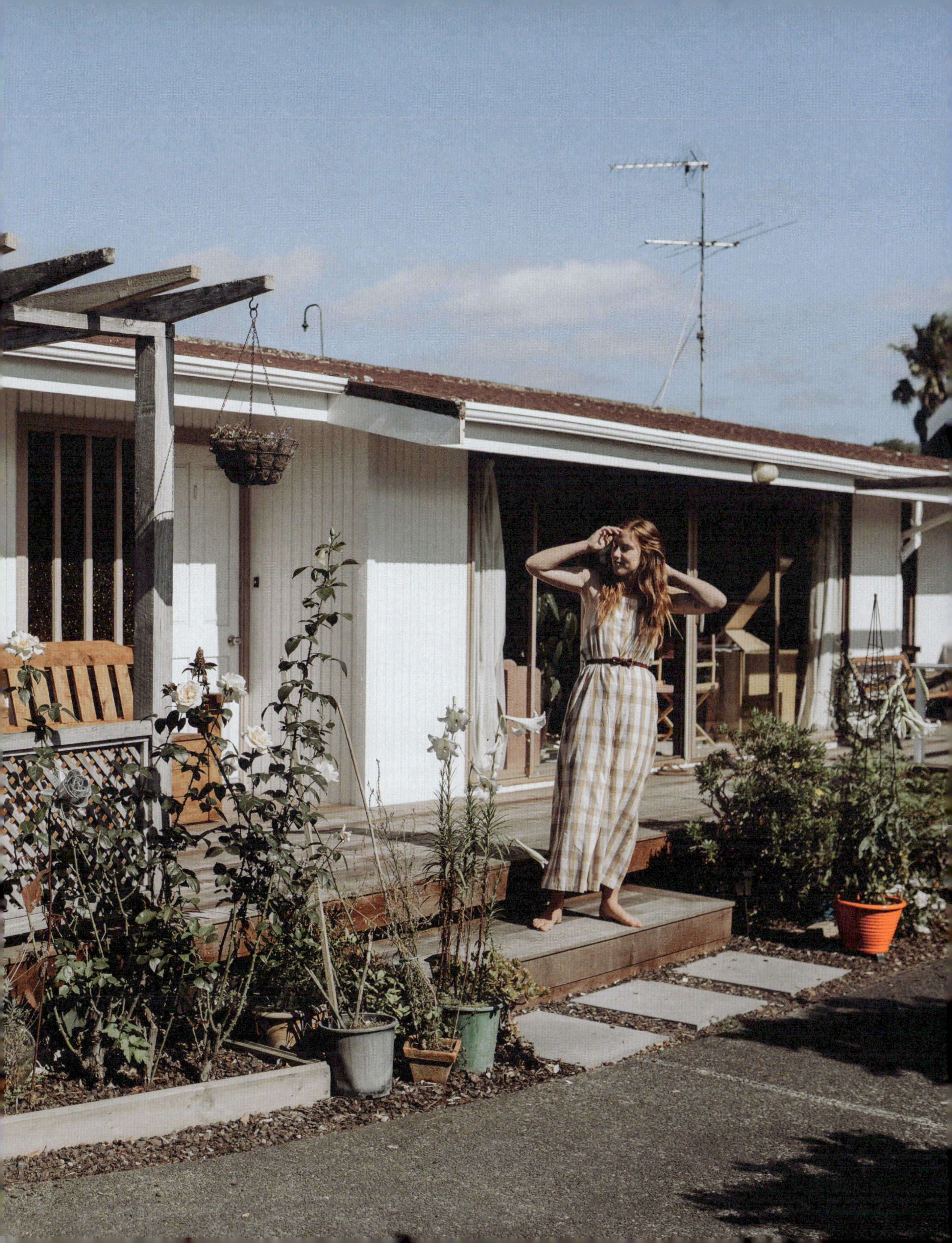

- What do you do with returns/samples/unsellable items? (This is a big waste stream for large companies!)
- How do you foster inclusion in your business? (A business has power and responsibility. I look out for brands with diverse teams, ranges of people represented, and brands who use their entity to make change.)

Getting dressed in the morning is special. Each garment I own comes with a story. Sure, I still have items in my wardrobe that were not ethically made, but they're old and loved; I've worn them many times and I fondly remember occasions they accompanied me to.

To be honest, when I watched *The True Cost* I wanted to throw my whole wardrobe away and disassociate myself from the toxicity of the fashion industry. I didn't want to remember the days when I only considered the cost and look of the garment on my body, without reading any garment tag or considering how the garment ended up in the store. But I realised that was not sustainable: using what you already have in your wardrobe is the best way to partake in sustainable fashion!

Knowing who made my clothes has helped me understand the true investment of clothing. Gone are the days when I viewed clothes as disposable skins that could easily be replaced. I know it's hard to grasp this mentality when ethically made fashion costs more, but that's the *true* cost of fashion without exploitation of people or planet somewhere along the supply chain. Clothes are pieces of art, made by clever humans. We must be conscious that the cost of clothes doesn't only refer to your pocket, it refers to the cost for other people and the planet, too.

I look after my clothes

Someone once said to me, 'You talk about your clothes like they're children.' I replied, 'If you mean I care for them like the wonderful investments and joy-givers they are, then yes, I do.'

We don't talk about how we look after our clothes enough. We have these things called washing machines, but we stop there. This attitude is ruining clothes quickly; costing us time, money and the loss of our favourite wardrobe pieces. You know that favourite shirt of yours that is starting to fray and fade? If you'd read the care label, spot-washed it and

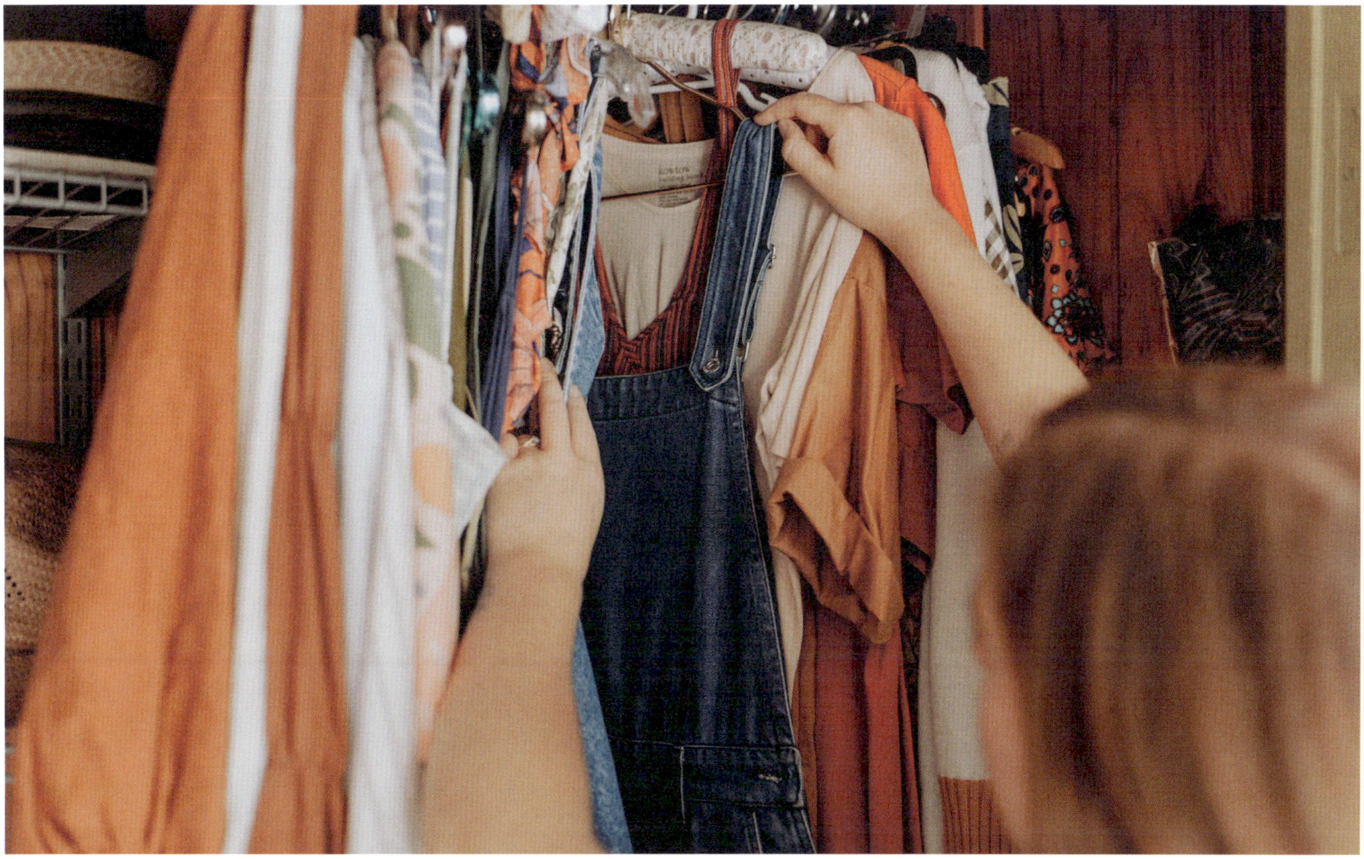

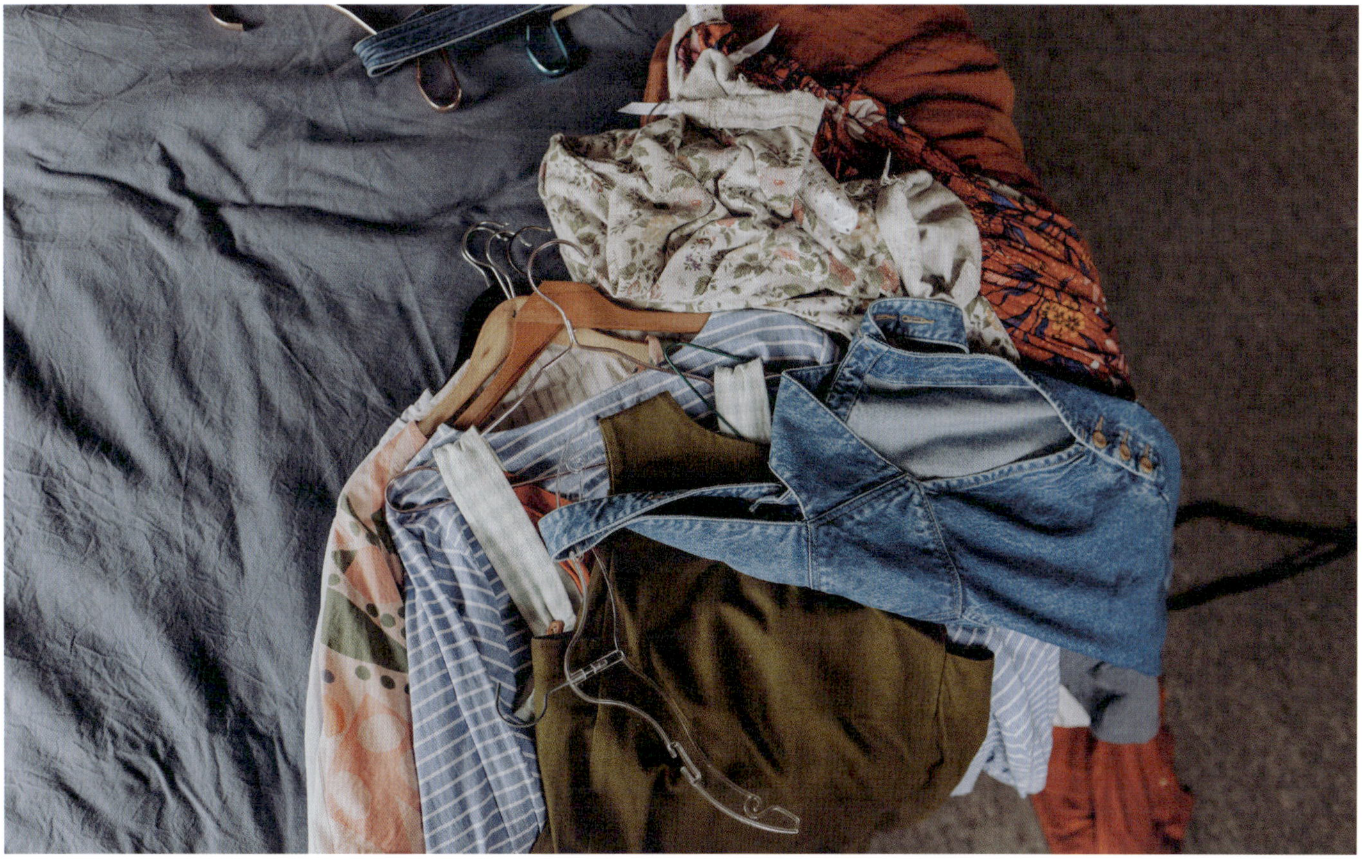

aired it in the sunshine instead of throwing it in the wash every time it was worn, it wouldn't be so dreary. I'm sure you want your favourite items to last forever, and if you treat them respectfully while they're in your care, they will!

On laundry day, you'll find Tim's shirts floating in the wind, my shoes catching stain-removing sun rays on the deck, a needle and thread waiting to fix the repair pile, and me, hunched over the laundry sink, hand-washing.

How to hand-wash

1. Separate your clothes into colours (lights and darks) and required washing temperatures. Read the care instructions for each garment before doing anything else. If you don't, you could ruin your garment instantly. If any of the items are new, hand-wash them separately in case dyes run during their first wash.
2. Pick a group of colours to begin with, and fill a bucket in your sink with water and laundry detergent. Make sure the water temperature matches what the care labels say. If the instructions are to wash with cold water, start with a small amount of hot water and your laundry liquid. Swirl it around so the liquid or powder dissolves completely before adding cold water. If you are using a powder, it's crucial that all the powder is dissolved before you put your clothes in the bucket. If it's not properly dissolved, the beads of powder can cause discoloration on your garments.
3. Dunk your clothes in. Push your clothes under the water so they are fully submerged, and start hand-washing. Stay away from twisting or rubbing, but make sure they're having a dance party in the bucket. The more movement, the more likely all fibres will get exposed to the cleaning product.
4. Some clothes require a short soaking. If that's the case, leave them for the specified time. If not, don't leave them to soak for longer than 5–10 minutes.
5. Squeeze the clothes gently and empty the bucket of water. If the laundry detergent is grey-water safe and no dyes have run, repurpose the water for things like watering plants. Fill the bucket back up with cold water. Submerge the clothes again and swish them around for

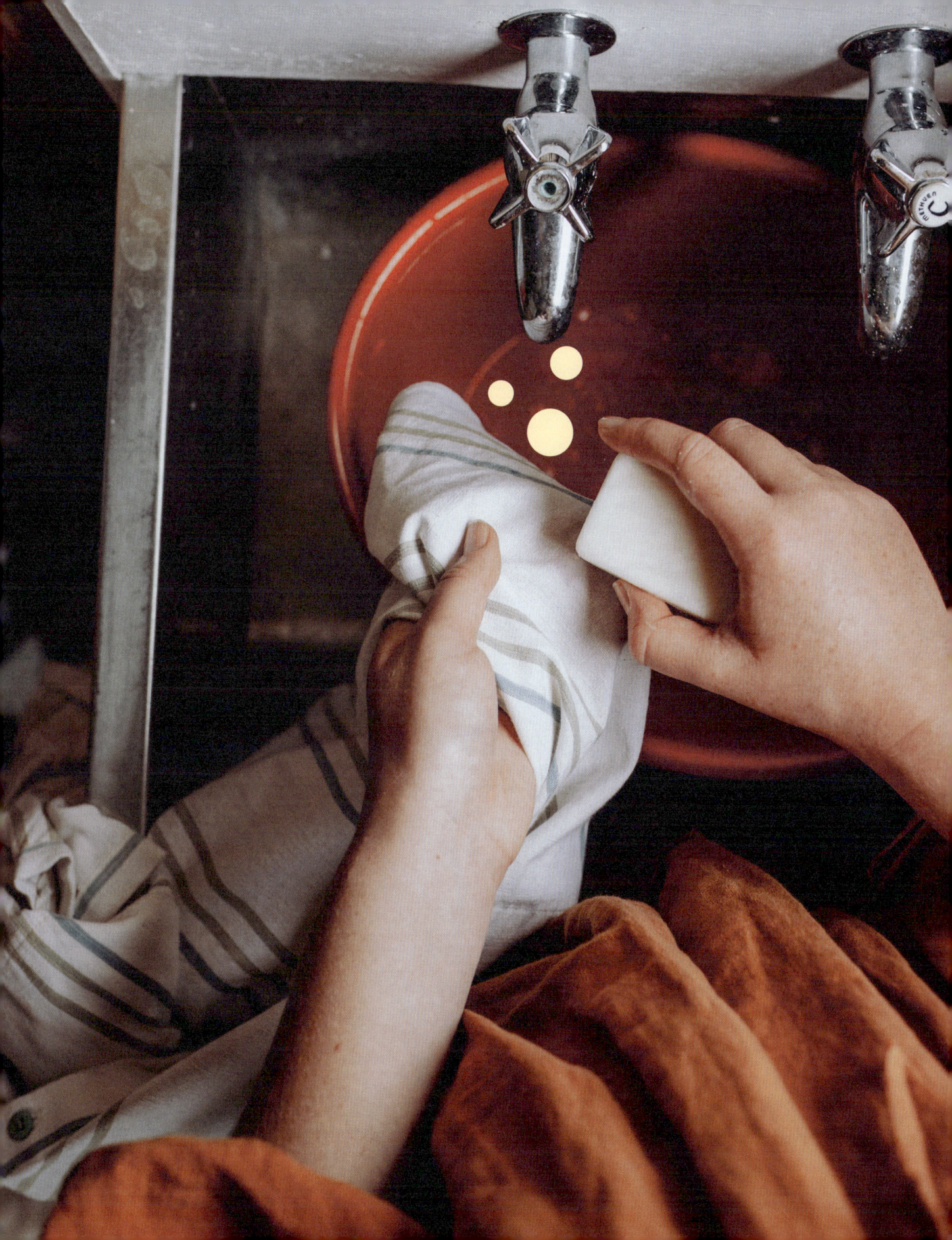

another bucket dance party. Do this until the soapy suds have been removed (if not, empty the bucket and rinse again).
6. If you have a gentle washing machine 'spin' cycle, use this to wring the clothes out properly. But only if you know it's slow and don't do it for incredibly delicate clothes. Otherwise, squeeze your clothes as much as you can without stretching their fibres and head straight to the washing line. Hang your clothes on the line, or lie things like sweaters on a flat surface.

Looking after my clothes is one of my hobbies. I do weird things that make me feel like I should have been born in the 1920s, like hand-washing my underwear, and actually enjoy my Saturday morning ritual of spending time with my clothes and reviving them. I wash my clothes properly, repair them when needed, or take them to my local seamstress if the repair goes beyond my basic sewing skills.

I'm not suggesting you give your washing machine away and become a full-time laundry maid. I'm encouraging you to take my lead; read the care labels and put a little more thought into how you care for your clothes so they have a longer life. If this feels unattainable because of your current time restraints, just do what you can. I guarantee this new mentality will lead to more satisfaction with what you already own. It will also encourage you to buy quality garments that respond well to washing and repairs (well-made clothes are often easier to care for).

Treating clothes with care (like you would treat a child!) means we can get more wear out of them and avoid demanding more resources from the planet than needed. Why buy new when your favourite shirt still looks gorgeous?

The way
we consume
clothes
is wild.

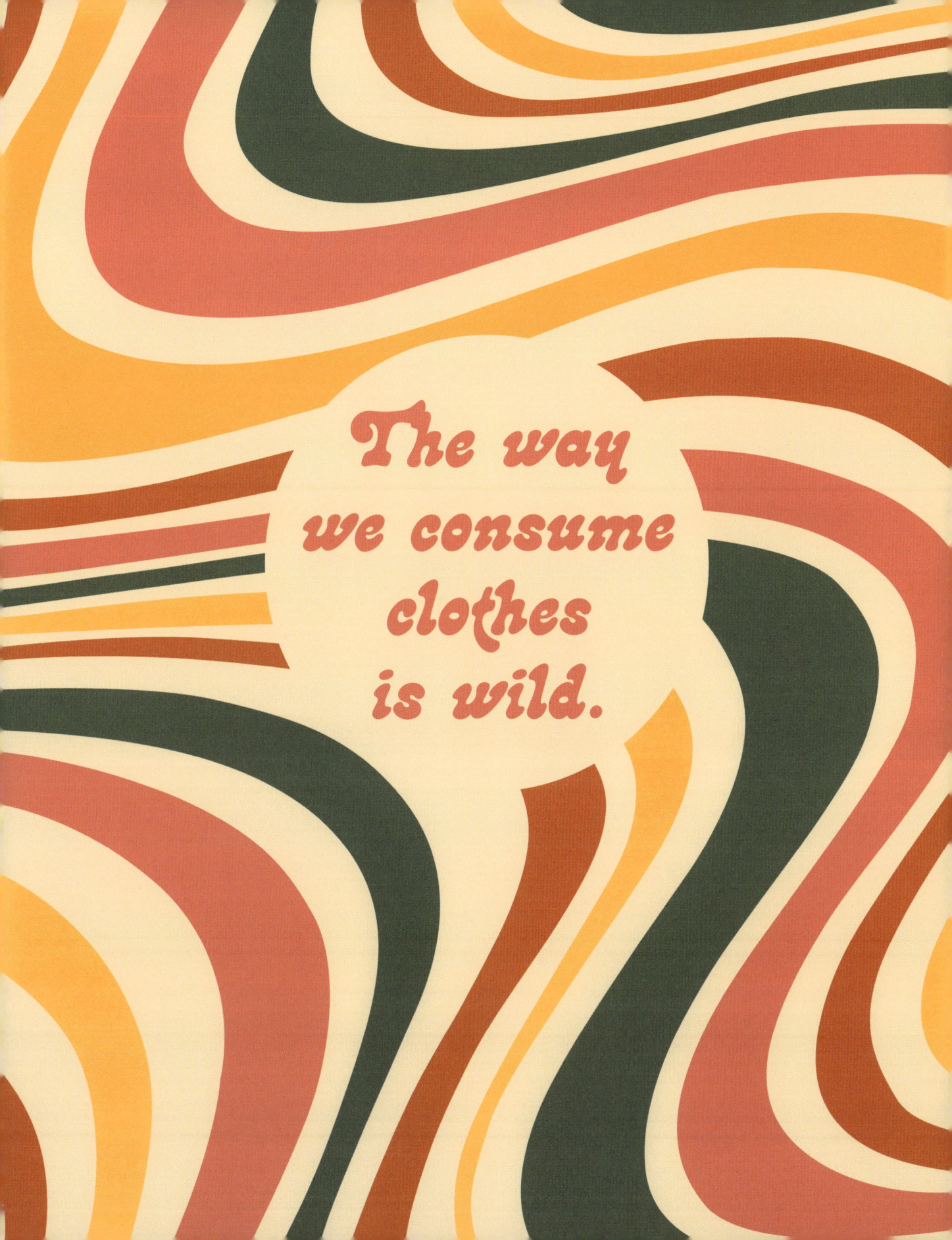

The world consumes 100 billion pieces of clothing a year.[2]

We consume 400 per cent more than what we were consuming 20 years ago.[3]

Approximately 54 billion litres of oil are required on an annual basis for the production of plastic fibres for the clothing industry.[4]

Garment workers are paid as low as US$0.39 per hour.[5]

Over half of the total amount of dyes expelled from the textile industry are highly toxic. These dyes affect the health of those who make the clothes and those who wear them, plus harm ocean habitats as the dyes bleed when washed.[6]

The average person purchases 27kg of new textiles each year and 23kg of those is discarded into landfill.[7]

I don't give in to consumerism

I have no attachment to trends, and it's the most liberating feeling. Presumably there is a subconscious trend-checker somewhere in my brain that influences the way I dress myself, but for the most part, I wear what I love and let my own creativity drive that.

I wear overalls that used to be my clown dress-ups as a kid. I am not scared of clashing colours. I don't buy things just because I'm moving into a new season, and I stay relatively far from understanding what the heck Gucci or anyone else in that sphere is up to. This doesn't mean I'm not a sucker for style. Spending a few hours in my wardrobe every month or so, gathering inspiration from outfits I see in movies, and admiring combinations in shop windows is fun. But if I were to keep up with fast-paced trends and give into the constant drone of BUY THIS, YOUR LIFE WILL BE BETTER marketing, I would buy way more than I need while still feeling unsatisfied with what I have.

Taking these three philosophies into reality, here's a simple way to shop and a helpful hierarchy to consider:

Less

Quality

Consciously

Less = Do I really need this? How can I avoid purchasing this? Does something else in my wardrobe already fulfill this purpose? I also ask the question: If I buy this garment, will I need to buy less in the long run (this is where styling and considering what other garments in my wardrobe will go with it comes in).

Quality = Will this garment last? Did you know that big fast-fashion retailers design their clothes to be worn fewer than ten times?[8] I was baffled when I first heard this, but it was re-emphasised to me when I walked through a mall recently. I touched the fabrics: stiff, easily held

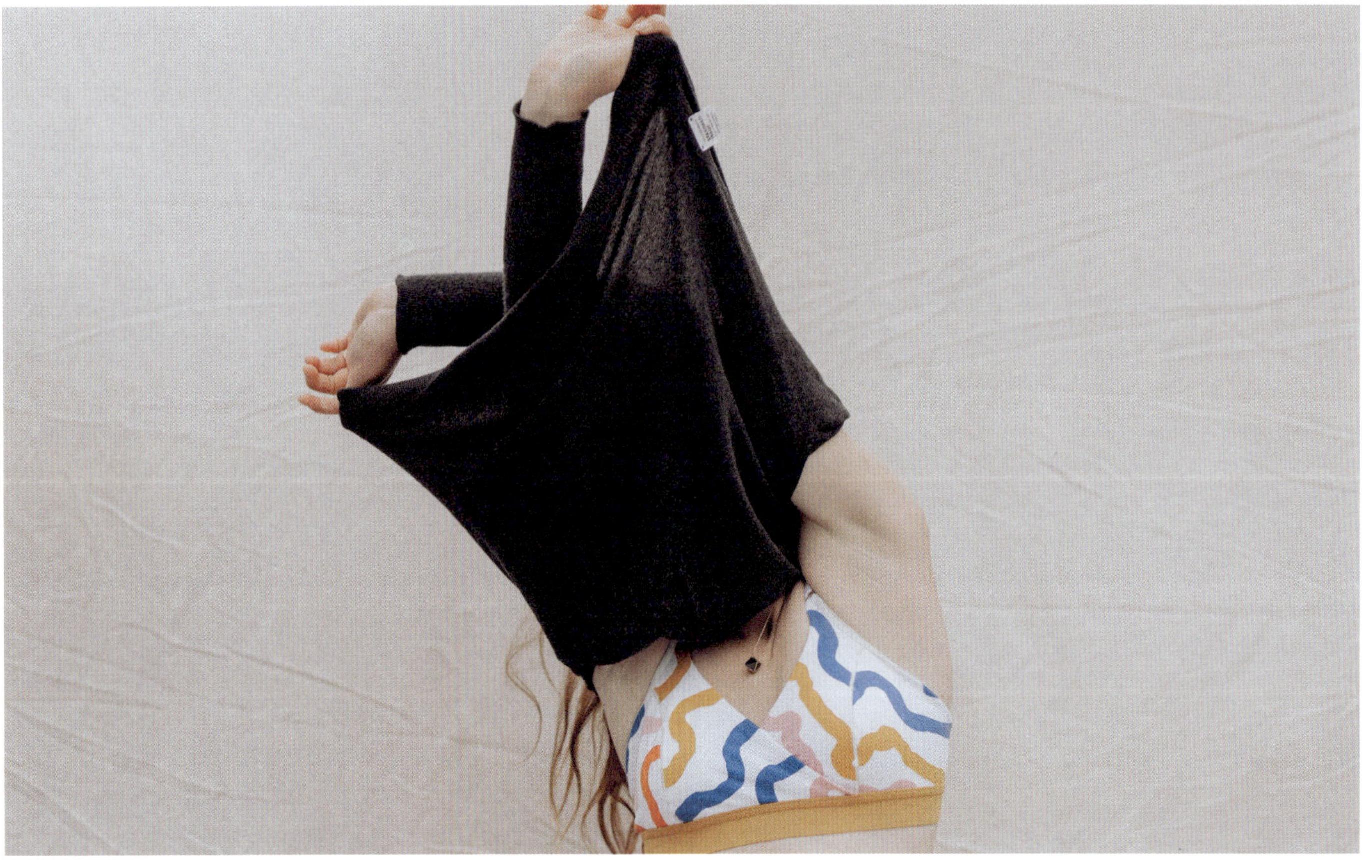

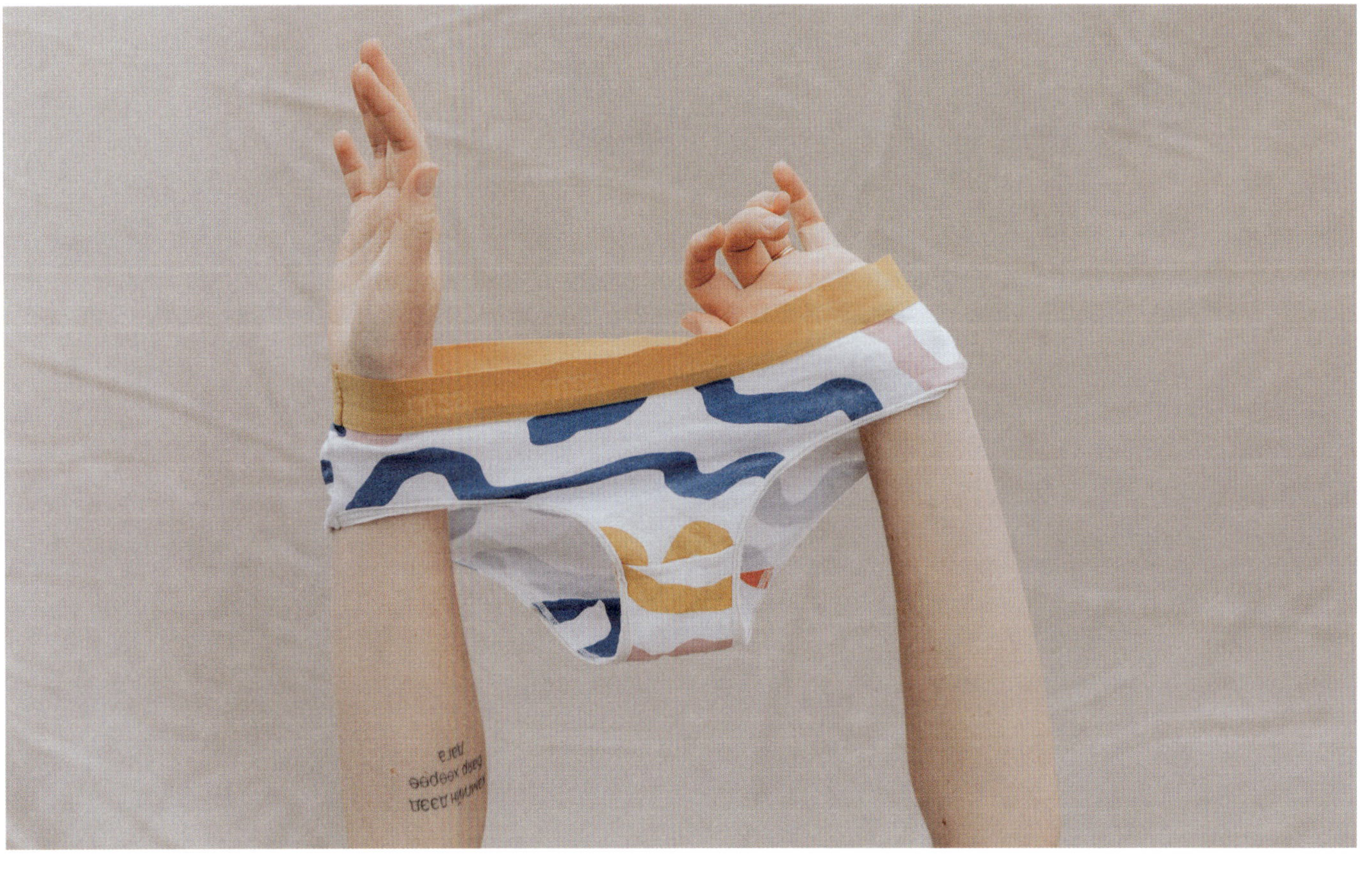

smells, thin, and probably quick to lose colour in the wash. I looked at the seams: loose, thin, easy to pull apart. There were even garments that were already torn and falling apart simply from sitting on a hanger that wasn't moving, sweating or living life.

Consciously = This is where the classic ethical fashion terms and values come in. I ask who made the garment; how those people were treated in their workplace; whether they were paid a fair wage; and are in a situation where they can have pride and joy in their work. We know fashion supply-chains are convoluted and sometimes impossible to trace back, but asking these questions is powerful. When I ask these of a brand, I don't look for perfection, I seek transparency and honesty.

With these three words in mind, in this order, I consume a lot less and a lot better. For anything to enter my wardrobe, it must be special. Through these three words I have avoided those I-have-nothing-to-wear moments. I've claimed back time, money and feelings of dissatisfaction with what I own and how I look.

I am aware not everyone loves clothes or relates to the artistry of fashion. But imagine if we all used those three words to shop. If we all repaired. If we had hooks outside for wafting away smells, instead of strange habits like throwing something in the wash just because it touched your skin once.

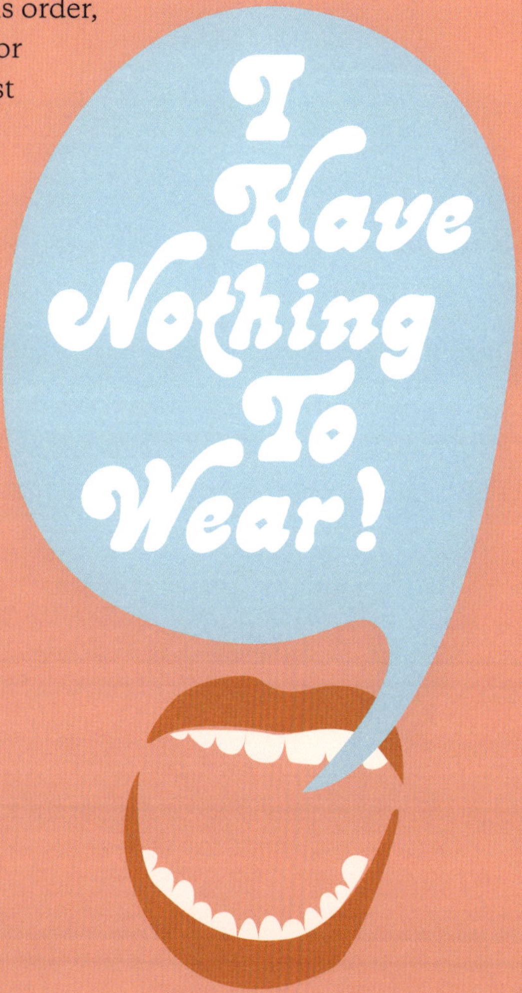
I Have Nothing To Wear!

How to buy less

The term 'less' comes first in my list, because it's so important. If everyone stuck to their frequency of purchasing but swapped their purchases with sustainable ones, we still wouldn't have a sustainable fashion industry.

It's time to introduce the eight tools that help me stick to 'less'.

1. Slow down

2. Repair

3. Upcycle

4. Think consciously

5. Rent

6. Borrow

7. Clothes-swap

8. Shop second-hand

Slow down

One of the best things I've done when it comes to my wardrobe is STOP. I've stopped mindless shopping. Instead, I sort through my wardrobe regularly and make a list of the garments I need — garments that would improve my wardrobe. When I visit shops with friends, or shop online, I have the list on my phone, or in my mind, and I look out for those items only. I've said goodbye to impulse buys and buying garments just because they are on sale, and I've realised that if I don't buy anything for several months or even a year at a time, I won't end

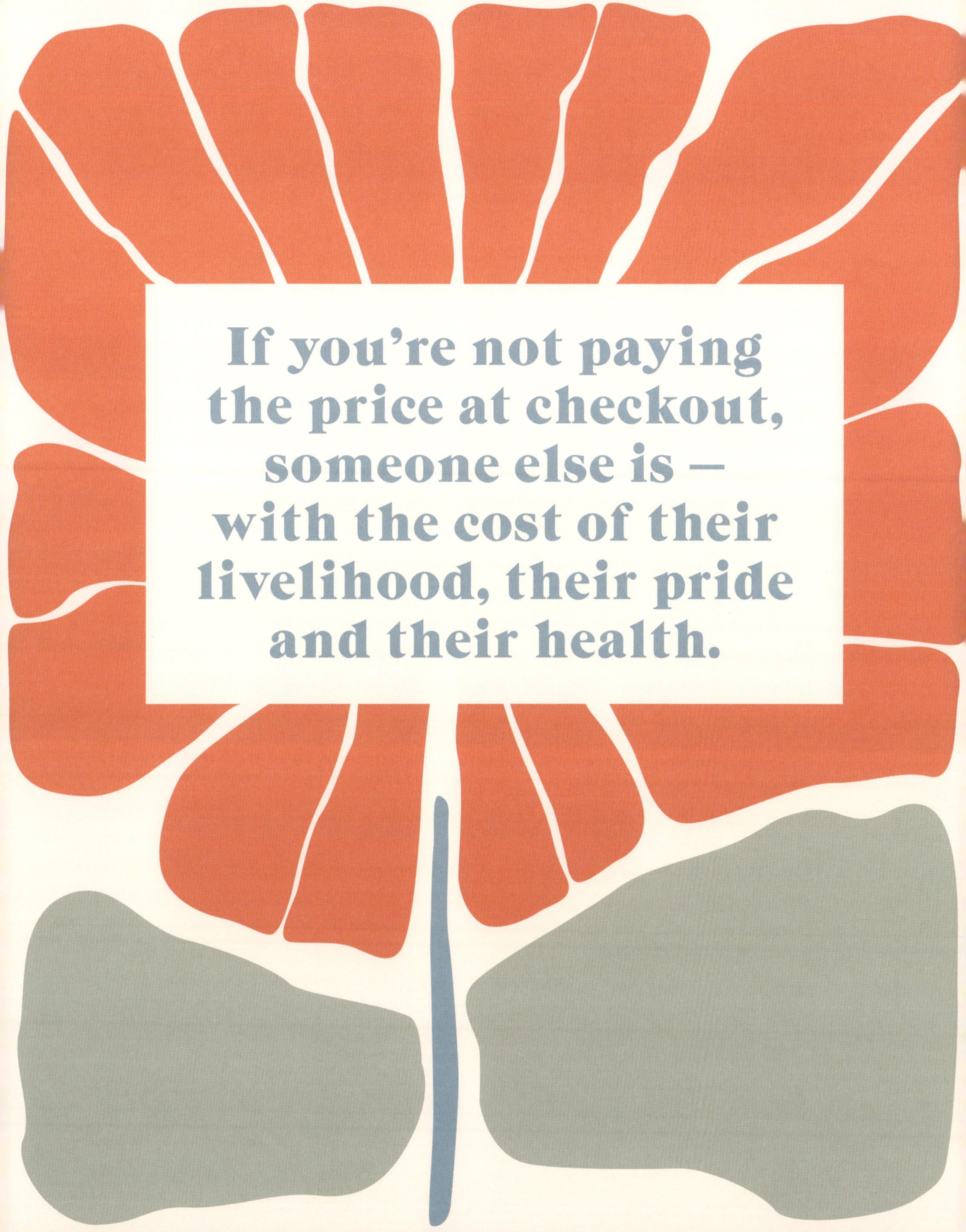

If you're not paying the price at checkout, someone else is – with the cost of their livelihood, their pride and their health.

up running around naked like the 4-year-old Kate I mentioned earlier.

I'm not asking everyone to do the same, and I'm certainly not perfect, but I'm suggesting you slow down. If you're likely to buy clothing every week, why not reduce it to every fortnight? If you buy something twice a month, how about shopping once a month instead? Start with where you are at, and make slow, but steady, changes.

To increase the chances of sticking to goals like this, find an accountability partner to hold you to your goal, or to join in with you. If you do not achieve your goal, the accountability partner can decide on a reprimand.

For example: My sister, Georgia, struggles with buying too many clothes. She's the best second-hand shopper I know. Even though 99 per cent of them are second-hand, her frequent purchases still cost money and involve constant wardrobe overhauls that take time and capacity. Georgia undertook a challenge: no clothing purchases for six months. I was her accountability partner. If she wanted something, she pitched me the reasons why she needed it, and I approved or denied the purchase.

Repair and upcycle

When it comes to the items I already have in my wardrobe, I try my best to keep them alive. I'm constantly resuscitating clothes, or turning them into new things. I repair rips and reattach buttons myself, and take the more complex repairs to my local seamstress. I never throw away old clothes! One of my coolest creations was my dog's bed. I sewed a square cover out of old sheets from the second-hand shop, and stuffed it with all our old garments (socks, underwear, ripped clothes) that were beyond repair. You can easily do the same thing with your old garments to make a cushion or a foot stool if you don't need a dog bed.

Ideas for resuscitating your clothes:
- Stains you cannot remove? Disguise them with a new colour using natural dyes.
- Learn to darn and fix small holes.[9]
- Try visible mending.
- Ask a local seamstress for ideas.

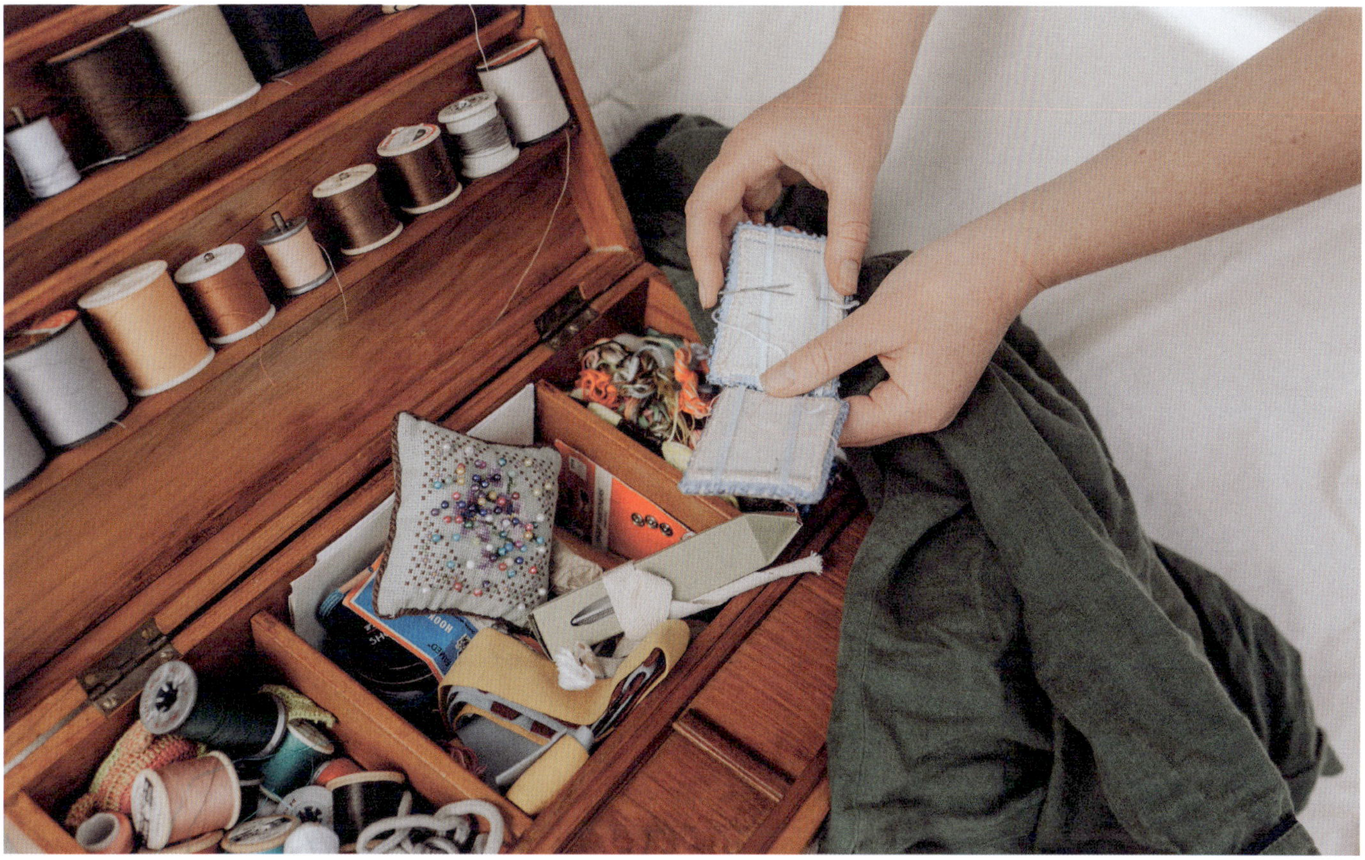

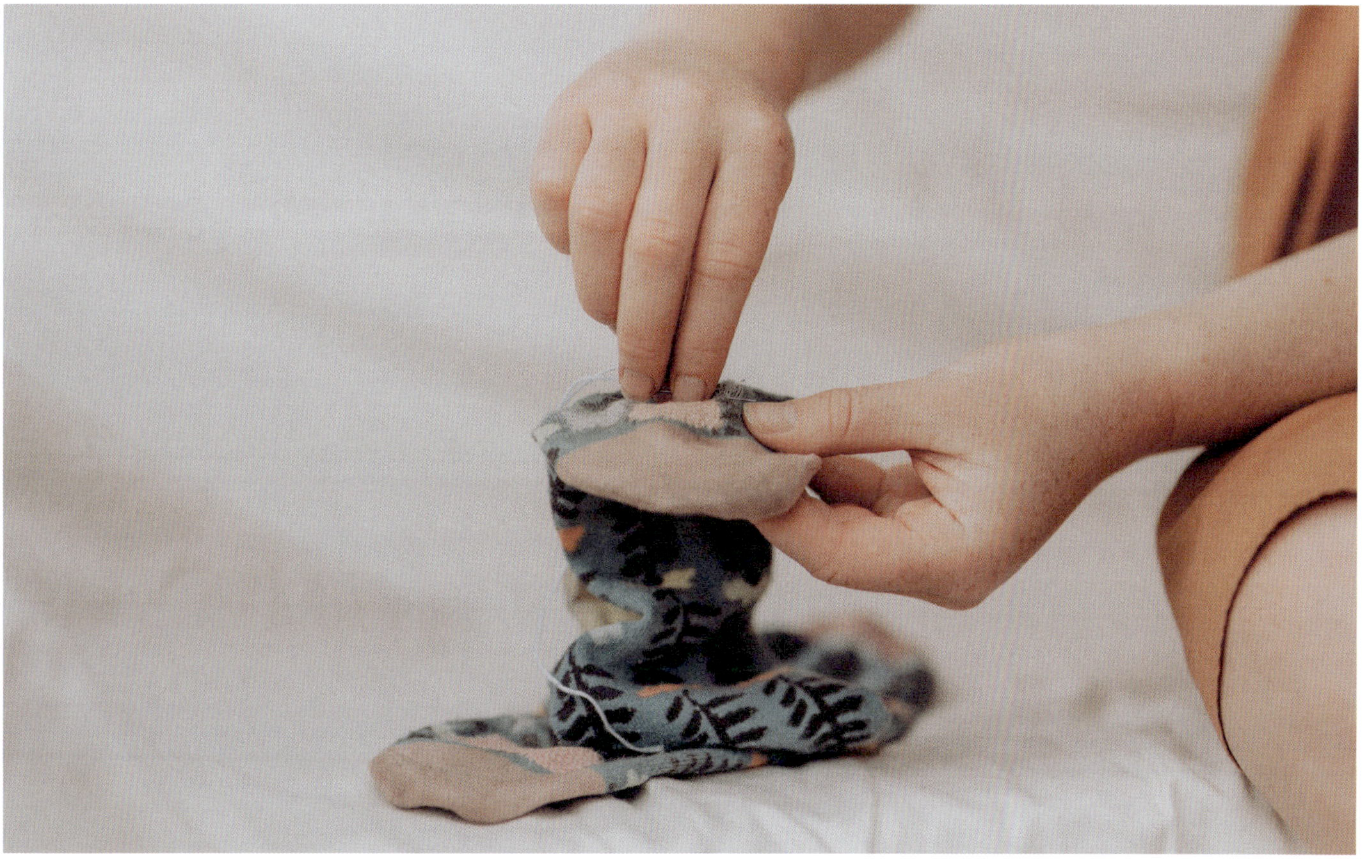

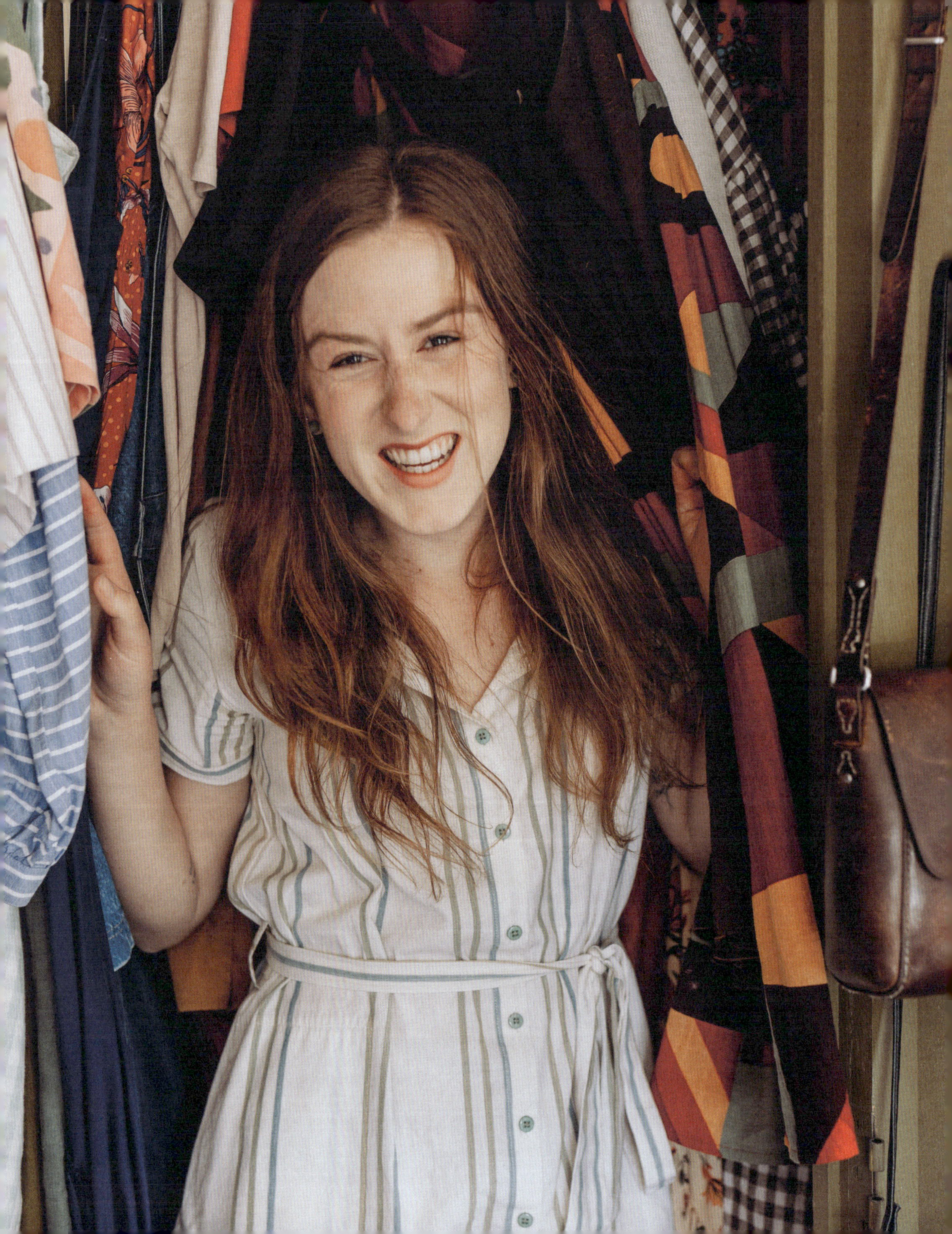

- Cut off the ripped part (e.g. turn jeans into shorts).
- Cover holes with embroidery and/or patches.

Think consciously

If there's an item on my wishlist, I think about it for at least a month before I buy it. By the end of the month I have either forgotten what it was, or I'm still thinking about it and have strategically assessed what it would go with in my wardrobe. I also consider if I will wear it 30+ times, a trick I learnt from sustainable fashion expert Livia Firth. Sometimes I ask my friends and family about the purchase first too: 'Can you imagine me wearing this often?' I consider every item in my wardrobe as an investment, and just like Marie Kondo says, 'If it doesn't spark joy, it shouldn't be in your life.'[10]

I also avoid malls. It helps that I hate them. Mainly because the music is terrible, the sterile lights give me a headache, and many of the clothes sold in them are made by literal modern-day slaves . . . but I also hate the temptation to buy stuff. It's the same reason I don't keep chocolate in my pantry often; if it's there, I'll eat all of it.

One in, one (or two!) out: if something comes into my wardrobe, I responsibly rehome another item less loved. Tim and I both follow this rule and keep each other accountable. This rule means I am less likely to grab a sale item just because it's cheap. I love my current wardrobe, so having to remove something means the new item coming in must be incredible.

Rent/borrow/clothes-swap

I know there will be many people reading who can't bear to hear me say 'slow down' or 'don't shop at all'. To you, I say: rent, borrow and swap. As we learnt in the Connection chapter, the social exchange of swapping and borrowing other people's clothes brings smiles and relationships. Plus, when you rent items, you have the opportunity to wear designer labels that, let's face it, you would never have been able to afford brand new.

Rent

Pay a certain amount of money to rent an item for a length of time. Rental stores are becoming more common for everyday clothes (not only ball dresses) and there are online rental stores, too. The fees are generally per item, or paid as a subscription per month with a cap on how many items you can borrow each month.

Borrow

I have 74 items in my wardrobe right now. I don't think it's humanly possible for me to wear all of them within the next month. I'd be happy to lend them to you! Find friends with similar styles, who are local (it's easiest to pick up rather than ship), and set some borrowing rules together — e.g. only wash as per garment instructions, no wearing the garment in dirty situations (like gardening), and a defined length of time you will borrow it for.

Clothes-swap

Clothes swaps are taking off! They can happen within a group of immediate friends, or on a larger scale. I've attended clothes swaps where hundreds of 'swappers' have participated and come away with helpful new wardrobe assets. Usually, the organisers implement a practical system that values your garment for a certain 'clothes-swap coin amount' and allows you to take home something that another clothes-swap attendee didn't vibe with. Some clothes swaps are less organised and are more of a free-for-all situation. I've even discovered garments from clothes swaps that have held little notes telling the garment's story. The benefits of clothes swaps extend beyond finding new garments and include new friendships, community resilience and fulfilling memories.

Another example of a mini clothes-swap system I've witnessed is a group of friends who live locally and have a shared wardrobe. The clothing wardrobe is open to anyone at any time, you simply write down what item you have taken, your name and the date. Tracking it helps to keep all items in circulation so nothing gets lost. This shared wardrobe system means they all consume far fewer items, saving money and time. They have a revolving array of options that is far greater than what one wardrobe could offer, and it's an enjoyable activity to do with mates.

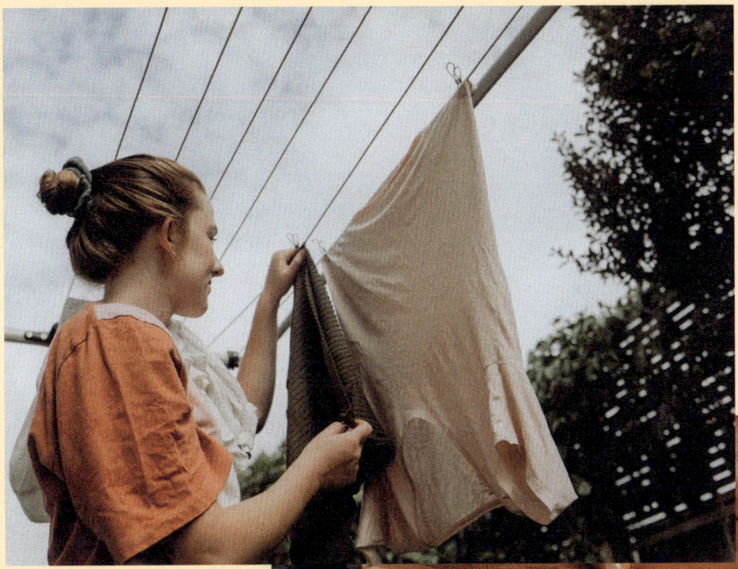
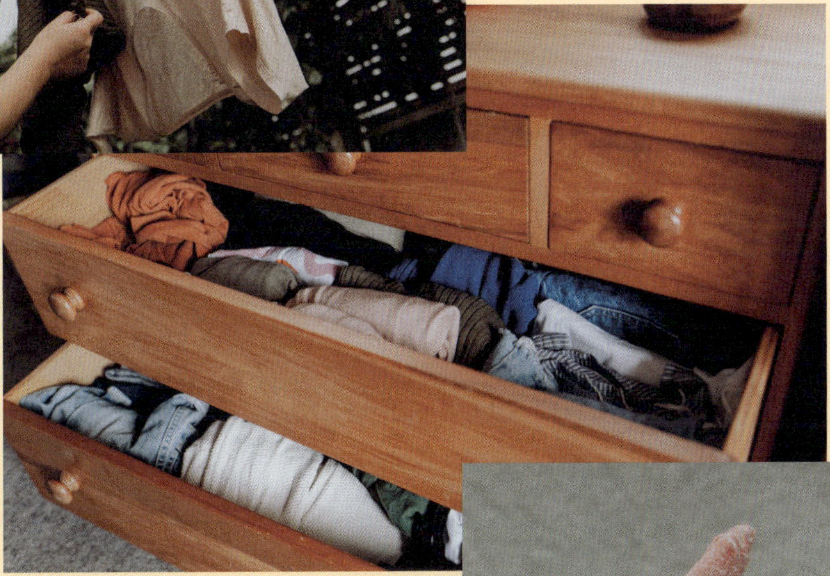
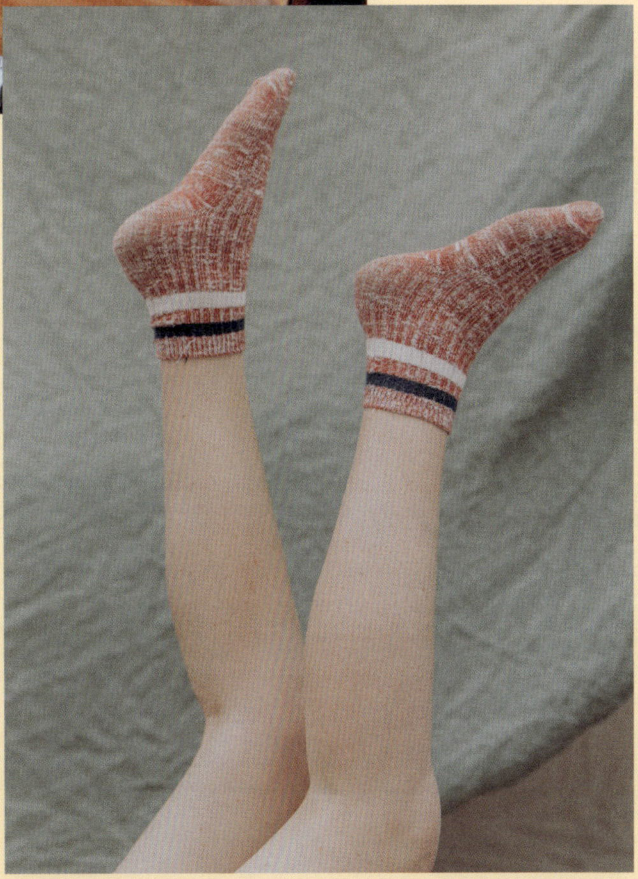

Shop second-hand

Imagine if there was a way to avoid demanding more clothing production, purchase good quality, support local charities, avoid plastic garment packaging, save money, boycott supporting the exploitation of garment-factory workers — and enjoy your shopping experience, too? Second-hand shops exist. Dreams do come true.

Shopping second-hand is a brilliant way to have a more sustainable and fulfilling wardrobe. Think of all the clothes you've ever worn in your lifetime. Chances are, the number of items that have come in and out of your wardrobe are in the thousands. I know mine would be! But just because you don't love or fit the garment, doesn't mean someone else won't.

Some of my favourite items in my wardrobe are second-hand. Some are from vintage stores, others found in the depths of quaint thrift shops, foraged from fancy second-hand shops in the middle of cities, or purchased online from what are essentially virtual second-hand shops.

Again, we all have different circumstances, sizes, preferences and styles that make some sustainable shopping tricks easier than others. But I believe most people could try slowing down, borrowing, renting, buying second-hand, repairing and upcycling. I also must re-emphasise that even though I started doing these things for environmental reasons, they've benefited me personally, too.

First, something everyone is always happy to hear: you will save money. I have saved so much money over the past few years. I've squirrelled it away in my savings, or spent it on more fulfilling experiences with my friends and family. You may not think you spend much money on clothes, but I can't count how many times someone has told me that, and with more thought they've realised they spend $200 a month on lots of little purchases. Even though I wasn't a massive consumer to begin with, being a conscious consumer has definitely saved me money.

I'm also happier. Studies have shown that most people do not wear more than 50 per cent of their wardrobes.[11] The rest sits unused, making us feel bad about the weight we put on, the pre-baby body we've lost, or the fashion phases we went through that we don't want to revisit.

The amount of clothes we consume as a global population is not sustainable for our wellbeing or the planet. It cannot continue, no matter what the clothes are made from or who made them.

Imagine if your entire wardrobe was made up of pieces you were thrilled to wear; garments that made you feel incredibly happy to put on in the morning! Remember that I-have-nothing-to-wear scenario? Well, when you are more present and conscious of the clothes you buy, you'll never have that problem again. Take it from me. Because I'm so careful about what comes into my wardrobe, I love what I have. I never have days when I struggle to find what to wear, and this helps me feel less emotionally and mentally strained when I get dressed.

I wish I could say that your wardrobe will automatically be easy after reading this chapter. You can take on my three principles and write my list of eight tools on your fridge, but we are humans and change doesn't come that easy.

Continue to mull over these lists and practical tools, and start with a simple wardrobe audit.

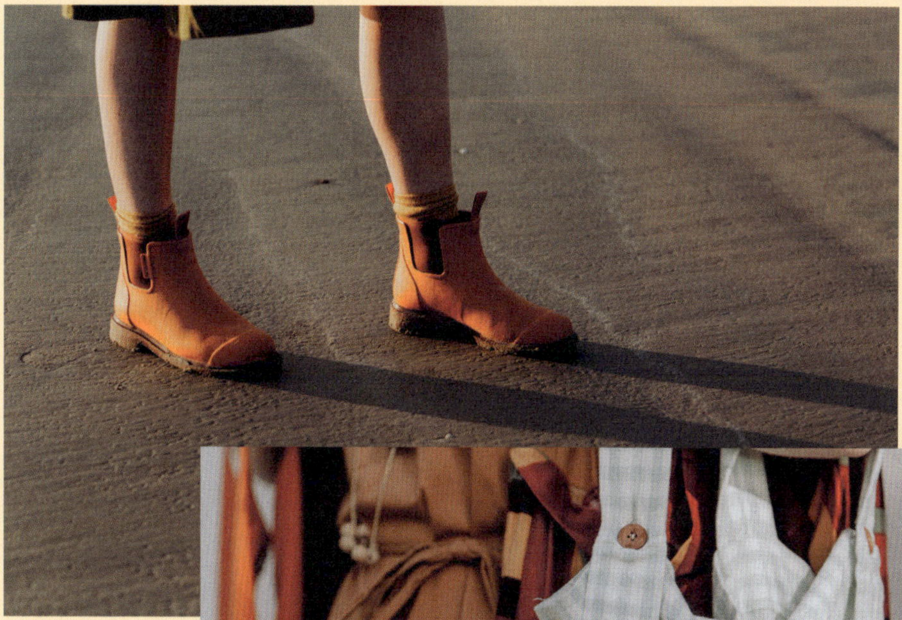

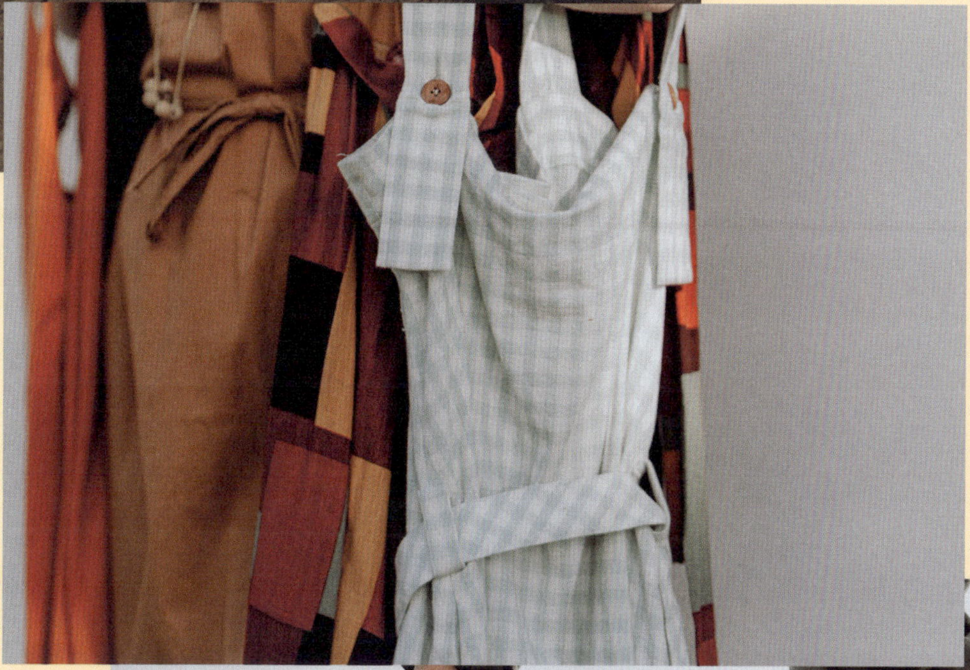

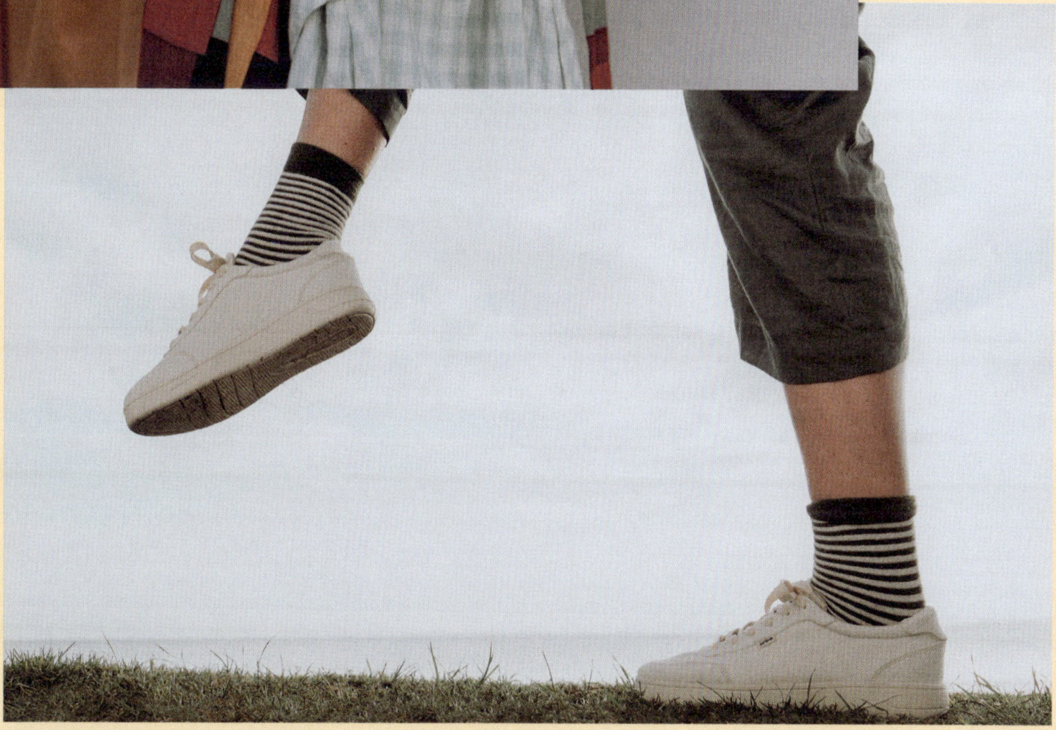

How to do a wardrobe audit

Or, how to effectively spend two hours in your wardrobe instead of two hours at the shopping mall.

I am a firm believer that two hours in your own wardrobe is far more cost-effective, enjoyable and productive than spending that same amount of time at a shopping mall. It pains me to think of all the beautiful clothes hanging up in wardrobes around the world, lonely, afraid of never seeing sunshine again. Doing a wardobe audit is a great way to maximise everything you own and avoid pointless mall trips.

Two hours in your wardrobe could look like a styling session that involves your favourite fashion magazines, screenshots of outfits you love, or your laptop positioned on your bed with a thousand tabs open. Give yourself the challenge of creating five looks that you've never worn before. Alternatively, two hours in your wardrobe with the intent to organise it and remove items you don't need is another fruitful task.

Having adopted the 'less, quality, consciously' mantra for many years now, I don't often undertake big wardrobe cleanouts. But when I do, I use these helpful steps:

1. Pull out your entire wardrobe. This includes your pajamas and your activewear! Get everything out of the closet (literally and figuratively).
2. Make six piles: repair, wash, no, maybe, yes, for another season.
3. Start sorting everything into your piles.
4. Once every garment has a place, congratulate yourself on completing the first phase. Grab a snack, call a friend, stretch your body.
5. Work through each pile.

Maybe: Sort through this pile again with a critical pair of eyes. Now that you've finished going through your entire wardrobe, you know what you have and most of the 'maybes' will find clear destinies in the 'yes' or 'no' piles. If not, store the maybe pile in a place that is out of daily eyesight. Revisit the maybe pile to make final decisions in one month. It's highly likely you will forget what you've stored during that month. This indicates those items should go!

Yes: Now you've decided what you will keep, make garment groups based on type. Separate your cardigans, pants, shorts, dresses, etc. This will help you see any clear double-ups, like three pairs of near-identical shorts. Sometimes we own things that we love but do not wear enough because of wardrobe double-ups. There are only so many items of clothing a person can wear at once! Usually this second sort will result in bigger maybe and no piles.

As you re-hang and re-fold the pile of garments that made it through as yeses, think about why each item you're hanging up is staying in your wardrobe. If it's not a clear yes, it should be a no (or a maybe). After the pile is organised in your wardrobe, give your clothes a little pat of appreciation and tell them they rock.

Repair: If you can repair clothing yourself, block out a time in your calendar to repair those things. If not, find a friend or local seamstress who can do that for you.

Wash: Wash them thoughtfully. After everything is dry, go through this bundle of freshly washed clothes using the instructions above.

No: Use my guide on how to responsibly donate things. For example, some of the items you do not want to keep may end up in your repair pile before finding a home.

For another season: Store these clothes in a convenient place that doesn't clutter the things you use daily. Make sure they are washed and repaired before storing, and fold them with care. Avoid damp spaces for storage and address moth problems if you know that's a risk. Also ask yourself if they are definitely seasonal clothes. I wear summer dresses over turtlenecks and tights in winter.

Struggling to decide what piles things go in? Ask yourself these questions:
- How often do I wear it?
- Does it make me uncomfortable wearing it? (e.g. itchy fabric, too tight)
- Do I need another item to wear with it?

- Is the price you spent stopping you from parting with it? (It's easy to want to hold onto an expensive item even if you don't love it.)
- Would someone else enjoy this garment more than me?

This technique isn't a one-time thing. Carry out this wardrobe audit again in six months' time. If you truly take on the values in this chapter, one day you'll do this audit and end up with only a yes pile!

If I adjusted it, would I wear it more?
Will I notice it's gone?
Has it been hiding?
Ask your local seamstress to change it.
Pop it in the maybe pile and see.
Hang it in your wardobe for a month to see what you think.

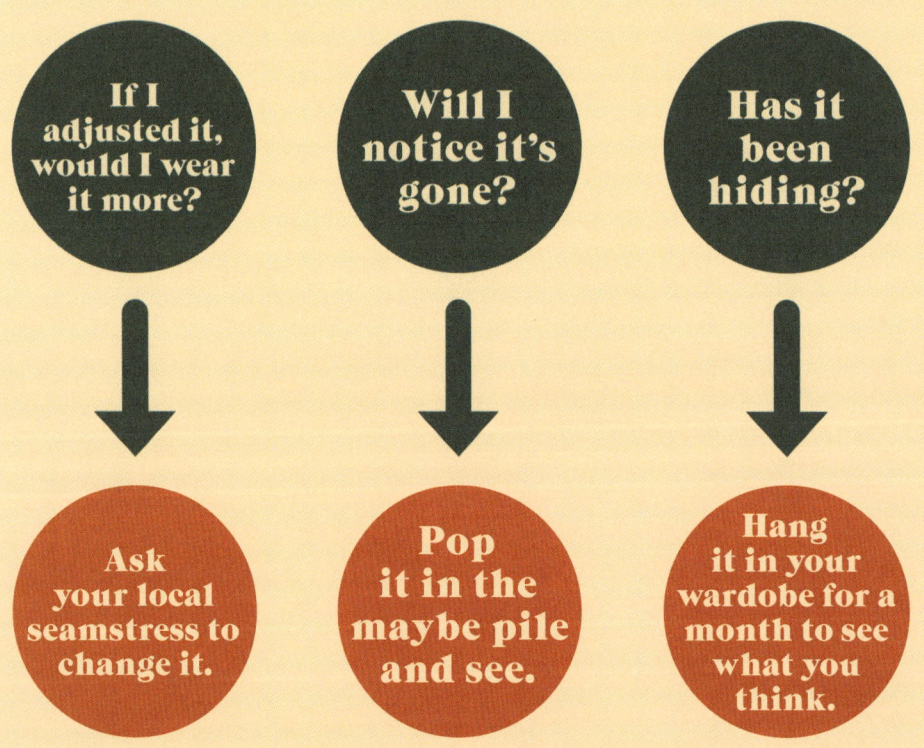

Dead clothes

In general, I think long and hard about an item before I throw it away, because there is no away. When we throw things away, it's only going to another part of the planet, and this planet has a finite amount of space. Unfortunately for us, there is no magical outer-space black hole that consumes our waste. I don't mean to freak you out, but all your old clothes are still sitting here on Earth somewhere.

For me, away means away to a better place. I haven't thrown a garment in the rubbish bin since I can remember. My first point of call, after asking friends and family, is to donate it to a second-hand shop. Sadly, second-hand stores, thrift stores, op-shops, opportunity stores or consignment stores, whatever you want to call them, spend millions of dollars a year on landfill fees.[12]

Before donating any clothes, use my 'op-shop etiquette' guidelines on pages 88-9. In short, fix rips, replace buttons and wash the garment. Assess if it is truly re-wearable by another human being. If not, here are some ideas around what to do with your undonatable clothing:

- Cut them up and use them as vegetables ties in your garden.
- Cut them up into little pieces and use them to stuff cushions, foot rests or even your dog's bed (like I did).
- If you can guarantee they are made with 100 per cent natural fibres (e.g. cotton, bamboo, hemp), cut them up put them in your home compost bin to decompose.
- Use them as cloths in your home to replace things like paper towels.
- Ask your local mechanic if they need rags (my old mechanic pays $35 for a bundle of rags that are essentially old T-shirts!).
- Ask your local pet shelter or vet clinic if they need textiles for anything.
- Cut old clothes into long strips and braid them into animal toys.

If you do not have a way to repurpose your clothes, ask people in your community if they know of a textile-recycling system.

You don't have to be a fashion connoisseur to apply sustainable values to your wardrobe. Heck, people who don't care about fashion are generally the ones who wear their clothes to death and consume a lot less. Don't throw out your wardrobe because it reminds you of your old fast-fashion ways, and don't expect your sustainable wardrobe mindset to happen overnight. Love what you have, and go from there.

In a nutshell:

- Know where your clothes come from.
- Don't let consumerism control you.
- Reduce the amount of clothes you purchase.
- Rent, borrow, clothes-swap.
- Wash your clothes thoughtfully.
- Repair your clothes or get someone else to.
- Shop second-hand, and donate clothes responsibly.
- Don't throw your old clothes in the rubbish bin.

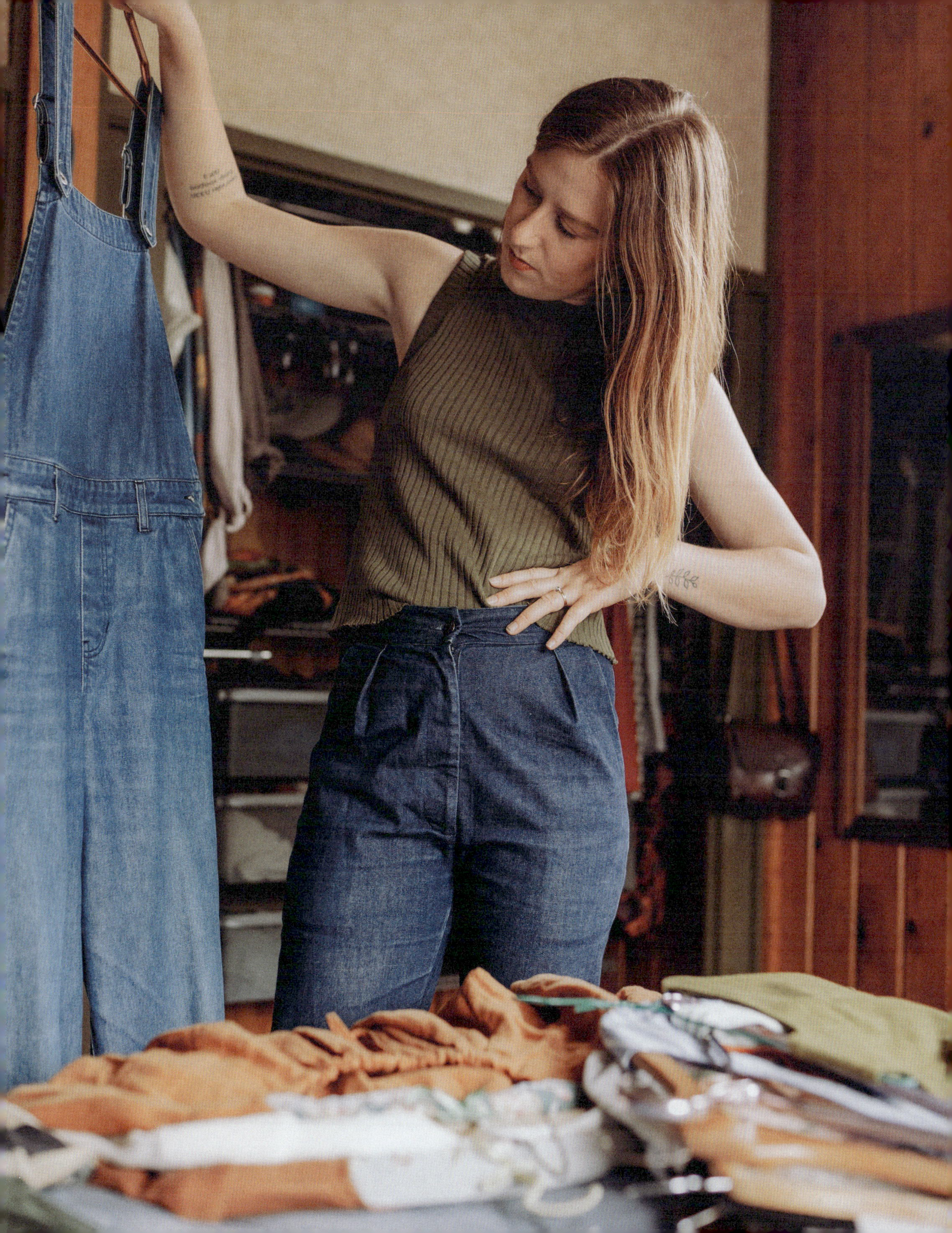

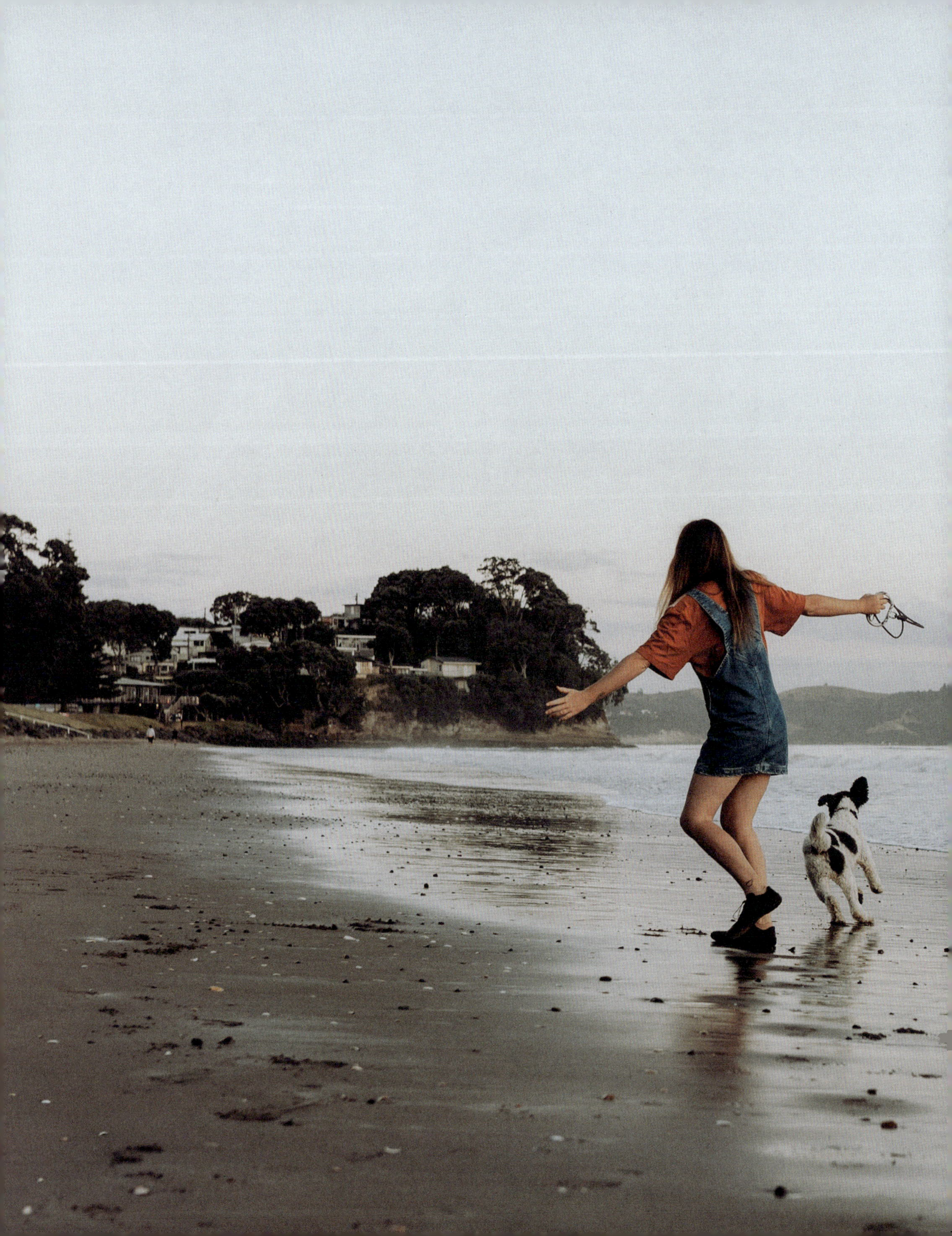

Conclusion

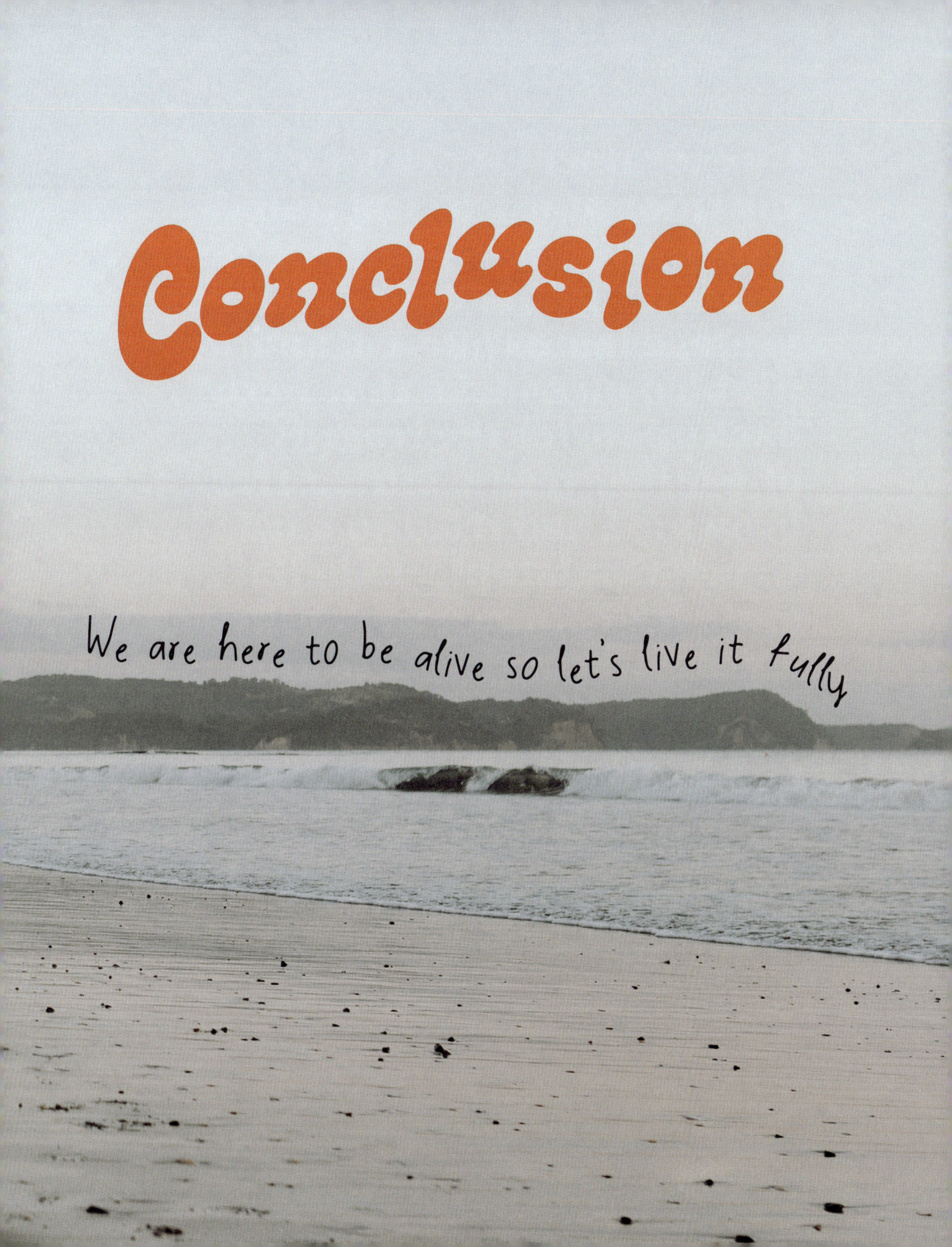

We are here to be alive so let's live it fully

One summer evening, I sat on the floor of my living room with one of my oldest friends. The fairy lights twinkled, the vintage lamps glowed, and we nibbled on snacks that were backups after the tragedy of a failed vegan, gluten-free brownie I had tried so hard to make palatable. Louella and I have known each other since we were six years old. You know those friends you don't see for years but when you meet you pick up exactly where you left off and there's zero awkward catching up? That's us.

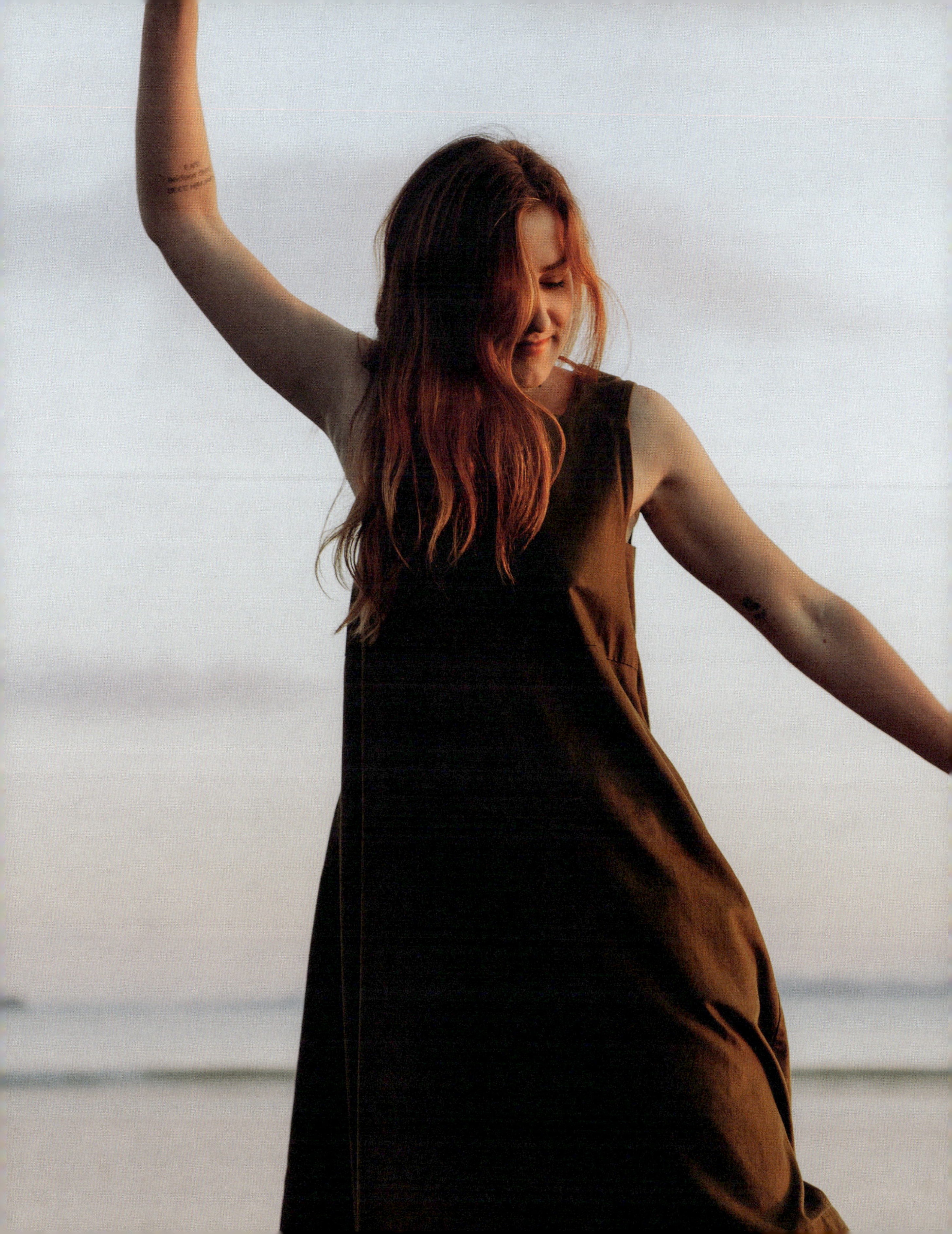

We share similar values, and conversation flows like a good wine on a Friday night. Naturally, the conversation that evening led to sustainable living and our personal efforts to live with less impact on the planet. Louella turned to me and said, 'Kate, wouldn't life just be so much easier if we didn't give a shit about the world?' I agreed. We laughed, and then continued to go about our lives living to our values that respect people and the planet. But why? Why live with so much inconvenience and hardship?

I find it hard to answer that question when people seriously (and frequently) ask it. Sometimes when I arrive to meetings looking like a sweaty mess after biking in the heat, cut myself on the glass jar that broke in my bag during my bike ride to the bulk bin store, or find myself walking away from delicious food venues because they haven't accepted my BYO container, I struggle to find the answer.

But I live this way because I cannot help it. It feels right. I live this way because aligning your values with your actions is one of the most fulfilling aspects of life. I live this way not because my bike trip will change the world, but because it changes me — and I *can* impact the world. You are your habits. You are what you do. And even though society doesn't make it easy for us to be us all the time, trying our absolute best is what counts.

Throughout this book, I trust you've laughed at and with me, screwed your nose up at wild ideas, written some down to do later, and reflected on your own life and how you live it. I can picture you walking to the supermarket instead of taking the car because it's only two kilometres away. I imagine you removing things from your online shopping cart and feeling empowered as you walk to your wardrobe and whisper 'You're enough.' I can also picture you dancing while you cook dinner.

You don't have to live like me, but I hope you will live a little better, a little bolder and a lot different. Who knows, maybe sleeping upside down on Thursday nights might just save us all.

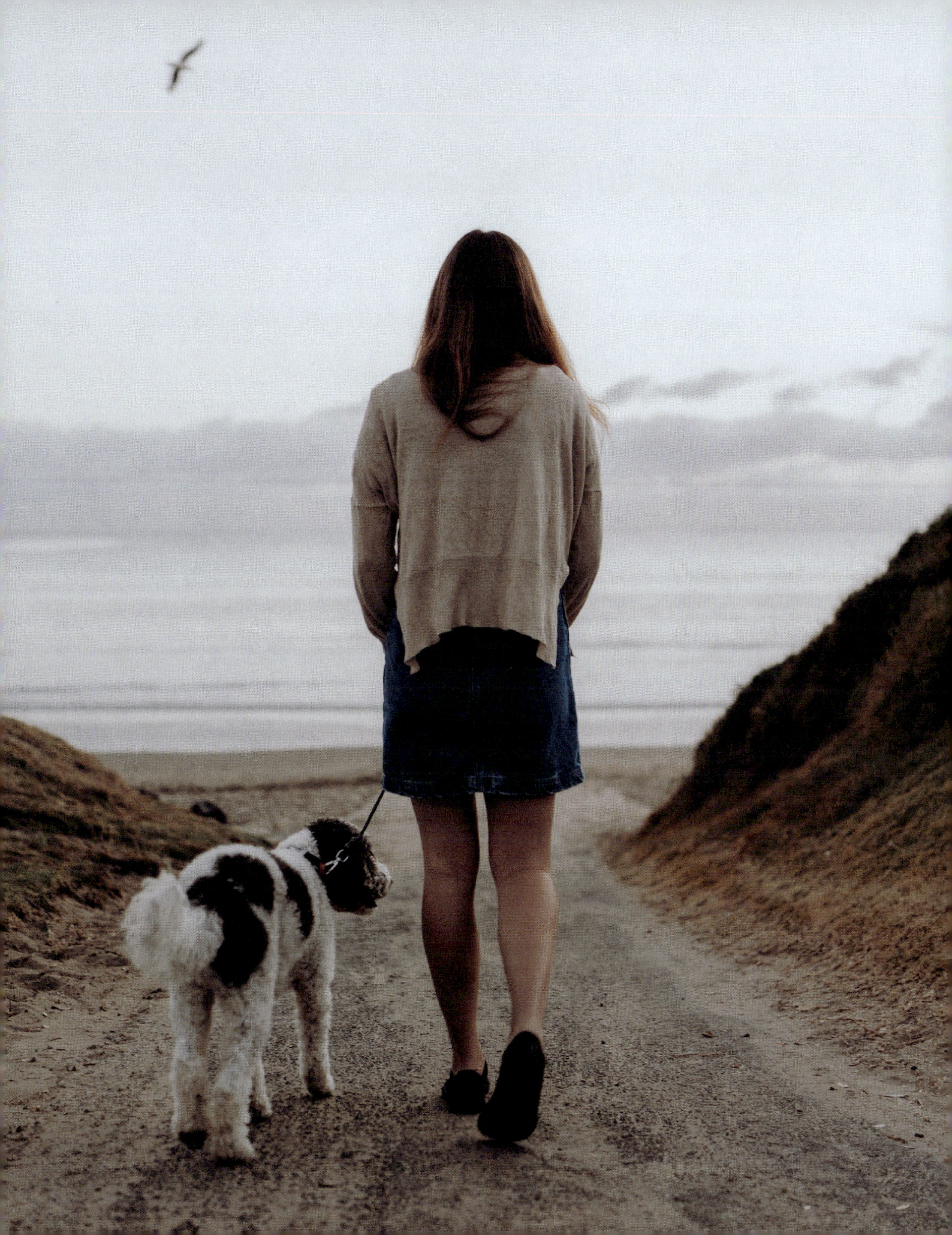

Thank you, so much

I'm often asked how I stay so positive, how I still jump out of bed in the morning wearing a smile and live joyfully when there is so much hurt in the world. One of my key reasons is you, the reader. I'm so thankful for your desire to live life better, bolder and differently. I am so thankful that you have taken the time to not only read this book and support my work, but also take action. Thank you.

Thank you to Nancy, Holly and Heidi for being my epic 'frienditors' (friends who edit). When you're so close to something, particularly a book, it's easy to get lost in the words and question everything. Your feedback helped me to stay grounded.

Thank you to Megan, who not only designed and pieced this book together, but also saw a book in me from the beginning! Without meeting me in person, you took my words, photos and vibe, and threw them together in a way that has honestly left me baffled. I could not have asked for a more talented designer.

Melissa. This book was written in solitude with many cups of tea, but the images were captured during moments bursting with energy while you pointed your camera at me. Although I'm stoked this book is in the hot little hands of many wonderful readers, I'm sad those photoshoots are over. Capturing photos with you will forever be one of my favourite pastimes. You rolled around in wet sand, woke up at strange hours of the morning and never said no to any of my ideas. Thank you.

Thank you to the Allen & Unwin team and editors: Jenny, Leonie, Tess, Abba and the other shining faces in the office who I had the pleasure of working with over the past year. I was hesitant to write a book with a publisher when I am so used to marching to the beat of my own drum. You truly let me run wild while crafting this book in a way I couldn't have done myself.

Thank you to my Patreons, for being there through my Patreon post ramblings and listening to my internal dialogue while I wrote the book. Your messages of celebration at milestones and support of my work were little firecrackers under my butt that kept me going!

I must also acknowledge the feathery friends who sat on my body while I wrote. Zugda, my hand-raised cockatiel, and Buddy, Tim's family bird, who passed away at 24 years old while this book was in the editing phase. These two creatures kept me company and made me laugh while I wrote a book during a pandemic. No one else saw the endless hours of writing. They did. Aside from pooping all over my desk and ripping my laptop keys off, they were helpful companions.

Mum, Dad, the older I get, the more I realise how much I've taken you for granted. I didn't have parents who told me what I 'should be' or stopped me from doing a single thing. Mum, I remember when you took me to get my nose pierced even when you didn't support the idea, and dropped me off at the airport for all sorts of adventures. Dad, you somehow came to all my school camps, joined us for dance parties after dinner, and spent many hours gardening with me — all while working 24/7 as a vet. Without these things, living better, bolder, differently, wouldn't have crossed my mind. Let alone writing a book about it. Thank you for reading my chapters, making the correct 'ooh' and 'ahhh' sounds at book drafts, and always checking in.

Georgia and Isaac. I don't know how to thank you without you mocking my heartfelt words like the good siblings that you are, but just let me say one thing: I might not say it enough, and you probably won't believe me, but who you are as people and what you do in your daily life inspires me (and in turn, this book) more than you know.

Thank you to my Rose Gardeners, especially those who made the 'sharing party' the wonderful night that it was — you know who you are. Thank you Clare and Brianne for your mentorship and leadership. Thank you to Stef, for lending your incredible researching skills. Thank you also to the hundreds of sustainable companies who have entrusted me with representing your products and services for so many years. You may have spotted your work throughout this book! Thank you for the sustainable tools you offer people and all that you do to use your business for good.

Finally, thank you to the person who sleeps upside down on Thursday nights with me. Who thinks I'm more capable than I actually am and tells me this every day. Who doesn't throw out my kombucha concoctions or roll his eyes when I try new strange sustainable things. Who provides constant styling advice and spends hours making our suburban homestead flourish. Thank you, Tim. Your support while I wrote this book was, unsurprisingly, legendary.

Wellbeing

1. www.limber.nz
2. 'Environmenstrual Fact Sheet', Wen (website), wen.org.uk/wp-content/uploads/Fact-Sheet-Environmenstrual.pdf, p. 1.
3. L. Briden, *Period Repair Manual*, Lara Briden, 2017.
4. 'Natural Family Planning (Fertility Awareness)', NHS, last reviewed 13 April 2021, nhs.uk/conditions/contraception/natural-family-planning/.
5. E. Rhoads, *Waste Not: Make a Big Difference by Throwing Away Less*, Hardie Grant, 2019.
6. See sustainablesalons.org for more about this.
7. unep.org/interactive/beat-plastic-pollution/

The 3 Ss: sleep, stuff, self

1. M. Walker, *Why We Sleep: Unlocking the power of sleep and dreams*, Scribner, 2017, p. 4.
2. Ibid, p. 164.
3. Ibid, p. 164.
4. Ibid, p. 134.
5. J. Wallman, *Stuffocated: Living more with less*, Penguin, 2015.
6. J. F. Millburn & R. Nicodemus, 'Play the 30-day Minimalism Game', theminimalists.com/game/.

Connection

1. E. Seppala, T. Rossomando and J. R. Doty, 'Social Connection and Compassion: Important predictors of health and well-being', *Social Research: An International Quarterly*, 80(2), Summer 2013, pp. 411–30, www.muse.jhu.edu/article/528212.
2. 'How much would a typical New Zealand wedding cost?', My Kiwi Wedding (website), 19 April 2017, mykiwiwedding.co.nz/typical-wedding-cost/
3. See www.takeawaythrowaways.nz to learn more about this.

Food

1. ecowithem.com.
2. A. Lard, *Root to Stem: A seasonal guide to natural recipes and remedies for everyday life*, Penguin Books, London, 2019, pp. XV.
3. C. Saunders and A. Barber, 'Carbon Footprints, Life Cycle Analysis, Food Miles: Global trade trends and market issues', *Political Science*, 60(1), 2008, pp. 73–88, doi.org/10.1177/003231870806000107.
4. K. Buchholz, 'How Has the World's Population Changed from 1950 to Today?', World Economic Forum, 4 November 2020, weforum.org/agenda/2020/11/global-continent-urban-population-urbanisation-percent/.
5. You can find out more about this at blueborage.teachable.com/p/foundations-of-edible-gardening.
6. 'The Food Miles Report: The dangers of long-distance food transport', Sustain (website), 2011, sustainweb.org/publications/the_food_miles_report/
7. WasteMINZ, 'New Zealand Food Waste Audits', October 2018, p. 2, lovefoodhatewaste.co.nz/wp-content/uploads/2019/02/Final-New-Zealand-Food-Waste-Audits-2018.pdf

8   S. Stoll-Kleemann and U. J. Schmidt, 'Reducing Meat Consumption in Developed and Transition Countries to Counter Climate Change and Biodiversity Loss: A review of influence factors', *Regional Environmental Change*, 17(5), 2016, pp. 1261–77.
9   E. Röös et al., 'Less meat, more legumes: prospects and challenges in the transition toward sustainable diets in Sweden', *Renewable Agriculture and Food Systems*, 35(2), 2018, pp. 192–205, doi.org/10.1017/s1742170518000443.
10 A. Siegfried, 'Insight into Regenerative Agriculture in New Zealand: The good, the bad, and the opportunity', PureAdvantage (website), 30 April 2020, pureadvantage.org/insight-into-regenerative-agriculture-in-new-zealand-the-good-the-bad-and-the-opportunity/.
11 'Easy homemade five seed crackers', Quite Good Food (website), quitegoodfood.co.nz/easy-home-made-five-seed-crackers
12 A. and J. Gallagher, 'Easy Hummus', Inspired Taste (website), inspiredtaste.net/15938/easy-and-smooth-hummus-recipe/?fbclid=IwAR1DJTPODguG01AF1My3izSS20cIGQoCArVqHf1MTiUC5yYyeUoQ7aeIi1I
13 'Auckland's Waste Assessment 2017', Auckland Council, p. 51, aucklandcouncil.govt.nz/plans-projects-policies-reports-bylaws/our-plans-strategies/topic-based-plans-strategies/environmental-plans-strategies/docswastemanagementplan/waste-assessment-2017.pdf
14 See sharewaste.org.nz for more on this.

Clothes

1   Morgan (director), *The True Cost*, 2015, truecostmovie.com
2   https://www.textilereuse.com/wp-content/uploads/2021/06/Usedfully_Government-Recommendations-Report-Final-May2021-Updated.pdf
3   X. Chen, H. A. Memon, Y. Wang, I. Marriam, and M. Tebyetekerwa, 'Circular Economy and Sustainability of the Clothing and Textile Industry, Materials Circular Economy, 3(1), 2021, https://doi.org/10.1007/s42824-021-00026-2.
4   Ellen MacArthur Foundation and Circular Fibres Initiative, 'A New Textiles Economy: Redesigning fashion's future', Ellen MacArthur Foundation, December 2017, https://ellenmacarthurfoundation.org/a-new-textiles-economy.
5   M. Anner, 'Squeezing workers' rights in global supply chains: Purchasing practices in the Bangladesh garment export sector in comparative perspective', Review of International Political Economy, 27(2), 2019, pp. 320–47, https://doi.org/10.1080/09692290.2019.1625426.
6   K. Vikrant et al., 'Recent advancements in bioremediation of dye: Current status and challenges', Bioresource Technology, 253, 2018, pp. 355–67, https://doi.org/10.1016/j.biortech.2018.01.029.
7   K. Shirvanimoghaddam, B. Motamed, S. Ramakrishna, S. and M. Naebe, 'Death by waste: Fashion and textile circular economy case', Science of The Total Environment, 718, 137317, 2020, doi.org/10.1016/j.scitotenv.2020.137317.
8   A. McAfee, A. Sjoman and V. Dessain, 'Zara: IT for fast fashion', Harvard Business School, June 2004, hbsp.harvard.edu/product/604081-PDF-ENG.
9   See repairredefined.com for ideas.
10 See konmari.com for more on Marie Kondo's philosophy.
11 M. van Elven, 'People Do Not Wear At Least 50 percent of Their Wardrobes, says study', Fashion United, 16 August 2018, fashionunited.uk/news/fashion/people-do-not-wear-at-least-50-percent-of-their-wardrobes-according-to-study/2018081638356.
12 A. Bainbridge and P. Timms, 'Charities Spending Millions Cleaning Up Fast Fashion Graveyard', ABC News, 4 October 2018, abc.net.au/news/2018-10-04/charities-spending-millions-cleaning-up-fast-fashion-graveyard/10328758.

Sharing chart

After reading this book, please fill in this chart with one thing you're excited to do. Pass the book on to someone who'll enjoy it. I want this book to be used by as many people as possible. Share it! Thank you, Kate

Date	Name	I am inspired to . . .